ELEMENTS OF
Literature
FIRST COURSE

The Holt Reader: An Interactive WorkText

Instruction in Reading Literature and Informational Materials

Standardized Test Practice

HOLT, RINEHART AND WINSTON

A Harcourt Education Company

Austin • Orlando • Chicago • New York • Toronto • London • San Diego

CREDITS

Supervisory Editors: Juliana Koenig, Fannie Safier

Managing Editor: Mike Topp

Administrative Managing Editor: Michael Neibergall

Senior Product Manager: Don Wulbrecht

Editors: Susan Kent Cakars, Michael Zakhar

Copyediting Supervisor: Mary Malone

Senior Copyeditor: Elizabeth Dickson

Copyeditors: Christine Altgelt, Joel Bourgeois, Emily Force, Julie A. Hill, Julia Thomas Hu, Jennifer Kirkland, Millicent Ondras, Dennis Scharnberg

Project Administration: Elizabeth LaManna

Editorial Support: Bret Isaacs, Brian Kachmar, Erik Netcher

Editorial Permissions: David Smith, Carrie Jones

Design: Bruce Bond, *Design Director, Book Design*

Electronic Publishing: Nanda Patel, JoAnn Stringer, *Project Coordinators;* Sally Dewhirst, *Quality Control Team Leader;* Angela Priddy, Barry Bishop, Becky Golden-Harrell, Ellen Rees, *Quality Control;* Juan Baquera, *Electronic Publishing Technology Services Team Leader;* Christopher Lucas, *Team Leader;* Lana Kaupp, Kim Orne, Susan Savkov; *Senior Production Artists;* Ellen Kennedy, Patricia Zepeda, *Production Artists;* Heather Jernt, *Electronic Publishing Supervisor;* Robert Franklin, *Electronic Publishing Director*

Production/Manufacturing: Michael Roche, *Senior Production Coordinator;* Belinda Barbosa Lopez, *Senior Production Coordinator;* Carol Trammel, *Production Manager;* Beth Prevelige, *Senior Production Manager*

Contents

PART 1 Reading Literature

Part 2 Reading Informational Materials

PART 3 Standardized Test Practice

Literature

Informational Materials

The Holt Reader:
An Interactive WorkText

Instruction in Reading Literature and Informational Materials

Standardized Test Practice

Skills Contents

Literary Skills

Reading Skills for Literary Texts

Reading Skills for Informational Texts

To the Student

A Book for You

Imagine this. A book full of stories you want to read and informational articles that are really interesting. Make it a book that actually tells you to write in it, circling, underlining, jotting down responses. Fill it with graphic organizers that encourage you to think a different way. Make it a size that's easy to carry around. That's *The Holt Reader: An Interactive WorkText*—a book created especially for you.

The Holt Reader: An Interactive WorkText is designed to accompany *Elements of Literature.* Like *Elements of Literature,* it's designed to help you interact with the literature and informational materials you read. The chart below shows you what's in your book and how the book is organized.

PART 1 Reading Literature	PART 2 Reading Informational Materials	PART 3 Standardized Test Practice
Literary selections from *Elements of Literature*	Informational texts topically or thematically linked to literary selections	Standardized test practice of literature and informational reading

Learning to Read Literary and Informational Materials

When you read informational materials like a social studies textbook or a newspaper article, you usually read to get the facts. You read mainly to get information that is stated directly on the page. When you read literature, you need to go beyond understanding what the words mean and getting the facts straight. You need to read between the lines of a poem or story to discover the writer's meaning. No matter what kind of reading you do—literary or informational—*The Holt Reader: An Interactive WorkText* will help you practice the skills and strategies you need to become an active and successful reader.

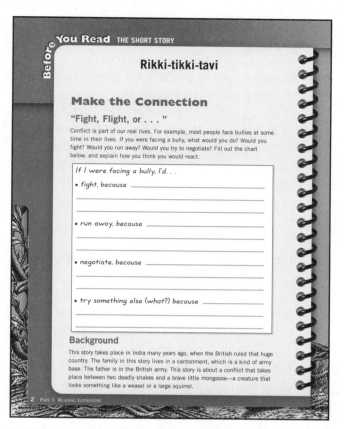

Setting the Stage: Before You Read

In Part 1, the Before-You-Read activity helps you make a personal connection with the selection you are about to read. It helps you sharpen your awareness of what you already know by asking you to think and write about a topic before you read. The more you know about the topic of a text, of course, the easier it is to understand the text. Sometimes this page will provide background information you need to know before you read the text.

Interactive Selections from *Elements of Literature*

The literary selections in Part 1 are many of the same selections that appear in *Elements of Literature,* First Course. The selections are reprinted in a single column and in larger type to give you the room you need to mark up the text.

PART 1 Reading Literature

Strategies to Guide Your Reading: Side Notes

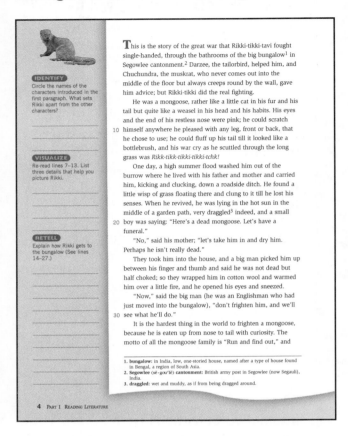

IDENTIFY
Circle the names of the characters introduced in the first paragraph. What sets Rikki apart from the other characters?

_____
_____
_____

VISUALIZE
Re-read lines 7–13. List three details that help you picture Rikki.

_____
_____
_____

RETELL
Explain how Rikki gets to the bungalow (See lines 14–27.)

_____
_____
_____
_____
_____
_____
_____
_____

This is the story of the great war that Rikki-tikki-tavi fought single-handed, through the bathrooms of the big bungalow[1] in Segowlee cantonment.[2] Darzee, the tailorbird, helped him, and Chuchundra, the muskrat, who never comes out into the middle of the floor but always creeps round by the wall, gave him advice; but Rikki-tikki did the real fighting.

He was a mongoose, rather like a little cat in his fur and his tail but quite like a weasel in his head and his habits. His eyes 10 and the end of his restless nose were pink; he could scratch himself anywhere he pleased with any leg, front or back, that he chose to use; he could fluff up his tail till it looked like a bottlebrush, and his war cry as he scuttled through the long grass was *Rikk-tikk-tikki-tikki-tchk!*

One day, a high summer flood washed him out of the burrow where he lived with his father and mother and carried him, kicking and clucking, down a roadside ditch. He found a little wisp of grass floating there and clung to it till he lost his senses. When he revived, he was lying in the hot sun in the 20 middle of a garden path, very draggled[3] indeed, and a small boy was saying: "Here's a dead mongoose. Let's have a funeral."

"No," said his mother; "let's take him in and dry him. Perhaps he isn't really dead."

They took him into the house, and a big man picked him up between his finger and thumb and said he was not dead but half choked; so they wrapped him in cotton wool and warmed him over a little fire, and he opened his eyes and sneezed.

"Now," said the big man (he was an Englishman who had just moved into the bungalow), "don't frighten him, and we'll 30 see what he'll do."

It is the hardest thing in the world to frighten a mongoose, because he is eaten up from nose to tail with curiosity. The motto of all the mongoose family is "Run and find out," and

---

1. **bungalow:** in India, low, one-storied house, named after a type of house found in Bengal, a region of South Asia.
2. **Segowlee** (sē·gou´lē) **cantonment:** British army post in Segowlee (now Segauli), India.
3. **draggled:** wet and muddy, as if from being dragged around.

Notes in the side column accompany each selection. They guide your interaction with the text and help you unlock meaning. Many notes ask you to circle or underline in the text itself. Others provide lines on which you can write. Here are the kinds of notes you will work with as you read the selections: identify, retell, infer, predict, interpret, evaluate, visualize, and build fluency.

Identify asks you to find information (like the name of a character or a description of the setting) that is stated directly in the text. You will often be asked to circle or underline the information in the text.

Retell asks you to restate or explain in your own words something that has just happened.

Rikki-tikki was a true mongoose. He looked at the cotton wool, decided that it was not good to eat, ran all round the table, sat up and put his fur in order, scratched himself, and jumped on the small boy's shoulder.

"Don't be frightened, Teddy," said his father. "That's his way of making friends."

40 "Ouch! He's tickling under my chin," said Teddy.

Rikki-tikki looked down between the boy's collar and neck, snuffed at his ear, and climbed down to the floor, where he sat rubbing his nose.

"Good gracious," said Teddy's mother, "and that's a wild creature! I suppose he's so tame because we've been kind to him."

"All mongooses are like that," said her husband. "If Teddy doesn't pick him up by the tail or try to put him in a cage, he'll run in and out of the house all day long. Let's give him

50 something to eat."

They gave him a little piece of raw meat. Rikki-tikki liked it <u>immensely</u>, and when it was finished, he went out into the veranda[4] and sat in the sunshine and fluffed up his fur to make it dry to the roots. Then he felt better.

"There are more things to find out about in this house," he said to himself, "than all my family could find out in all their lives. I shall certainly stay and find out."

He spent all that day roaming over the house. He nearly drowned himself in the bathtubs, put his nose into the ink on a

60 writing table, and burnt it on the end of the big man's cigar, for he climbed up in the big man's lap to see how writing was done. At nightfall he ran into Teddy's nursery to watch how kerosene lamps were lighted, and when Teddy went to bed, Rikki-tikki climbed up too; but he was a restless companion, because he had to get up and attend to every noise all through the night and find out what made it. Teddy's mother and father came in, the last thing, to look at their boy, and Rikki-tikki was awake on the pillow. "I don't like that," said Teddy's mother;

---

4. **veranda:** open porch covered by a roof, running along the outside of a building.

IDENTIFY

Circle the motto of the mongoose family on page 4. List three things that Rikki does to live up to the motto.

INTERPRET

Read lines 55–57. Underline the reason Rikki decides to stay at the bungalow. How does his decision to stay show that he is a true mongoose?

WORDS TO OWN
immensely (i-mens'lē) *adv.*: exactly.

PREDICT

Pause at line 71. What do you think would happen if a snake came into Teddy's room? Finish Teddy's father's sentence.

INFER

Re-read lines 73–80. Underline the lines that show how the people feel about animals.

VISUALIZE

Underline the details that help you picture the garden setting (lines 81–93).

WORDS TO OWN
cowered (kou'ərd) *v.*: crouched and trembled in fear.

"he may bite the child." "He'll do no such thing," said the father.

70 "Teddy's safer with that little beast than if he had a bloodhound to watch him. If a snake came into the nursery now—"

But Teddy's mother wouldn't think of anything so awful.

Early in the morning, Rikki-tikki came to early breakfast in the veranda riding on Teddy's shoulder, and they gave him banana and some boiled egg; and he sat on all their laps one after the other, because every well-brought-up mongoose always hopes to be a house mongoose someday and have rooms to run about in; and Rikki-tikki's mother (she used to live in the General's house at Segowlee) had carefully told Rikki what to

80 do if ever he came across white men.

Then Rikki-tikki went out into the garden to see what was to be seen. It was a large garden, only half cultivated, with bushes, as big as summerhouses, of Marshal Niel roses; lime and orange trees; clumps of bamboos; and thickets of high grass. Rikki-tikki licked his lips. "This is a splendid hunting ground," he said, and his tail grew bottlebrushy at the thought of it, and he scuttled up and down the garden, snuffing here and there till he heard very sorrowful voices in a thorn bush. It was Darzee, the tailorbird, and his wife. They had made a

90 beautiful nest by pulling two big leaves together and stitching them up the edges with fibers and had filled the hollow with cotton and downy fluff. The nest swayed to and fro as they sat on the rim and cried.

"What is the matter?" asked Rikki-tikki.

"We are very miserable," said Darzee. "One of our babies fell out of the nest yesterday and Nag ate him."

"H'm!" said Rikki-tikki, "that is very sad—but I am a stranger here. Who is Nag?"

Darzee and his wife only <u>cowered</u> down in the nest without

100 answering, for from the thick grass at the foot of the bush there came a low hiss—a horrid, cold sound that made Rikki-tikki jump back two clear feet. Then inch by inch out of the grass rose up the head and spread hood of Nag, the big black cobra, and he was five feet long from tongue to tail. When he had lifted one third of himself clear of the ground, he stayed

---

Infer asks you to make an **inference,** or an educated guess. You make inferences on the basis of clues writers give you and on experiences from your own life. When you make an inference, you read between the lines to figure out what the writer suggests but does not say directly.

Predict asks you to figure out what will happen next. Making predictions as you read helps you think about and understand what you are reading. To make predictions, look for clues that the writer gives you. Connect those clues with other things you've read, as well as your own experience. You'll probably find yourself adjusting predictions as you read.

Interpret asks you to explain the meaning of something. When you make an interpretation of a character, for example, you look at what the character says or does, and then you think about what the character's words and actions mean. You ask yourself why the character said those words and did those things. Your answer is the interpretation. Interpretations help you get at the main idea of a selection, the discovery about life you take away from it.

balancing to and fro exactly as a dandelion tuft balances in the wind, and he looked at Rikki-tikki with the wicked snake's eyes that never change their expression, whatever the snake may be thinking of.

110 "Who is Nag," said he. "*I am Nag.* The great God Brahm[5] put his mark upon all our people, when the first cobra spread his hood to keep the sun off Brahm as he slept. Look, and be afraid!"

He spread out his hood more than ever, and Rikki-tikki saw the spectacle mark on the back of it that looks exactly like the eye part of a hook-and-eye fastening. He was afraid for the minute; but it is impossible for a mongoose to stay frightened for any length of time, and though Rikki-tikki had never met a live cobra before, his mother had fed him on dead ones, and he
120 knew that all a grown mongoose's business in life was to fight and eat snakes. Nag knew that too, and at the bottom of his cold heart, he was afraid.

"Well," said Rikki-tikki, and his tail began to fluff up again, "marks or no marks, do you think it is right for you to eat fledglings out of a nest?"

Nag was thinking to himself and watching the least little movement in the grass behind Rikki-tikki. He knew that mongooses in the garden meant death sooner or later for him and his family, but he wanted to get Rikki-tikki off his guard. So
130 he dropped his head a little and put it on one side.

"Let us talk," he said. "You eat eggs. Why should not I eat birds?"

"Behind you! Look behind you!" sang Darzee.

Rikki-tikki knew better than to waste time in staring. He jumped up in the air as high as he could go, and just under him whizzed by the head of Nagaina, Nag's wicked wife. She had crept up behind him as he was talking, to make an end of him; and he heard her savage hiss as the stroke missed. He came down almost across her back, and if he had been an old
140 mongoose, he would have known that then was the time to

---

5. **Brahm** (bräm): in the Hindu religion, the creator (also called Brahma).

RIKKI-TIKKI-TAVI **7**

Pretend that you are Nag. Read the boxed passage out loud. Try to use a voice "that makes the tailorbirds cower."

Pause at line 123. Do you think a **conflict**, or struggle, will develop between Rikki and Nag? Why?

---

break her back with one bite; but he was afraid of the terrible lashing return stroke of the cobra. He bit, indeed, but did not bite long enough, and he jumped clear of the whisking tail, leaving Nagaina torn and angry.

"Wicked, wicked Darzee!" said Nag, lashing up as high as he could reach toward the nest in the thorn bush; but Darzee had built it out of reach of snakes, and it only swayed to and fro.

Rikki-tikki felt his eyes growing red and hot (when a mongoose's eyes grow red, he is angry), and he sat back on his
150 tail and hind legs like a little kangaroo, and looked all round him, and chattered with rage. But Nag and Nagaina had disappeared into the grass. When a snake misses its stroke, it never says anything or gives any sign of what it means to do next. Rikki-tikki did not care to follow them, for he did not feel sure that he could manage two snakes at once. So he trotted off to the gravel path near the house and sat down to think. It was a serious matter for him. If you read the old books of natural history, you will find they say that when the mongoose fights the snake and happens to get bitten, he runs off and eats some
160 herb that cures him. That is not true. The victory is only a matter of quickness of eye and quickness of foot—snake's blow against the mongoose's jump—and as no eye can follow the motion of a snake's head when it strikes, this makes things much more wonderful than any magic herb. Rikki-tikki knew he was a young mongoose, and it made him all the more pleased to think that he had managed to escape a blow from behind. It gave him confidence in himself, and when Teddy came running down the path, Rikki-tikki was ready to be petted. But just as Teddy was stooping, something wriggled a
170 little in the dust and a tiny voice said: "Be careful. I am Death!" It was Karait, the dusty brown snakeling that lies for choice on the dusty earth; and his bite is as dangerous as the cobra's. But he is so small that nobody thinks of him, and so he does the more harm to people.

Rikki-tikki's eyes grew red again, and he danced up to Karait with the peculiar rocking, swaying motion that he had inherited from his family. It looks very funny, but it is so perfectly

Re-read lines 131–156. **Retell** what happens between Rikki and the snakes.

8 PART 1 READING LITERATURE

Evaluate asks you to form opinions about what you read. For example, you might see the following note at the end of a story: "How satisfying is the ending of this story? Give two reasons for your answer."

Visualize asks you to picture the characters, settings, and events being described in a selection. As you read, look for details that help you make a mental picture. Think of visualizing as making your own mental movie of a selection.

Build Fluency asks you to read a poem or passages from a story. It lets you practice phrasing, expression, and reading in meaningful chunks. Sometimes hearing text read aloud makes the text easier to understand.

Words to Own lists words for you to learn and own. These words are underlined in the selection, letting you see the words in context. The words are defined for you right there in the side column.

xiv TO THE STUDENT

PART 1 Reading Literature

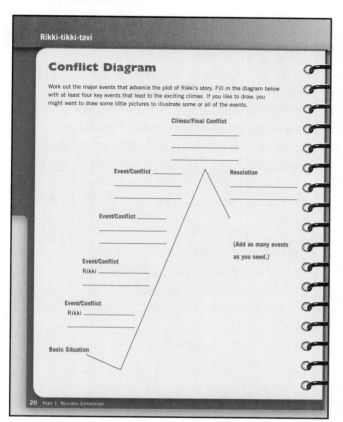

After You Read: Graphic Organizers

After each selection, **graphic organizers** give you a visual way to organize, interpret, and understand the reading or literary focus of the selection. You might be asked to chart the main events of the plot or complete a cause-and-effect chain.

After You Read: Vocabulary and Comprehension

Vocabulary and Comprehension worksheets at the end of literary selections check your knowledge of the Words to Own and your understanding of the selection.

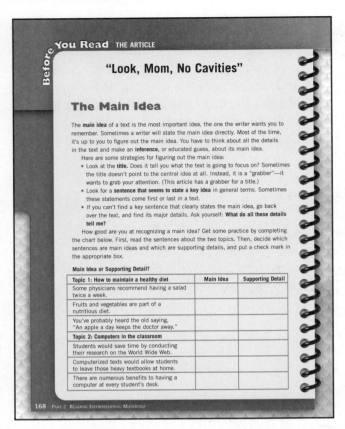

Focus on Skills: Before You Read

The Before-You-Read page in Part 2 teaches skills and strategies you'll need to read informational materials like textbooks, newspaper and magazine articles, and instructional manuals. You'll learn how to recognize text structure, find the main idea, and determine an author's perspective or point of view on these Before-You-Read pages.

Interactive Informational Texts

The informational texts in Part 2 are linked by theme or by topic to the literature selections that appear in *Elements of Literature,* First Course and *The Holt Reader: An Interactive WorkText,* First Course. For example, the text you see on the example pages reproduced here comes from an informational text on cobras that you might want to read after you've finished "Rikki-tikki-tavi," Rudyard Kipling's classic story about a little mongoose who battles several ferocious cobras. The informational selections are printed in a single column and in larger type to give you the room you need to mark up the text.

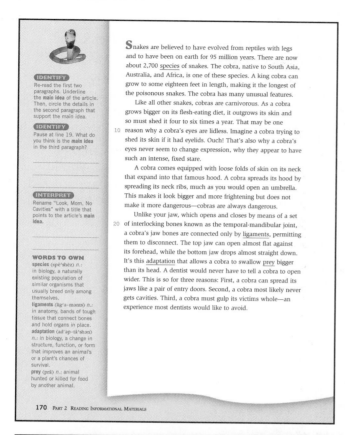

IDENTIFY
Re-read the first two paragraphs. Underline the **main idea** of the article. Then, circle the details in the second paragraph that support the main idea.

IDENTIFY
Pause at line 19. What do you think is the **main idea** in the third paragraph?

INTERPRET
Rename "Look, Mom, No Cavities" with a title that points to the article's **main idea.**

WORDS TO OWN
species (spē'shēz) *n.*: in biology, a naturally existing population of similar organisms that usually breed only among themselves.
ligaments (lig'ə·mənts) *n.*: in anatomy, bands of tough tissue that connect bones and hold organs in place.
adaptation (ad'əp·tā'shən) *n.*: in biology, a change in structure, function, or form that improves an animal's or a plant's chances of survival.
prey (prā) *n.*: animal hunted or killed for food by another animal.

Snakes are believed to have evolved from reptiles with legs and to have been on earth for 95 million years. There are now about 2,700 species of snakes. The cobra, native to South Asia, Australia, and Africa, is one of these species. A king cobra can grow to some eighteen feet in length, making it the longest of the poisonous snakes. The cobra has many unusual features.

Like all other snakes, cobras are carnivorous. As a cobra grows bigger on its flesh-eating diet, it outgrows its skin and so must shed it four to six times a year. That may be one reason why a cobra's eyes are lidless. Imagine a cobra trying to shed its skin if it had eyelids. Ouch! That's also why a cobra's eyes never seem to change expression, why they appear to have such an intense, fixed stare.

A cobra comes equipped with loose folds of skin on its neck that expand into that famous hood. A cobra spreads its hood by spreading its neck ribs, much as you would open an umbrella. This makes it look bigger and more frightening but does not make it more dangerous—cobras are always dangerous.

Unlike your jaw, which opens and closes by means of a set of interlocking bones known as the temporal-mandibular joint, a cobra's jaw bones are connected only by ligaments, permitting them to disconnect. The top jaw can open almost flat against its forehead, while the bottom jaw drops almost straight down. It's this adaptation that allows a cobra to swallow prey bigger than its head. A dentist would never have to tell a cobra to open wider. This is so for three reasons: First, a cobra can spread its jaws like a pair of entry doors. Second, a cobra most likely never gets cavities. Third, a cobra must gulp its victims whole—an experience most dentists would like to avoid.

Strategies to Guide Your Reading: Side Notes

As in Part 1, **notes** in the side column accompany each selection. They guide your interaction with the text and help you unlock meaning. Many notes ask you to circle or underline in the text itself. Others provide lines on which you can write. Here are the kinds of notes you will work with as you read the informational materials in Part 2: identify, retell, infer, predict, interpret, evaluate, visualize, and build fluency. See pages xii–xiv for an explanation of each note.

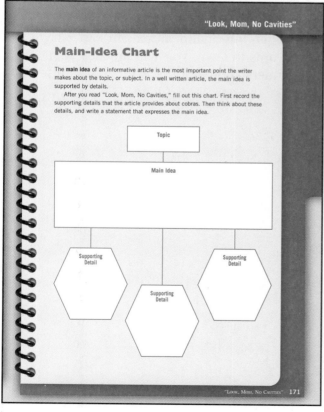

"Look, Mom, No Cavities"

Main-Idea Chart

The **main idea** of an informative article is the most important point the writer makes about the topic, or subject. In a well written article, the main idea is supported by details.

After you read "Look, Mom, No Cavities," fill out this chart. First record the supporting details that the article provides about cobras. Then think about these details, and write a statement that expresses the main idea.

Topic

Main Idea

Supporting Detail

Supporting Detail

Supporting Detail

"LOOK, MOM, NO CAVITIES" 171

After You Read: Graphic Organizers

After each selection, a **graphic organizer** gives you a visual way to organize, interpret, and understand the selection. These organizers focus on the strategy introduced on the Before-You-Read page. You might be asked to collect supporting details that point to a main idea or to complete a comparison chart.

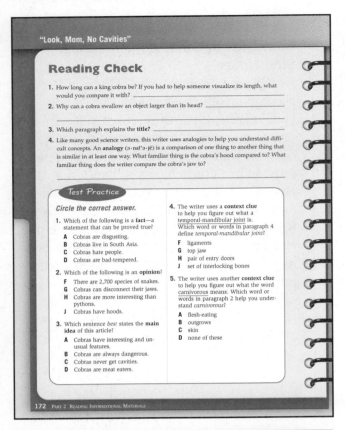

"Look, Mom, No Cavities"

Reading Check

1. How long can a king cobra be? If you had to help someone visualize its length, what would you compare it with? _____

2. Why can a cobra swallow an object larger than its head? _____

3. Which paragraph explains the **title**? _____

4. Like many good science writers, this writer uses analogies to help you understand difficult concepts. An **analogy** (ə‧nal′ə‧jē) is a comparison of one thing to another thing that is similar in at least one way. What familiar thing is the cobra's hood compared to? What familiar thing does the writer compare the cobra's jaw to? _____

Test Practice

Circle the correct answer.

1. Which of the following is a **fact**—a statement that can be proved true?
   A Cobras are disgusting.
   B Cobras live in South Asia.
   C Cobras hate people.
   D Cobras are bad-tempered.

2. Which of the following is an **opinion**?
   F There are 2,700 species of snakes.
   G Cobras can disconnect their jaws.
   H Cobras are more interesting than pythons.
   J Cobras have hoods.

3. Which sentence *best* states the **main idea** of this article?
   A Cobras have interesting and unusual features.
   B Cobras are always dangerous.
   C Cobras never get cavities.
   D Cobras are meat eaters.

4. The writer uses a **context clue** to help you figure out what a temporal-mandibular joint is. Which word or words in paragraph 4 define *temporal-mandibular joint*?
   F ligaments
   G top jaw
   H pair of entry doors
   J set of interlocking bones

5. The writer uses another **context clue** to help you figure out what the word carnivorous means. Which word or words in paragraph 2 help you understand *carnivorous*?
   A flesh-eating
   B outgrows
   C skin
   D none of these

After You Read: Reading Check and Test Practice

Reading Check and Test Practice worksheets at the end of informational selections check your understanding of the selection with short-answer and multiple-choice questions. The multiple-choice questions are similar to the ones you'll answer on state and national standardized tests.

"Look, Mom, No Cavities"

Vocabulary: Words to Own

Words from Latin

Doctors and other scientists used to study Latin because much of the vocabulary of science (including the vocabulary words from "Look, Mom, No Cavities") is derived from Latin.

1. Match the letter of the vocabulary word in the left column with the Latin word it comes from in the right column.

   Word Bank
   species
   ligaments
   adaptation
   prey

   a. species   _____ *adaptare* (to fit)
   b. ligaments   _____ *ligare* (to tie)
   c. adaptation   _____ *prehendere* (to seize)
   d. prey   _____ *specere* (to see)

2. How is the meaning of the Latin word reflected in the meaning of the English word?

   species _____
   ligaments _____
   adaptation _____
   prey _____

3. Below, write down which Latin word each English word comes from. Then, write how the Latin word is reflected in the meaning of each word.

   spectacles _____ ligature _____
   prehensile _____ adapter _____

4. Fill out the chart by writing in the third column an English word derived from the Latin word in the first column.

Latin Word	English Meaning	English Word
credere	to believe	
ignire	to light	
jus	law	
locus	place	
pedis	of the foot	

Vocabulary: Words to Own

When informational texts in Part 2 have Words to Own, you will practice your understanding of the words in exercises like the one shown here.

STANDARDIZED TEST PRACTICE   INFORMATIONAL MATERIALS

DIRECTIONS
Read the following article. Then, read each question on page 245 and circle the letter of the best response.

Mongoose on the Loose
Larry Luxner

In 1872, a Jamaican sugar planter imported nine furry little mongooses from India to eat the rats that were devouring his crops. They did such a good job, the planter started breeding his exotic animals and selling them to eager farmers on neighboring islands.

With no natural predators—like wolves, coyotes, or poisonous snakes—the mongoose population exploded, and within a few years, they were killing not just rats but pigs, lambs, chickens, puppies, and kittens. Dr. G. Roy Horst, a U.S. expert on mongooses, says that today mongooses live on seventeen Caribbean islands as well as Hawaii and Fiji, where they have attacked small animals, threatened endangered species, and have even spread minor rabies epidemics.

In Puerto Rico there are from 800,000 to one million of them. That is about one mongoose for every four humans. In St. Croix, there are 100,000 mongooses, about twice as many as the human population. "It's impossible to eliminate the mongoose population, short of nuclear war," says Horst. "You can't poison them, because cats, dogs, and chickens get poisoned, too. I'm not a prophet crying in the wilderness, but the potential for real trouble is there," says Horst.

According to Horst, great efforts have been made to rid the islands of mongooses, which have killed off a number of species, including the Amevia lizard on St. Croix, presumed extinct for several decades. On Hawaii, the combination of mongooses and sports hunting has reduced the Hawaiian goose, or nene, to less than two dozen individuals. . . .

Horst says his research will provide local and federal health officials with extremely valuable information if they ever decide to launch a campaign against rabies in Puerto Rico or the U.S. Virgin Islands.

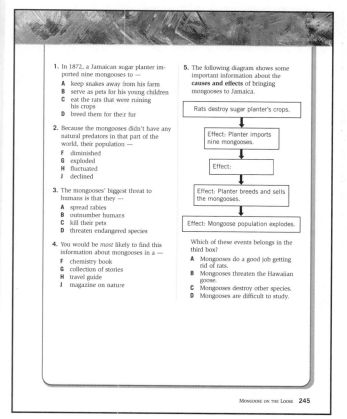

1. In 1872, a Jamaican sugar planter imported nine mongooses to —
   A keep snakes away from his farm
   B serve as pets for his young children
   C eat the rats that were ruining his crops
   D breed them for their fur

2. Because the mongooses didn't have any natural predators in that part of the world, their population —
   F diminished
   G exploded
   H fluctuated
   J declined

3. The mongooses' biggest threat to humans is that they —
   A spread rabies
   B outnumber humans
   C kill their pets
   D threaten endangered species

4. You would be *most* likely to find this information about mongooses in a —
   F chemistry book
   G collection of stories
   H travel guide
   J magazine on nature

5. The following diagram shows some important information about the **causes and effects** of bringing mongooses to Jamaica.

   > Rats destroy sugar planter's crops.
   > ↓
   > Effect: Planter imports nine mongooses.
   > ↓
   > Effect:
   > ↓
   > Effect: Planter breeds and sells the mongooses.
   > ↓
   > Effect: Mongoose population explodes.

   Which of these events belongs in the third box?
   A Mongooses do a good job getting rid of rats.
   B Mongooses threaten the Hawaiian goose.
   C Mongooses destroy other species.
   D Mongooses are difficult to study.

Putting Your Skill as a Reader to the Test
The last part of this book gives you practice in reading and responding to the kinds of literary and informational selections you read in Parts 1 and 2. The selections and multiple-choice questions are similar to the ones you'll see on state and national standardized tests.

PART 1   READING LITERATURE

Rikki-tikki-tavi

Make the Connection

"Fight, Flight, or . . . "

Conflict is part of our real lives. For example, most people face bullies at some time in their lives. If you were facing a bully, what would you do? Would you fight? Would you run away? Would you try to negotiate? Fill out the chart below, and explain how you think you would react.

If I were facing a bully, I'd. . .

- *fight, because* _____
  _____
  _____

- *run away, because* _____
  _____
  _____

- *negotiate, because* _____
  _____
  _____

- *try something else (what?) because* _____
  _____
  _____

Background

This story takes place in India many years ago, when the British ruled that huge country. The family in this story lives in a cantonment, which is a kind of army base. The father is in the British army. This story is about a conflict that takes place between two deadly snakes and a brave little mongoose—a creature that looks something like a weasel or a large squirrel.

Rikki-tikki-tavi

Rudyard Kipling

IDENTIFY

Circle the names of the characters introduced in the first paragraph. What sets Rikki apart from the other characters?

_____

_____

_____

VISUALIZE

Re-read lines 7–13. List three details that help you picture Rikki.

_____

_____

_____

RETELL

Explain how Rikki gets to the bungalow (See lines 14–27.)

_____

_____

_____

_____

_____

_____

_____

_____

This is the story of the great war that Rikki-tikki-tavi fought single-handed, through the bathrooms of the big bungalow[1] in Segowlee cantonment.[2] Darzee, the tailorbird, helped him, and Chuchundra, the muskrat, who never comes out into the middle of the floor but always creeps round by the wall, gave him advice; but Rikki-tikki did the real fighting.

He was a mongoose, rather like a little cat in his fur and his tail but quite like a weasel in his head and his habits. His eyes and the end of his restless nose were pink; he could scratch
10 himself anywhere he pleased with any leg, front or back, that he chose to use; he could fluff up his tail till it looked like a bottlebrush, and his war cry as he scuttled through the long grass was *Rikk-tikk-tikki-tikki-tchk!*

One day, a high summer flood washed him out of the burrow where he lived with his father and mother and carried him, kicking and clucking, down a roadside ditch. He found a little wisp of grass floating there and clung to it till he lost his senses. When he revived, he was lying in the hot sun in the middle of a garden path, very draggled[3] indeed, and a small
20 boy was saying: "Here's a dead mongoose. Let's have a funeral."

"No," said his mother; "let's take him in and dry him. Perhaps he isn't really dead."

They took him into the house, and a big man picked him up between his finger and thumb and said he was not dead but half choked; so they wrapped him in cotton wool and warmed him over a little fire, and he opened his eyes and sneezed.

"Now," said the big man (he was an Englishman who had just moved into the bungalow), "don't frighten him, and we'll
30 see what he'll do."

It is the hardest thing in the world to frighten a mongoose, because he is eaten up from nose to tail with curiosity. The motto of all the mongoose family is "Run and find out," and

---

1. **bungalow:** in India, low, one-storied house, named after a type of house found in Bengal, a region of South Asia.
2. **Segowlee** (sē·gou′lē) **cantonment:** British army post in Segowlee (now Segauli), India.
3. **draggled:** wet and muddy, as if from being dragged around.

Rikki-tikki was a true mongoose. He looked at the cotton wool, decided that it was not good to eat, ran all round the table, sat up and put his fur in order, scratched himself, and jumped on the small boy's shoulder.

"Don't be frightened, Teddy," said his father. "That's his way of making friends."

40   "Ouch! He's tickling under my chin," said Teddy.

Rikki-tikki looked down between the boy's collar and neck, snuffed at his ear, and climbed down to the floor, where he sat rubbing his nose.

"Good gracious," said Teddy's mother, "and that's a wild creature! I suppose he's so tame because we've been kind to him."

"All mongooses are like that," said her husband. "If Teddy doesn't pick him up by the tail or try to put him in a cage, he'll run in and out of the house all day long. Let's give him

50 something to eat."

They gave him a little piece of raw meat. Rikki-tikki liked it <u>immensely</u>, and when it was finished, he went out into the veranda[4] and sat in the sunshine and fluffed up his fur to make it dry to the roots. Then he felt better.

"There are more things to find out about in this house," he said to himself, "than all my family could find out in all their lives. I shall certainly stay and find out."

He spent all that day roaming over the house. He nearly drowned himself in the bathtubs, put his nose into the ink on a

60 writing table, and burnt it on the end of the big man's cigar, for he climbed up in the big man's lap to see how writing was done. At nightfall he ran into Teddy's nursery to watch how kerosene lamps were lighted, and when Teddy went to bed, Rikki-tikki climbed up too; but he was a restless companion, because he had to get up and attend to every noise all through the night and find out what made it. Teddy's mother and father came in, the last thing, to look at their boy, and Rikki-tikki was awake on the pillow. "I don't like that," said Teddy's mother;

---

4. **veranda:** open porch covered by a roof, running along the outside of a building.

IDENTIFY

Circle the motto of the mongoose family on page 4. List three things that Rikki does to live up to the motto.

INTERPRET

Read lines 55–57. Underline the reason Rikki decides to stay at the bungalow. How does his decision to stay show that he is a true mongoose?

WORDS TO OWN
immensely (i·mens′lē) *adv.:* exactly.

PREDICT

Pause at line 71. What do you think would happen if a snake came into Teddy's room? Finish Teddy's father's sentence.

_____

_____

_____

_____

_____

_____

_____

_____

INFER

Re-read lines 73–80. Underline the lines that show how the people feel about animals.

_____

_____

VISUALIZE

Underline the details that help you picture the garden **setting** (lines 81–93).

_____

_____

WORDS TO OWN

cowered (kou′ərd) *v.:* crouched and trembled in fear.

"he may bite the child." "He'll do no such thing," said the father.
70 "Teddy's safer with that little beast than if he had a bloodhound to watch him. If a snake came into the nursery now—"

But Teddy's mother wouldn't think of anything so awful.

Early in the morning, Rikki-tikki came to early breakfast in the veranda riding on Teddy's shoulder, and they gave him banana and some boiled egg; and he sat on all their laps one after the other, because every well-brought-up mongoose always hopes to be a house mongoose someday and have rooms to run about in; and Rikki-tikki's mother (she used to live in the General's house at Segowlee) had carefully told Rikki what to
80 do if ever he came across white men.

Then Rikki-tikki went out into the garden to see what was to be seen. It was a large garden, only half cultivated, with bushes, as big as summerhouses, of Marshal Niel roses; lime and orange trees; clumps of bamboos; and thickets of high grass. Rikki-tikki licked his lips. "This is a splendid hunting ground," he said, and his tail grew bottlebrushy at the thought of it, and he scuttled up and down the garden, snuffing here and there till he heard very sorrowful voices in a thorn bush. It was Darzee, the tailorbird, and his wife. They had made a
90 beautiful nest by pulling two big leaves together and stitching them up the edges with fibers and had filled the hollow with cotton and downy fluff. The nest swayed to and fro as they sat on the rim and cried.

"What is the matter?" asked Rikki-tikki.

"We are very miserable," said Darzee. "One of our babies fell out of the nest yesterday and Nag ate him."

"H'm!" said Rikki-tikki, "that is very sad—but I am a stranger here. Who is Nag?"

Darzee and his wife only <u>cowered</u> down in the nest without
100 answering, for from the thick grass at the foot of the bush there came a low hiss—a horrid, cold sound that made Rikki-tikki jump back two clear feet. Then inch by inch out of the grass rose up the head and spread hood of Nag, the big black cobra, and he was five feet long from tongue to tail. When he had lifted one third of himself clear of the ground, he stayed

balancing to and fro exactly as a dandelion tuft balances in the wind, and he looked at Rikki-tikki with the wicked snake's eyes that never change their expression, whatever the snake may be thinking of.

110   "Who is Nag," said he. "*I* am Nag. The great God Brahm[5] put his mark upon all our people, when the first cobra spread his hood to keep the sun off Brahm as he slept. Look, and be afraid!"

He spread out his hood more than ever, and Rikki-tikki saw the spectacle mark on the back of it that looks exactly like the eye part of a hook-and-eye fastening. He was afraid for the minute; but it is impossible for a mongoose to stay frightened for any length of time, and though Rikki-tikki had never met a live cobra before, his mother had fed him on dead ones, and he
120 knew that all a grown mongoose's business in life was to fight and eat snakes. Nag knew that too, and at the bottom of his cold heart, he was afraid.

"Well," said Rikki-tikki, and his tail began to fluff up again, "marks or no marks, do you think it is right for you to eat fledglings out of a nest?"

Nag was thinking to himself and watching the least little movement in the grass behind Rikki-tikki. He knew that mongooses in the garden meant death sooner or later for him and his family, but he wanted to get Rikki-tikki off his guard. So
130 he dropped his head a little and put it on one side.

"Let us talk," he said. "You eat eggs. Why should not I eat birds?"

"Behind you! Look behind you!" sang Darzee.

Rikki-tikki knew better than to waste time in staring. He jumped up in the air as high as he could go, and just under him whizzed by the head of Nagaina, Nag's wicked wife. She had crept up behind him as he was talking, to make an end of him; and he heard her savage hiss as the stroke missed. He came down almost across her back, and if he had been an old
140 mongoose, he would have known that then was the time to

---

5. **Brahm** (bräm): in the Hindu religion, the creator (also called Brahma).

BUILD FLUENCY

Pretend that you are Nag. Read the boxed passage out loud. Try to use a voice "that makes the tailorbirds cower."

PREDICT

Pause at line 123. Do you think a **conflict,** or struggle, will develop between Rikki and Nag? Why?

RETELL

Re-read lines 131–156.
Retell what happens
between Rikki and the
snakes.

break her back with one bite; but he was afraid of the terrible lashing return stroke of the cobra. He bit, indeed, but did not bite long enough, and he jumped clear of the whisking tail, leaving Nagaina torn and angry.

"Wicked, wicked Darzee!" said Nag, lashing up as high as he could reach toward the nest in the thorn bush; but Darzee had built it out of reach of snakes, and it only swayed to and fro.

Rikki-tikki felt his eyes growing red and hot (when a mongoose's eyes grow red, he is angry), and he sat back on his
150 tail and hind legs like a little kangaroo, and looked all round him, and chattered with rage. But Nag and Nagaina had disappeared into the grass. When a snake misses its stroke, it never says anything or gives any sign of what it means to do next. Rikki-tikki did not care to follow them, for he did not feel sure that he could manage two snakes at once. So he trotted off to the gravel path near the house and sat down to think. It was a serious matter for him. If you read the old books of natural history, you will find they say that when the mongoose fights the snake and happens to get bitten, he runs off and eats some
160 herb that cures him. That is not true. The victory is only a matter of quickness of eye and quickness of foot—snake's blow against the mongoose's jump—and as no eye can follow the motion of a snake's head when it strikes, this makes things much more wonderful than any magic herb. Rikki-tikki knew he was a young mongoose, and it made him all the more pleased to think that he had managed to escape a blow from behind. It gave him confidence in himself, and when Teddy came running down the path, Rikki-tikki was ready to be petted. But just as Teddy was stooping, something wriggled a
170 little in the dust and a tiny voice said: "Be careful. I am Death!" It was Karait, the dusty brown snakeling that lies for choice on the dusty earth; and his bite is as dangerous as the cobra's. But he is so small that nobody thinks of him, and so he does the more harm to people.

Rikki-tikki's eyes grew red again, and he danced up to Karait with the peculiar rocking, swaying motion that he had inherited from his family. It looks very funny, but it is so perfectly

balanced a <u>gait</u> that you can fly off from it at any angle you please; and in dealing with snakes this is an advantage. If Rikki-
180 tikki had only known, he was doing a much more dangerous thing than fighting Nag, for Karait is so small and can turn so quickly that unless Rikki bit him close to the back of the head, he would get the return stroke in his eye or his lip. But Rikki did not know; his eyes were all red, and he rocked back and forth, looking for a good place to hold. Karait struck out, Rikki jumped sideways and tried to run in, but the wicked little dusty gray head lashed within a fraction of his shoulder, and he had to jump over the body, and the head followed his heels close.

Teddy shouted to the house: "Oh, look here! Our mongoose
190 is killing a snake," and Rikki-tikki heard a scream from Teddy's mother. His father ran out with a stick, but by the time he came up, Karait had lunged out once too far, and Rikki-tikki had sprung, jumped on the snake's back, dropped his head far between his forelegs, bitten as high up the back as he could get hold, and rolled away. That bite paralyzed Karait, and Rikki-tikki was just going to eat him up from the tail, after the custom of his family at dinner, when he remembered that a full meal makes a slow mongoose, and if he wanted all his strength and quickness ready, he must keep himself thin. He went away
200 for a dust bath under the castor-oil bushes, while Teddy's father beat the dead Karait. "What is the use of that?" thought Rikki-tikki; "I have settled it all"; and then Teddy's mother picked him up from the dust and hugged him, crying that he had saved Teddy from death, and Teddy's father said that he was a providence,[6] and Teddy looked on with big, scared eyes. Rikki-tikki was rather amused at all the fuss, which, of course, he did not understand. Teddy's mother might just as well have petted Teddy for playing in the dust. Rikki was thoroughly enjoying himself.

210 That night at dinner, walking to and fro among the wineglasses on the table, he might have stuffed himself three times over with nice things; but he remembered Nag and

---

6. **providence:** favor or gift from God or nature.

IDENTIFY

Underline the part of the story that tells why Karait is more dangerous than the cobras.

RETELL

Retell what happens during Rikki's **conflict** with Karait (lines 169–199).

_____

_____

_____

_____

_____

_____

_____

_____

IDENTIFY

Circle the word *fuss* in line 206. How does Rikki feel about being fussed over?

_____

_____

_____

WORDS TO OWN

gait (gāt) *n.:* way of walking or running.

INTERPRET

Re-read the dialogue between Rikki and Chuchundra in lines 225–244. Underline at least two or three lines that add a feeling of **suspense** or uncertainty.

IDENTIFY

What does Rikki hear when the house is "as still as still" (line 245)? Who does he think it is?

Nagaina, and though it was very pleasant to be patted and petted by Teddy's mother and to sit on Teddy's shoulder, his eyes would get red from time to time, and he would go off into his long war cry of *Rikk-tikk-tikki-tikki-tchk!*

Teddy carried him off to bed and insisted on Rikki-tikki's sleeping under his chin. Rikki-tikki was too well bred to bite or scratch, but as soon as Teddy was asleep, he went off for his
220 nightly walk round the house, and in the dark he ran up against Chuchundra, the muskrat, creeping round by the wall. Chuchundra is a brokenhearted little beast. He whimpers and cheeps all night, trying to make up his mind to run into the middle of the room; but he never gets there.

"Don't kill me," said Chuchundra, almost weeping. "Rikki-tikki, don't kill me!"

"Do you think a snake killer kills muskrats?" said Rikki-tikki scornfully.

"Those who kill snakes get killed by snakes," said
230 Chuchundra, more sorrowfully than ever. "And how am I to be sure that Nag won't mistake me for you some dark night?"

"There's not the least danger," said Rikki-tikki, "but Nag is in the garden, and I know you don't go there."

"My cousin Chua, the rat, told me—" said Chuchundra, and then he stopped.

"Told you what?"

"H'sh! Nag is everywhere, Rikki-tikki. You should have talked to Chua in the garden."

"I didn't—so you must tell me. Quick, Chuchundra, or I'll
240 bite you!"

Chuchundra sat down and cried till the tears rolled off his whiskers. "I am a very poor man," he sobbed. "I never had spirit enough to run out into the middle of the room. H'sh! I mustn't tell you anything. Can't you *hear*, Rikki-tikki?"

Rikki-tikki listened. The house was as still as still, but he thought he could just catch the faintest *scratch-scratch* in the world—a noise as faint as that of a wasp walking on a windowpane—the dry scratch of a snake's scales on brickwork.

"That's Nag or Nagaina," he said to himself, "and he is
250 crawling into the bathroom sluice.[7] You're right, Chuchundra; I
should have talked to Chua."

He stole off to Teddy's bathroom, but there was nothing
there, and then to Teddy's mother's bathroom. At the bottom of
the smooth plaster wall there was a brick pulled out to make a
sluice for the bathwater, and as Rikki-tikki stole in by the
masonry[8] curb where the bath is put, he heard Nag and
Nagaina whispering together outside in the moonlight.

"When the house is emptied of people," said Nagaina to her
husband, "*he* will have to go away, and then the garden will be
260 our own again. Go in quietly, and remember that the big man
who killed Karait is the first one to bite. Then come out and tell
me, and we will hunt for Rikki-tikki together."

"But are you sure that there is anything to be gained by
killing the people?" said Nag.

"Everything. When there were no people in the bungalow,
did we have any mongoose in the garden? So long as the
bungalow is empty, we are king and queen of the garden; and
remember that as soon as our eggs in the melon bed hatch (as
they may tomorrow), our children will need room and quiet."

270 "I had not thought of that," said Nag. "I will go, but there is no
need that we should hunt for Rikki-tikki afterward. I will kill the
big man and his wife, and the child if I can, and come away
quietly. Then the bungalow will be empty, and Rikki-tikki
will go."

Rikki-tikki tingled all over with rage and hatred at this, and
then Nag's head came through the sluice, and his five feet of
cold body followed it. Angry as he was, Rikki-tikki was very
frightened as he saw the size of the big cobra. Nag coiled
himself up, raised his head, and looked into the bathroom in
280 the dark, and Rikki could see his eyes glitter.

"Now, if I kill him here, Nagaina will know; and if I fight
him on the open floor, the odds are in his favor. What am I to
do?" said Rikki-tikki-tavi.

---

7. **sluice** (slo͞os): drain.
8. **masonry:** built of stone or brick.

RETELL

Explain how Nag and Nagaina plan to become king and queen of the garden (lines 258–262).

_____

_____

_____

_____

_____

_____

_____

_____

_____

EVALUATE

Do you think Nag and Nagaina's plan of attack will work? Why or why not?

_____

_____

_____

_____

_____

_____

_____

_____

_____

PREDICT

What do you think will happen between Rikki and Nag? Give at least one reason for your answer.

_____

_____

_____

_____

_____

_____

_____

_____

_____

_____

_____

_____

INTERPRET

Re-read lines 302–320. Write down three or four words that describe Rikki's personality.

_____

_____

_____

_____

Nag waved to and fro, and then Rikki-tikki heard him drinking from the biggest water jar that was used to fill the bath. "That is good," said the snake. "Now, when Karait was killed, the big man had a stick. He may have that stick still, but when he comes in to bathe in the morning, he will not have a stick. I shall wait here till he comes. Nagaina—do you hear
290   me?—I shall wait here in the cool till daytime."

There was no answer from outside, so Rikki-tikki knew Nagaina had gone away. Nag coiled himself down, coil by coil, round the bulge at the bottom of the water jar, and Rikki-tikki stayed still as death. After an hour he began to move, muscle by muscle, toward the jar. Nag was asleep, and Rikki-tikki looked at his big back, wondering which would be the best place for a good hold. "If I don't break his back at the first jump," said Rikki, "he can still fight; and if he fights—O Rikki!" He looked at the thickness of the neck below the hood, but that
300   was too much for him; and a bite near the tail would only make Nag savage.

"It must be the head," he said at last, "the head above the hood; and when I am once there, I must not let go."

Then he jumped. The head was lying a little clear of the water jar, under the curve of it; and as his teeth met, Rikki braced his back against the bulge of the red earthenware to hold down the head. This gave him just one second's purchase,[9] and he made the most of it. Then he was battered to and fro as a rat is shaken by a dog—to and fro on the floor, up
310   and down, and round in great circles, but his eyes were red and he held on as the body cartwhipped over the floor, upsetting the tin dipper and the soap dish and the flesh brush, and banged against the tin side of the bath. As he held, he closed his jaws tighter and tighter, for he made sure[10] he would be banged to death, and for the honor of his family, he preferred to be found with his teeth locked. He was dizzy, aching, and felt shaken to pieces, when something went off like a thunderclap just behind him; a hot wind knocked him senseless and red fire

---

9. **purchase:** firm hold.
10. **made sure:** here, felt sure.

singed his fur. The big man had been wakened by the noise and
320 had fired both barrels of a shotgun into Nag just behind the hood.

Rikki-tikki held on with his eyes shut, for now he was quite
sure he was dead; but the head did not move, and the big man
picked him up and said: "It's the mongoose again, Alice; the
little chap has saved *our* lives now." Then Teddy's mother came
in with a very white face and saw what was left of Nag, and
Rikki-tikki dragged himself to Teddy's bedroom and spent half
the rest of the night shaking himself tenderly to find out
whether he really was broken into forty pieces, as he fancied.

When morning came, he was very stiff but well pleased
330 with his doings. "Now I have Nagaina to settle with, and she
will be worse than five Nags, and there's no knowing when the
eggs she spoke of will hatch. Goodness! I must go and see
Darzee," he said.

Without waiting for breakfast, Rikki-tikki ran to the thorn
bush, where Darzee was singing a song of triumph at the top of
his voice. The news of Nag's death was all over the garden, for
the sweeper had thrown the body on the rubbish heap.

"Oh, you stupid tuft of feathers!" said Rikki-tikki angrily. "Is
this the time to sing?"

340 "Nag is dead—is dead—is dead!" sang Darzee. "The <u>valiant</u>
Rikki-tikki caught him by the head and held fast. The big man
brought the bang-stick, and Nag fell in two pieces! He will
never eat my babies again."

"All that's true enough, but where's Nagaina?" said Rikki-
tikki, looking carefully round him.

"Nagaina came to the bathroom sluice and called for Nag,"
Darzee went on; "and Nag came out on the end of a stick—the
sweeper picked him up on the end of a stick and threw him
upon the rubbish heap. Let us sing about the great, the red-
350 eyed Rikki-tikki!" and Darzee filled his throat and sang.

"If I could get up to your nest, I'd roll your babies out!" said
Rikki-tikki. "You don't know when to do the right thing at the
right time. You're safe enough in your nest there, but it's war
for me down here. Stop singing a minute, Darzee."

INFER

What does Rikki mean
when he says that Nagaina
will be "worse than five
Nags" (line 331)?

_____

_____

_____

_____

_____

_____

_____

_____

_____

_____

_____

IDENTIFY

Re-read lines 340–363.
Circle the words that Darzee
uses to describe Rikki.
Then underline two things
Rikki wants to learn from
Darzee.

WORDS TO OWN
valiant (val'yǝnt) *adj.:* brave
and determined.

PREDICT

Rikki asks where Nagaina keeps her eggs (lines 360–361). What do you think Rikki will do with Nagaina's eggs?

_____

_____

_____

_____

_____

_____

_____

IDENTIFY

Kipling calls Darzee's wife "a sensible bird" (line 375). Underline what she does that is sensible.

_____

_____

_____

_____

_____

_____

WORDS TO OWN
consolation (kän'sə-lā'shən)
_n.:_ comfort.

"For the great, beautiful Rikki-tikki's sake I will stop," said Darzee. "What is it, O Killer of the terrible Nag?"

"Where is Nagaina, for the third time?"

"On the rubbish heap by the stables, mourning for Nag. Great is Rikki-tikki with the white teeth."

360 "Bother[11] my white teeth! Have you ever heard where she keeps her eggs?"

"In the melon bed, on the end nearest the wall, where the sun strikes nearly all day. She hid them there weeks ago."

"And you never thought it worthwhile to tell me? The end nearest the wall, you said?"

"Rikki-tikki, you are not going to eat her eggs?"

"Not eat exactly; no. Darzee, if you have a grain of sense, you will fly off to the stables and pretend that your wing is broken and let Nagaina chase you away to this bush. I must get

370 to the melon bed, and if I went there now, she'd see me."

Darzee was a featherbrained little fellow who could never hold more than one idea at a time in his head, and just because he knew that Nagaina's children were born in eggs like his own, he didn't think at first that it was fair to kill them. But his wife was a sensible bird, and she knew that cobra's eggs meant young cobras later on; so she flew off from the nest and left Darzee to keep the babies warm and continue his song about the death of Nag. Darzee was very like a man in some ways.

She fluttered in front of Nagaina by the rubbish heap and

380 cried out, "Oh, my wing is broken! The boy in the house threw a stone at me and broke it." Then she fluttered more desperately than ever.

Nagaina lifted up her head and hissed, "You warned Rikki-tikki when I would have killed him. Indeed and truly, you've chosen a bad place to be lame in." And she moved toward Darzee's wife, slipping along over the dust.

"The boy broke it with a stone!" shrieked Darzee's wife.

"Well! It may be some <u>consolation</u> to you when you're dead to know that I shall settle accounts with the boy. My husband

---

11. **bother:** here, never mind.

390 lies on the rubbish heap this morning, but before night the boy in the house will lie very still. What is the use of running away? I am sure to catch you. Little fool, look at me!"

Darzee's wife knew better than to do *that*, for a bird who looks at a snake's eyes gets so frightened that she cannot move. Darzee's wife fluttered on, piping sorrowfully and never leaving the ground, and Nagaina quickened her pace.

Rikki-tikki heard them going up the path from the stables, and he raced for the end of the melon patch near the wall. There, in the warm litter above the melons, very cunningly

400 hidden, he found twenty-five eggs about the size of a bantam's[12] eggs but with whitish skins instead of shells.

"I was not a day too soon," he said, for he could see the baby cobras curled up inside the skin, and he knew that the minute they were hatched, they could each kill a man or a mongoose. He bit off the tops of the eggs as fast as he could, taking care to crush the young cobras, and turned over the litter from time to time to see whether he had missed any. At last there were only three eggs left, and Rikki-tikki began to chuckle to himself, when he heard Darzee's wife screaming:

410 "Rikki-tikki, I led Nagaina toward the house, and she has gone into the veranda, and—oh, come quickly—she means killing!"

Rikki-tikki smashed two eggs, and tumbled backward down the melon bed with the third egg in his mouth, and scuttled to the veranda as hard as he could put foot to the ground. Teddy and his mother and father were there at early breakfast, but Rikki-tikki saw that they were not eating anything. They sat stone still, and their faces were white. Nagaina was coiled up on the matting by Teddy's chair, within easy striking distance of

420 Teddy's bare leg, and she was swaying to and fro, singing a song of triumph.

"Son of the big man that killed Nag," she hissed, "stay still. I am not ready yet. Wait a little. Keep very still, all you three! If

---

12. **bantam's:** small chicken's.

INTERPRET

What does Nagaina mean when she says, "the boy in the house will lie very still" (line 391)? What does she plan to do to Teddy?

_____

_____

_____

_____

_____

_____

_____

_____

_____

_____

PREDICT

Why do you think Rikki takes the last egg with him to the veranda?

_____

_____

_____

_____

_____

_____

INTERPRET

Re-read Rikki's words in lines 435–436. Why do you think they make Nagaina turn around?

_____

_____

_____

_____

_____

_____

_____

_____

INTERPRET

Do you believe Nagaina when she says that she'll go away and never come back lines (457–458)? Why or why not?

_____

_____

_____

_____

_____

_____

_____

_____

_____

you move, I strike, and if you do not move, I strike. Oh, foolish people, who killed my Nag!"

Teddy's eyes were fixed on his father, and all his father could do was to whisper, "Sit still, Teddy. You mustn't move. Teddy, keep still."

Then Rikki-tikki came up and cried: "Turn round, Nagaina;
430 turn and fight!"

"All in good time," said she, without moving her eyes. "I will settle my account with *you* presently. Look at your friends, Rikki-tikki. They are still and white. They are afraid. They dare not move, and if you come a step nearer, I strike."

"Look at your eggs," said Rikki-tikki, "in the melon bed near the wall. Go and look, Nagaina!"

The big snake turned half round and saw the egg on the veranda. "Ah-h! Give it to me," she said.

Rikki-tikki put his paws one on each side of the egg, and his
440 eyes were blood-red. "What price for a snake's egg? For a young cobra? For a young king cobra? For the last—the very last of the brood? The ants are eating all the others down by the melon bed."

Nagaina spun clear round, forgetting everything for the sake of the one egg; and Rikki-tikki saw Teddy's father shoot out a big hand, catch Teddy by the shoulder, and drag him across the little table with the teacups, safe and out of reach of Nagaina.

"Tricked! Tricked! Tricked! *Rikk-tck-tck!*" chuckled Rikki-tikki. "The boy is safe, and it was I—I—I—that caught Nag by the hood last night in the bathroom." Then he began to jump
450 up and down, all four feet together, his head close to the floor. "He threw me to and fro, but he could not shake me off. He was dead before the big man blew him in two. I did it! *Rikki-tikki-tck-tck!* Come then, Nagaina. Come and fight with me. You shall not be a widow long."

Nagaina saw that she had lost her chance of killing Teddy, and the egg lay between Rikki-tikki's paws. "Give me the egg, Rikki-tikki. Give me the last of my eggs, and I will go away and never come back," she said, lowering her hood.

"Yes, you will go away, and you will never come back; for
you will go to the rubbish heap with Nag. Fight, widow! The
big man has gone for his gun! Fight!"

Rikki-tikki was bounding all round Nagaina, keeping just
out of reach of her stroke, his little eyes like hot coals. Nagaina
gathered herself together and flung out at him. Rikki-tikki
jumped up and backwards. Again and again and again she
struck, and each time her head came with a whack on the
matting of the veranda and she gathered herself together like a
watch spring. Then Rikki-tikki danced in a circle to get behind
her, and Nagaina spun round to keep her head to his head, so
that the rustle of her tail on the matting sounded like dry leaves
blown along by the wind.

He had forgotten the egg. It still lay on the veranda, and
Nagaina came nearer and nearer to it, till at last, while Rikki-tikki
was drawing breath, she caught it in her mouth, turned to the
veranda steps, and flew like an arrow down the path, with Rikki-
tikki behind her. When the cobra runs for her life, she goes like a
whiplash flicked across a horse's neck. Rikki-tikki knew that he
must catch her or all the trouble would begin again. She headed
straight for the long grass by the thorn bush, and as he was
running, Rikki-tikki heard Darzee still singing his foolish little song
of triumph. But Darzee's wife was wiser. She flew off her nest as
Nagaina came along and flapped her wings about Nagaina's head.
If Darzee had helped, they might have turned her, but Nagaina
only lowered her hood and went on. Still, the instant's delay
brought Rikki-tikki up to her, and as she plunged into the rat hole
where she and Nag used to live, his little white teeth were
clenched on her tail and he went down with her—and very few
mongooses, however wise and old they may be, care to follow a
cobra into its hole. It was dark in the hole, and Rikki-tikki never
knew when it might open out and give Nagaina room to turn and
strike at him. He held on savagely and stuck out his feet to act as
brakes on the dark slope of the hot, moist earth. Then the grass by
the mouth of the hole stopped waving, and Darzee said: "It is all
over with Rikki-tikki! We must sing his death song. Valiant Rikki-
tikki is dead! For Nagaina will surely kill him underground."

460

470

480

490

RETELL

Make a list of what happens
in lines 472–495.

PREDICT

Do you agree with Darzee
that Rikki is dead? Why or
why not?

INFER

What do you think happened to Nagaina's last egg?

_____

_____

_____

_____

_____

_____

_____

_____

_____

INFER

In the last paragraph (top of page 19) Kipling says, "Rikki had a right to be proud of himself, but he did not grow too proud." What do you think kept Rikki from becoming proud?

_____

_____

_____

_____

_____

_____

So he sang a very mournful song that he made up on the spur of the minute, and just as he got to the most touching part, the grass quivered again, and Rikki-tikki, covered with dirt, dragged himself out of the hole leg by leg, licking his 500 whiskers. Darzee stopped with a little shout. Rikki-tikki shook some of the dust out of his fur and sneezed. "It is all over," he said. "The widow will never come out again." And the red ants that live between the grass stems heard him and began to troop down one after another to see if he had spoken the truth.

Rikki-tikki curled himself up in the grass and slept where he was—slept and slept till it was late in the afternoon, for he had done a hard day's work.

"Now," he said, when he awoke, "I will go back to the house. Tell the Coppersmith, Darzee, and he will tell the garden 510 that Nagaina is dead."

The Coppersmith is a bird who makes a noise exactly like the beating of a little hammer on a copper pot; and the reason he is always making it is because he is the town crier to every Indian garden and tells all the news to everybody who cares to listen. As Rikki-tikki went up the path, he heard his "attention" notes like a tiny dinner gong and then the steady "_Ding-dong-tock!_ Nag is dead—_dong!_ Nagaina is dead! _Ding-dong-tock!_" That set all the birds in the garden singing and the frogs croaking, for Nag and Nagaina used to eat frogs as well as 520 little birds.

When Rikki got to the house, Teddy and Teddy's mother (she looked very white still, for she had been fainting) and Teddy's father came out and almost cried over him; and that night he ate all that was given him till he could eat no more and went to bed on Teddy's shoulder, where Teddy's mother saw him when she came to look late at night.

"He saved our lives and Teddy's life," she said to her husband. "Just think, he saved all our lives."

Rikki-tikki woke up with a jump, for the mongooses are 530 light sleepers.

"Oh, it's you," said he. "What are you bothering for? All the cobras are dead; and if they weren't, I'm here."

Rikki-tikki had a right to be proud of himself, but he did not grow too proud, and he kept that garden as a mongoose should keep it, with tooth and jump and spring and bite, till never a cobra dared show its head inside the walls.

Darzee's Chant

Sung in honor of Rikki-tikki-tavi

Singer and tailor am I—
540   Doubled the joys that I know—
Proud of my lilt[13] to the sky,
    Proud of the house that I sew.
Over and under, so weave I my music—
    so weave I the house that I sew.

Sing to your fledglings again,
    Mother, O lift up your head!
Evil that plagued us is slain,
    Death in the garden lies dead.
Terror that hid in the roses is impotent[14]—
550   flung on the dunghill and dead!

Who has delivered us, who?
    Tell me his nest and his name.
Rikki, the valiant, the true,
    Tikki, with eyeballs of flame—
Rikk-tikki-tikki, the ivory-fanged,
    the hunter with eyeballs of flame!

Give him the Thanks of the Birds,
    Bowing with tail feathers spread,
Praise him with nightingale words—
560   Nay, I will praise him instead.
Hear! I will sing you the praise of the bottle-
    tailed Rikki with eyeballs of red!
(*Here Rikki-tikki interrupted, so the rest of the song is lost.*)

---

13. **lilt:** light, graceful way of singing or speaking.
14. **impotent** (im′pə·tənt): powerless.

IDENTIFY
Underline the words in Darzee's chant that show he is grateful to Rikki.

INFER
Knowing Rikki's relationship with Darzee, what might Rikki have said as he interrupted him?

Conflict Diagram

Work out the major events that advance the plot of Rikki's story. Fill in the diagram below with at least four key events that lead to the exciting climax. If you like to draw, you might want to draw some little pictures to illustrate some or all of the events.

Climax/Final Conflict

_____

_____

_____

Event/Conflict _____   **Resolution**

_____   _____

_____   _____

Event/Conflict _____

_____

_____   **[Add as many events**

as you need.]

Event/Conflict
Rikki _____

_____

Event/Conflict
Rikki _____

_____

Basic Situation

Vocabulary and Comprehension

A. Match words and definitions. Write the letter of the correct definition next to each word.

_____ **1.** immensely

_____ **2.** cowered

_____ **3.** valiant

_____ **4.** gait

_____ **5.** consolation

a. comfort

b. way of walking or running

c. crouched and trembled in fear

d. enormously

e. brave and determined

Word Bank
immensely
cowered
valiant
gait
consolation

B. Choose three words from above. Use each word in a sentence.

1. _____

_____

2. _____

_____

3. _____

_____

C. Answer each question below.

1. How does Rikki-tikki-tavi come to live with the family? _____

_____

_____

2. Describe what happens when Nag and Nagaina enter the house. _____

_____

_____

3. How does Rikki-tikki-tavi save Teddy's life? _____

_____

_____

The Runaway

Make the Connection

That's Life

In "The Runaway" a colt experiences snow for the first time. All living things face new experiences from time to time. What is it like to meet a new situation? Maybe you remember when you first saw your new baby sister or moved to a new town or pitched your first game. Record your experience and your reactions to it on the chart below.

The Book of Life

A New Experience	Reactions

Background

The subject of "The Runaway" is a Morgan colt. Morgans are a breed of swift, strong horses named for Justin Morgan (1747–1798), a Vermont schoolteacher who owned the stallion that founded the line.

The Runaway

Robert Frost

BUILD FLUENCY

Read the poem aloud at least once. Listen to its sounds, and think about its sense. Be aware of punctuation, especially periods and commas. If a line doesn't end with punctuation, don't pause. Continue reading until you see some form of punctuation. Then, read the poem again and draw a line at the places you think you should pause. Some of your pauses may come in the middle of a line.

_____

_____

INTERPRET

Underline the details that show the colt is frightened.

_____

_____

INFER

Re-read lines 19–21. Explain how you think the **speaker** feels about the colt's owner.

_____

_____

_____

_____

_____

O̲nce when the snow of the year was beginning to fall,
We stopped by a mountain pasture to say, "Whose colt?"
A little Morgan had one forefoot on the wall,
The other curled at his breast. He dipped his head

5 And snorted at us. And then he had to bolt.
We heard the miniature thunder where he fled,
And we saw him, or thought we saw him, dim and gray,
Like a shadow against the curtain of falling flakes.
"I think the little fellow's afraid of the snow.

10 He isn't winter-broken. It isn't play
With the little fellow at all. He's running away.
I doubt if even his mother could tell him, 'Sakes,
It's only weather.' He'd think she didn't know!
Where is his mother? He can't be out alone."

15 And now he comes again with clatter of stone,
And mounts the wall again with whited eyes
And all his tail that isn't hair up straight.
He shudders his coat as if to throw off flies.
"Whoever it is that leaves him out so late,

20 When other creatures have gone to stall and bin,
Ought to be told to come and take him in."

Thinking About a Poem's Message

Some people think that the colt in "The Runaway" **symbolizes,** or represents, a lost child or someone who is too innocent to understand what he or she is experiencing. Do you agree with this interpretation, or do you have another one? Collect ideas to support your interpretation of the poem in the organizer below. Then, state the poem's message in a sentence or two.

The Speaker	The Colt
What the speaker does	How the colt looks
_____	_____
_____	_____
What the speaker says	_____
_____	How the colt acts
_____	_____
How the speaker feels	_____
_____	_____
_____	_____

The Poem's Message

_____

_____

A Day's Wait

Make the Connection

Fear Factor

Everyone feels fear at one time or another. Whether you've been startled by an unexpected tap on the shoulder, heard an eerie clanking sound coming from the basement, or jumped at the sight of a spider, fear can be a powerful—and memorable—emotion. Using the graphic organizer below, list several fears that you or someone you know may have experienced, and then think of advice you might give a child if he or she was feeling afraid.

Reasons Someone Might Feel Afraid	Advice I'd Give (Start your advice like this: Whenever I feel afraid I . . .)
1.	1.
2.	2.
3.	3.

Background

The events in this story really happened to Hemingway and his nine-year-old son Bumby. (In this story Bumby is called Schatz, a German word meaning "treasure.") Hemingway and his family lived in France for many years; in this story they are back in the United States.

A
Day's
Wait

Ernest Hemingway

IDENTIFY

Circle all the words in lines 1–3 that show how ill Schatz is.

_____

_____

INTERPRET

Schatz is dressed and out of bed when his father comes downstairs. What does this tell you about Schatz's **character**?

_____

_____

_____

_____

_____

_____

IDENTIFY

According to the doctor in lines 17–25, what is wrong with Schatz? Underline what the doctor says about the danger of the illness.

_____

_____

_____

_____

WORDS TO OWN

detached (dē·tacht′) *adj.*: not involved emotionally; indifferent.

He came into the room to shut the windows while we were still in bed and I saw he looked ill. He was shivering, his face was white, and he walked slowly as though it ached to move.

"What's the matter, Schatz?"

"I've got a headache."

"You better go back to bed."

"No. I'm all right."

"You go to bed. I'll see you when I'm dressed."

But when I came downstairs he was dressed, sitting by the
10 fire, looking a very sick and miserable boy of nine years. When I put my hand on his forehead I knew he had a fever.

"You go up to bed," I said, "you're sick."

"I'm all right," he said.

When the doctor came he took the boy's temperature.

"What is it?" I asked him.

"One hundred and two."

Downstairs, the doctor left three different medicines in different-colored capsules with instructions for giving them. One was to bring down the fever, another a purgative,[1] the
20 third to overcome an acid condition. The germs of influenza can only exist in an acid condition, he explained. He seemed to know all about influenza and said there was nothing to worry about if the fever did not go above one hundred and four degrees. This was a light epidemic of flu and there was no danger if you avoided pneumonia.

Back in the room I wrote the boy's temperature down and made a note of the time to give the various capsules.

"Do you want me to read to you?"

"All right. If you want to," said the boy. His face was very
30 white and there were dark areas under his eyes. He lay still in the bed and seemed very <u>detached</u> from what was going on.

I read aloud from Howard Pyle's *Book of Pirates;* but I could see he was not following what I was reading.

"How do you feel, Schatz?" I asked him.

"Just the same, so far," he said.

---

1. **purgative** (pur′gə·tiv): laxative.

I sat at the foot of the bed and read to myself while I waited for it to be time to give another capsule. It would have been natural for him to go to sleep, but when I looked up he was looking at the foot of the bed, looking very strangely.

40   "Why don't you try to go to sleep? I'll wake you up for the medicine."

"I'd rather stay awake."

After a while he said to me, "You don't have to stay in here with me, Papa, if it bothers you."

"It doesn't bother me."

"No, I mean you don't have to stay if it's going to bother you."

I thought perhaps he was a little lightheaded and after giving him the prescribed capsules at eleven o'clock I went
50 out for a while.

It was a bright, cold day, the ground covered with a sleet that had frozen so that it seemed as if all the bare trees, the bushes, the cut brush, and all the grass and the bare ground had been varnished with ice. I took the young Irish setter for a little walk up the road and along a frozen creek, but it was difficult to stand or walk on the glassy surface and the red dog slipped and slithered and I fell twice, hard, once dropping my gun and having it slide away over the ice.

We flushed a covey of quail[2] under a high clay bank with
60 overhanging brush and I killed two as they went out of sight over the top of the bank. Some of the covey lit in trees, but most of them scattered into brush piles and it was necessary to jump on the ice-coated mounds of brush several times before they would flush. Coming out while you were <u>poised</u> unsteadily on the icy, springy brush, they made difficult shooting and I killed two, missed five, and started back pleased to have found a covey close to the house and happy there were so many left to find on another day.

At the house they said the boy had refused to let anyone
70 come into the room.

---

2. **flushed a covey** (kuv′ē) **of quail:** frightened a small group of wild birds called quail from their hiding place.

INTERPRET
Underline the things that Schatz does in lines 29–50 that seem out of the ordinary to his father.

_____

_____

INFER
Pause at line 50. What do you suppose Schatz thinks is going to happen to him?

_____

_____

_____

_____

INTERPRET
What do the father's outdoor activities reveal about his **character**?

_____

_____

_____

_____

_____

WORDS TO OWN
poised (poizd) v.: balanced.

INTERPRET

In lines 95–105 you learn what's been troubling Schatz. How does this help to explain his behavior throughout the story? Now that you know what he's been thinking, what words would you use to describe his **character**?

WORDS TO OWN
commenced (kə·menst´) v.: began.

"You can't come in," he said. "You mustn't get what I have."

I went up to him and found him in exactly the position I had left him, white-faced, but with the tops of his cheeks flushed by the fever, staring still, as he had stared, at the foot of the bed.

I took his temperature.

"What is it?"

"Something like a hundred," I said. It was one hundred and
80   two and four tenths.

"It was a hundred and two," he said.

"Who said so?"

"The doctor."

"Your temperature is all right," I said. "It's nothing to worry about."

"I don't worry," he said, "but I can't keep from thinking."

"Don't think," I said. "Just take it easy."

"I'm taking it easy," he said and looked straight ahead. He was evidently holding tight onto himself about something.

90   "Take this with water."

"Do you think it will do any good?"

"Of course it will."

I sat down and opened the Pirate book and <u>commenced</u> to read, but I could see he was not following, so I stopped.

"About what time do you think I'm going to die?" he asked.

"What?"

"About how long will it be before I die?"

"You aren't going to die. What's the matter with you?"

"Oh, yes, I am. I heard him say a hundred and two."

100   "People don't die with a fever of one hundred and two. That's a silly way to talk."

"I know they do. At school in France the boys told me you can't live with forty-four degrees. I've got a hundred and two."

He had been waiting to die all day, ever since nine o'clock in the morning.

"You poor Schatz," I said. "Poor old Schatz. It's like miles and kilometers. You aren't going to die. That's a different thermometer. On that thermometer thirty-seven is normal. On this kind it's ninety-eight."

110 "Are you sure?"

"Absolutely," I said. "It's like miles and kilometers. You know, like how many kilometers we make when we do seventy miles in the car?"

"Oh," he said.

But his gaze at the foot of the bed relaxed slowly. The hold over himself relaxed too, finally, and the next day it was very slack and he cried very easily at little things that were of no importance.

IDENTIFY

Lines 106–109 offer an explanation for Schatz's fear. How has the misunderstanding been corrected?

_____

_____

_____

INTERPRET

Why do you suppose Schatz cries about things that according to his father weren't very important? How well do you think Schatz's father understands him?

_____

_____

_____

_____

_____

_____

_____

_____

_____

WORDS TO OWN
slack *adj.:* loose.

Character Questionnaire

You analyze a character by examining the character's actions, speech, appearance, thoughts, and effects on other people. When you analyze a character, you almost always also want to evaluate how realistic or believable the character is. You ask: Is this character like a person I might know in real life?

   Answering the questions in this Character-Analysis Questionnaire will help you analyze the character of Schatz.

Character: Schatz

1. What does Schatz do in the story?

2. What are Schatz's thoughts and feelings?

3. How do other characters respond to Schatz?

4. Is Schatz like people you know? Explain.

My Analysis of Schatz

_____

_____

_____

_____

Vocabulary and Comprehension

A. Match each word to own with its definition. Write the letter of the correct definition next to each word.

_____ **1.** detached   **a.** loose

_____ **2.** poised   **b.** indifferent

_____ **3.** commenced   **c.** began

_____ **4.** slack   **d.** balanced

Word Bank
detached
poised
commenced
slack

B. Choose three words from above. Use each word in a sentence.

1. _____

_____

2. _____

_____

3. _____

_____

C. Answer each question below.

1. Who is telling the story?

_____

_____

2. Why does Schatz refuse to let visitors into his room?

_____

_____

3. What does Schatz learn at the end of the story?

_____

_____

Fish Cheeks

Make the Connection

"Stunned into Silence"

What makes someone feel embarrassed? Perhaps it's a bad hair day or having to wear that strange-looking shirt that was a gift from a relative. Think of an embarrassing situation that might make someone want to run and hide. In the middle of the circle below, tell what the embarrassing situation is. Then, inside the burning rays coming out of the circle, write words and phrases that describe how someone might feel about the situation.

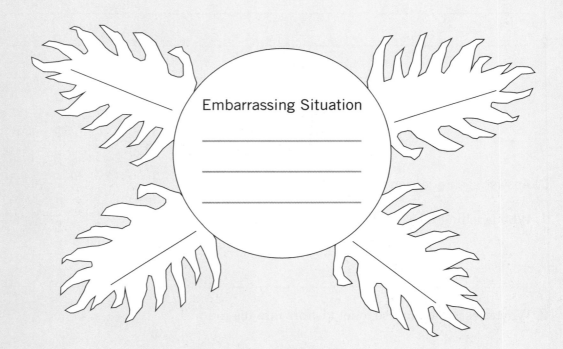

Embarrassing Situation

_____

_____

_____

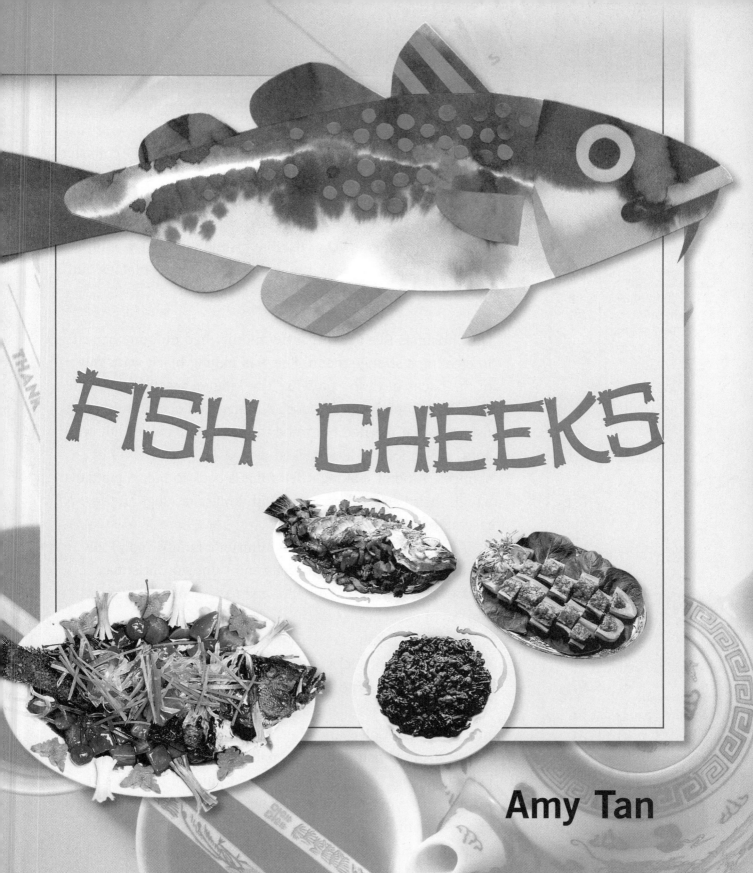

FISH CHEEKS

Amy Tan

IDENTIFY

Re-read lines 5–11.
Underline the phrases that
tell why Amy cries when
she finds out her parents
have invited the minister's
family to Christmas Eve
dinner.

EVALUATE

Do you think Amy is right
to feel so embarrassed?
Why or why not?

_____

_____

_____

_____

_____

_____

IDENTIFY

In lines 25–39, place the
letter "A" over the actions
of Amy's family at the
dinner table, and Amy's
reactions to what happens.
Place the letter "R" over
the actions and reactions
of Robert and his family.

WORDS TO OWN
appalling (ə·pôl′iŋ) *adj.:*
shocking.
wedges (wej′iz) *n.:* pieces
of material, tapering from
thick to thin.
clamor (klam′ər) *n.:* loud,
confused noise.
rumpled (rum′pəld) *v. used
as adj.:* wrinkled, not neat.

I fell in love with the minister's son the winter I turned fourteen. He was not Chinese, but as white as Mary in the manger. For Christmas I prayed for this blond-haired boy, Robert, and a slim new American nose.

When I found out that my parents had invited the minister's family over for Christmas Eve dinner, I cried. What would Robert think of our shabby *Chinese* Christmas? What would he think of our noisy *Chinese* relatives who lacked proper American manners? What terrible disappointment would he 10 feel upon seeing not a roasted turkey and sweet potatoes but *Chinese* food?

On Christmas Eve I saw that my mother had outdone herself in creating a strange menu. She was pulling black veins out of the backs of fleshy prawns. The kitchen was littered with appalling mounds of raw food: A slimy rock cod with bulging fish eyes that pleaded not to be thrown into a pan of hot oil. Tofu, which looked like stacked wedges of rubbery white sponges. A bowl soaking dried fungus back to life. A plate of squid, their backs crisscrossed with knife markings so they 20 resembled bicycle tires.

And then they arrived—the minister's family and all my relatives in a clamor of doorbells and rumpled Christmas packages. Robert grunted hello, and I pretended he was not worthy of existence.

Dinner threw me deeper into despair. My relatives licked the ends of their chopsticks and reached across the table, dipping them into the dozen or so plates of food. Robert and his family waited patiently for platters to be passed to them. My relatives murmured with pleasure when my mother brought out the 30 whole steamed fish. Robert grimaced. Then my father poked his chopsticks just below the fish eye and plucked out the soft meat. "Amy, your favorite," he said, offering me the tender fish cheek. I wanted to disappear.

At the end of the meal my father leaned back and belched loudly, thanking my mother for her fine cooking. "It's a polite

Chinese custom to show you are satisfied," explained my father to our astonished guests. Robert was looking down at his plate with a reddened face. The minister managed to <u>muster</u> up a quiet burp. I was stunned into silence for the rest of the night.

40   After everyone had gone, my mother said to me, "You want to be the same as American girls on the outside." She handed me an early gift. It was a miniskirt in beige tweed. "But inside you must always be Chinese. You must be proud you are different. Your only shame is to have shame."

And even though I didn't agree with her then, I knew that she understood how much I had suffered during the evening's dinner. It wasn't until many years later—long after I had gotten over my crush on Robert—that I was able to fully appreciate her lesson and the true purpose behind our particular menu. For

50 Christmas Eve that year, she had chosen all my favorite foods.

INTERPRET

How do you think Amy feels about the gift of the miniskirt? What does the gift show about Amy's mother?

_____

_____

_____

INTERPRET

Re-read lines 40–50. Why had Amy's mother chosen the strange food items on the menu for that Christmas Eve dinner? Why do you think it takes many years for Amy to fully appreciate her mother's lesson?

_____

_____

_____

_____

_____

_____

_____

_____

_____

WORDS TO OWN
muster (mus′tər) v.: call forth.

Events Chart

In the essay "Fish Cheeks," the topic is a Christmas dinner. The events in this essay are told in **chronological order,** the order in which they happened. As with all essays, this one is told to make a point.

The narrator's mother invites Robert's family for Christmas dinner.

⬇

Event

⬇

Event

⬇

Event

⬇

Event

⬇

Event

⬇

Event

⬇

What is the writer's point?

Vocabulary and Comprehension

A. Complete each sentence with a word from the Word Bank.

Word Bank
rumpled
muster
clamor
appalling
wedges

1. I quickly ironed out the wrinkles in the
   _____ tablecloth.

2. My young cousins made a noisy
   _____ as they sat down to eat.

3. Robin thought that the squid looked too horrible and
   _____ to eat.

4. My uncle was able to _____ the courage to eat a small bite.

5. Instead of apple pie, my mother served _____ of tofu
   cheesecake for dessert.

B. Finish each sentence with a description that fits the underlined word.

1. If you are *appalled,* you are shocked and upset. An <u>appalling</u> amount of

   food would look _____

   _____

2. *Clamor* means "loud and confused." A <u>clamorous</u> crowd would sound

   _____

   _____

C. Answer each question below.

1. Why does Amy cry when she finds out the minister's family is coming

   over for Christmas?_____

   _____

2. How has Amy's view of the Christmas dinner changed over time?

   _____

   _____

Names/Nombres

Make the Connection

"Hello, My Name Is..."

Names and nicknames help identify people. They give strangers a window into someone's personality and allow family and friends a way to show affection. Ethnic names tell about heritage. A name passed down from another generation says something about a person's family. Use the graphic organizer below to explain what your name or nickname says about you. Tell how you got the name and how you feel about it. Would you like to have a different name? What would it be?

Hello, My Name Is

_____

Names/Nombres

Julie Alvarez

When we arrived in New York City, our names changed almost immediately. At Immigration, the officer asked my father, *Mister Elbures*, if he had anything to declare. My father shook his head no, and we were waved through. I was too afraid we wouldn't be let in if I corrected the man's pronunciation, but I said our name to myself, opening my mouth wide for the organ blast of the *a*, trilling my tongue for the drumroll of the *r, All-vah-rrr-es!* How could anyone get *Elbures* out of that orchestra of sound?

10   At the hotel my mother was Missus Alburest, and I was *little girl*, as in, "Hey, little girl, stop riding the elevator up and down. It's *not* a toy."

When we moved into our new apartment building, the super called my father *Mister Alberase*, and the neighbors who became mother's friends pronounced her name *Jew-lee-ah* instead of *Hoo-lee-ah*. I, her namesake, was known as *Hoo-lee-tah* at home. But at school I was *Judy* or *Judith*, and once an English teacher mistook me for *Juliet*.

It took a while to get used to my new names. I wondered
20   if I shouldn't correct my teachers and new friends. But my mother argued that it didn't matter. "You know what your friend Shakespeare said, *'A rose by any other name would smell as sweet.'*"[1] My family had gotten into the habit of calling any famous author "my friend" because I had begun to write poems and stories in English class.

By the time I was in high school, I was a popular kid, and it showed in my name. Friends called me *Jules* or *Hey Jude*, and once a group of troublemaking friends my mother forbade me to hang out with called me *Alcatraz*. I was *Hoo-lee-tah* only to
30   Mami and Papi and uncles and aunts who came over to eat sancocho[2] on Sunday afternoons—old world folk whom I would just as soon go back to where they came from and leave me to pursue whatever mischief I wanted to in America. *JUDY ALCATRAZ*, the name on the "Wanted" poster would read. Who would ever trace her to me?

---

1. *"A rose . . . as sweet":* Julia's mother is quoting from the play *Romeo and Juliet*.
2. **sancocho** (sän·kō′chō): stew of meats and fruit.

My older sister had the hardest time getting an American name for herself because *Mauricia* did not translate into English. Ironically, although she had the most foreign-sounding name, she and I were the Americans in the family. We had
40 been born in New York City when our parents had first tried immigration and then gone back "home," too homesick to stay. My mother often told the story of how she had almost changed my sister's name in the hospital.

After the delivery, Mami and some other new mothers were cooing over their new baby sons and daughters and exchanging names and weights and delivery stories. My mother was embarrassed among the Sallys and Janes and Georges and Johns to reveal the rich, noisy name of *Mauricia*, so when her turn came to brag, she gave her baby's name as *Maureen*.
50   "Why'd ya give her an Irish name with so many pretty Spanish names to choose from?" one of the women asked.

My mother blushed and admitted her baby's real name to the group. Her mother-in-law had recently died, she apologized, and her husband had insisted that the first daughter be named after his mother, *Mauran*. My mother thought it the ugliest name she had ever heard, and she talked my father into what she believed was an improvement, a combination of *Mauran* and her own mother's name, *Felicia*.

"Her name is M*ao-ree-shee-ah*," my mother said to the group
60 of women.

"Why, that's a beautiful name," the new mothers cried. "*Moor-ee-sha, Moor-ee-sha,*" they cooed into the pink blanket. *Moor-ee-sha* it was when we returned to the States eleven years later. Sometimes, American tongues found even that mispronunciation tough to say and called her *Maria* or *Marsha* or *Maudy* from her nickname *Maury*. I pitied her. What an awful name to have to transport across borders!

My little sister, Ana, had the easiest time of all. She was plain *Anne*—that is, only her name was plain, for she turned
70 out to be the pale, blond "American beauty" in the family. The only Hispanic thing about her was the affectionate nicknames her boyfriends sometimes gave her. *Anita*, or, as one goofy guy

INFER

How is Julia's sister Ana different from the others in the family? List two ways.

_____

_____

_____

_____

IDENTIFY

Julia says that, at first, she wanted to be known by her correct Dominican name. Underline the details that tell why she changed her mind (lines 83–90).

_____

_____

_____

INTERPRET

Why do you think Julia deliberately misspells *Puerto Rico* (line 97)? What details show that her classmates don't know much geography?

_____

_____

_____

_____

_____

used to sing to her to the tune of the banana advertisement, *Anita Banana.*

Later, during her college years in the late sixties, there was a push to pronounce Third World[3] names correctly. I remember calling her long distance at her group house and a roommate answering.

"Can I speak to Ana?" I asked, pronouncing her name the 80 American way.

"Ana?" The man's voice hesitated. "Oh! You must mean *Ah-nah*!"

Our first few years in the States, though, ethnicity was not yet "in." Those were the blond, blue-eyed, bobby-sock years of junior high and high school before the sixties ushered in peasant blouses, hoop earrings, serapes.[4] My initial desire to be known by my correct Dominican name faded. I just wanted to be Judy and merge with the Sallys and Janes in my class. But, inevitably, my accent and coloring gave me away. "So 90 where are you from, Judy?"

"New York," I told my classmates. After all, I had been born blocks away at Columbia-Presbyterian Hospital.

"I mean, *originally.*"

"From the Caribbean," I answered vaguely, for if I specified, no one was quite sure on what continent our island was located.

"Really? I've been to Bermuda. We went last April for spring vacation. I got the worst sunburn! So, are you from Portoriko?"

"No," I sighed. "From the Dominican Republic."

"Where's that?"

100 "South of Bermuda."

They were just being curious, I knew, but I burned with shame whenever they singled me out as a "foreigner," a rare, exotic friend.

"Say your name in Spanish, oh, please say it!" I had made mouths drop one day by rattling off my full name, which,

---

3. **Third World:** the developing countries of Latin America, Africa, and Asia.
4. **serapes** (sə·rä′pēz): brightly colored woolen shawls worn in Latin American countries.

according to Dominican custom, included my middle names, Mother's and Father's surnames for four generations back.

110 "Julia Altagracia María Teresa Álvarez Tavares Perello Espaillat Julia Pérez Rochet González." I pronounced it slowly, a name as chaotic with sounds as a Middle Eastern bazaar or market day in a South American village.

My Dominican heritage was never more apparent than when my extended family attended school occasions. For my graduation, they all came, the whole lot of aunts and uncles and the many little cousins who snuck in without tickets. They sat in the first row in order to better understand the Americans' fast-spoken English. But how could they listen when they were constantly speaking among themselves in florid-sounding[5]

120 phrases, rococo[6] consonants, rich, rhyming vowels?

Introducing them to my friends was a further trial to me. These relatives had such complicated names and there were so many of them, and their relationships to myself were so convoluted. There was my Tía[7] Josefina, who was not really an aunt but a much older cousin. And her daughter, Aida Margarita, who was adopted, una hija de crianza.[8] My uncle of affection, Tío José, brought my madrina[9] Tía Amelia and her comadre[10] Tía Pilar. My friends rarely had more than a "Mom and Dad" to introduce.

130 After the commencement ceremony, my family waited outside in the parking lot while my friends and I signed yearbooks with nicknames which recalled our high school good times: "Beans" and "Pepperoni" and "Alcatraz." We hugged and cried and promised to keep in touch.

Our goodbyes went on too long. I heard my father's voice calling out across the parking lot, *"Hoo-lee-tah! Vámonos!"*[11]

---

5. **florid-sounding:** flowery; using fancy words.
6. **rococo** (rǝ·kō′kō): fancy. Rococo is a style of art and architecture of the early eighteenth century known for its fancy ornamentation.
7. **Tía** (tē′ä): Spanish for "Aunt." **Tío** is "Uncle."
8. **una hija de crianza** (oo͞′nä ē′hä dä krē·än′sä): Spanish for "an adopted daughter." *Crianza* means "upbringing."
9. **madrina** (mä·drē′nä): Spanish for "godmother."
10. **comadre** (kô·mä′drä): Spanish for "close friend" (informal). *Comadre* is the name used by the mother and the godmother of a child for each other.
11. **Vámonos!** (vä′mô·nôs): Spanish for "Let's go!"

IDENTIFY

Re-read lines 109–112. Underline the **similes** that Julia uses to describe her full Dominican name. (Remember that a **simile** is a comparison between two unlike things using words such as *like* or *as*.)

INFER

How is Julia's family different from the families of her friends? How does she feel about the relatives who come to her graduation (lines 113–129)?

INFER

Do you think Julia's parents are happy that she might become a writer? Underline the detail that backs up your answer.

_____

_____

EVALUATE

How accurate was the family's prediction? Tell why you think the last sentence is or is not a good way for Julia to end "Names/Nombres." As an adult, what name did she decide to go by?

_____

_____

_____

_____

_____

_____

_____

_____

_____

_____

_____

_____

_____

Back home, my tíos and tías and primas,[12] Mami and Papi, and mis hermanas[13] had a party for me with sancocho and a store-bought pudín,[14] inscribed with *Happy Graduation, Julie.* 140 There were many gifts—that was a plus to a large family! I got several wallets and a suitcase with my initials and a graduation charm from my godmother and money from my uncles. The biggest gift was a portable typewriter from my parents for writing my stories and poems.

Someday, the family predicted, my name would be well-known throughout the United States. I laughed to myself, wondering which one I would go by.

12. **primas** (prē′mäs): Spanish for "female cousins."
13. **mis hermanas** (mēs är·mä′näs): Spanish for "my sisters."
14. **pudín** (poo·dēn′): Spanish cake.

Main Idea and Details Map

Fill in the following map with details from "Names/Nombres." Then, review those details and identify the main idea.

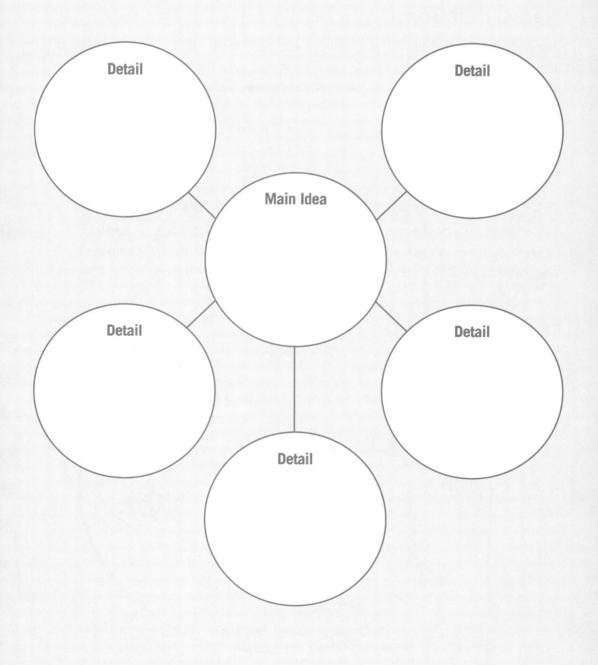

The Naming of Names

Make the Connection

Name that Town

Imagine that you travel with your family and several hundred other colonists to a faraway planet made up of islands. The rocket sets the colonists down on one of the islands. At the first all-island meeting, each family is asked to come up with names for

- the islands
- the ocean
- the town
- the river
- the mountain range

What would you say at this meeting? You might want to name the islands after stars since you've traveled through outer space to get there. You could name the town after something that was important to you back on earth. Or you could name each place after your favorite science fiction characters. What names would you suggest? Write them on the map below.

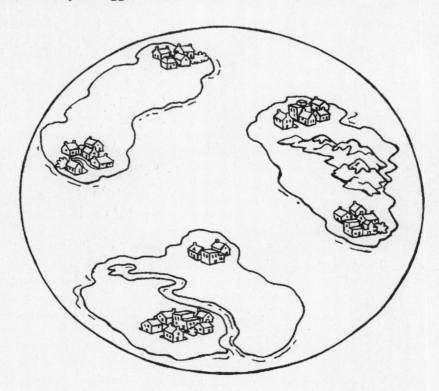

The Naming of Names

Ray Bradbury

IDENTIFY

Where in the world does this story take place? In lines 1–9, underline the words that tell you the **setting**.

_____

_____

_____

_____

_____

_____

VISUALIZE

Re-read lines 16–32. List at least three details that help you picture the setting.

_____

_____

_____

_____

_____

_____

_____

_____

WORDS TO OWN

interior (in·tir′ē·ər) *n.*: inside.
submerged (səb·murjd′) *v.* used as *adj.*: sunk.

The rocket metal cooled in the meadow winds. Its lid gave a bulging *pop*. From its clock interior stepped a man, a woman, and three children. The other passengers whispered away across the Martian meadow, leaving the man alone among his family.

The man felt his hair flutter and the tissues of his body draw tight as if he were standing at the center of a vacuum.[1] His wife, before him, seemed almost to whirl away in smoke. The children, small seeds, might at any instant be sown to all the Martian climes.[2]

The children looked up at him, as people look to the sun to tell what time of their life it is. His face was cold.

"What's wrong?" asked his wife.

"Let's get back on the rocket."

"Go back to Earth?"

"Yes! Listen!"

The wind blew as if to flake away their identities. At any moment the Martian air might draw his soul from him, as marrow comes from a white bone. He felt submerged in a chemical that could dissolve his intellect and burn away his past.

They looked at Martian hills that time had worn with a crushing pressure of years. They saw the old cities, lost in their meadows, lying like children's delicate bones among the blowing lakes of grass.

"Chin up, Harry," said his wife. "It's too late. We've come over sixty million miles."

The children with their yellow hair hollered at the deep dome of Martian sky. There was no answer but the racing hiss of wind through the stiff grass.

He picked up the luggage in his cold hands. "Here we go," he said—a man standing on the edge of a sea, ready to wade in and be drowned.

They walked into town.

Their name was Bittering. Harry and his wife, Cora; Dan, Laura, and David. They built a small white cottage and ate good breakfasts there, but the fear was never gone. It lay with

---

1. **vacuum:** closed space with the air sucked out.
2. **climes:** regions.

Mr. Bittering and Mrs. Bittering, a third, unbidden partner at every midnight talk, at every dawn awakening.

"I feel like a salt crystal," he said, "in a mountain stream, being washed away. We don't belong here. We're Earth people. This is Mars. It was meant for Martians. For heaven's sake, Cora, let's buy tickets for home!"

But she only shook her head. "One day the atom bomb will fix Earth. Then we'll be safe here."

"Safe and insane!"

Tick-tock, seven o'clock, sang the voice-clock; *time to get up.* And they did.

Something made him check everything each morning—warm hearth, potted blood-geraniums—precisely as if he expected something to be amiss. The morning paper was toast-warm from the 6:00 A.M. Earth rocket. He broke its seal and tilted it at his breakfast place. He forced himself to be convivial.

"Colonial days all over again," he declared. "Why, in ten years there'll be a million Earthmen on Mars. Big cities, everything! They said we'd fail. Said the Martians would resent our invasion. But did we find any Martians? Not a living soul! Oh, we found their empty cities, but no one in them. Right?"

A river of wind submerged the house. When the windows ceased rattling, Mr. Bittering swallowed and looked at the children.

"I don't know," said David. "Maybe there're Martians around we don't see. Sometimes nights I think I hear 'em. I hear the wind. The sand hits my window. I get scared. And I see those towns way up in the mountains where the Martians lived a long time ago. And I think I see things moving around those towns, Papa. And I wonder if those Martians *mind* us living here. I wonder if they won't do something to us for coming here."

"Nonsense!" Mr. Bittering looked out the windows. "We're clean, decent people." He looked at his children. "All dead cities have some kind of ghosts in them. Memories, I mean." He stared at the hills. "You see a staircase and you wonder what Martians looked like climbing it. You see Martian paintings and you wonder what the painter was like. You make a little ghost

PREDICT

Pause at line 44. Mr. and Mrs. Bittering have different ideas about what's going to happen to them on Mars. What's your prediction? How safe do you think the Bittering family will be on Mars?

reference to atom bombs © 1949

IDENTIFY

Re-read lines 47–66. Circle the details that make the Bitterings feel that everything is going to be OK on Mars. Underline the details that make them worry that something might go wrong.

WORDS TO OWN
amiss (ə·mis′) *adj.:* wrong.
convivial (kən·viv′ē·əl) *adj.:* sociable.
ceased (sēst) *v.:* stopped.

IDENTIFY

Underline the words that tell about an event on Earth that will have a big effect on the Bitterings' lives.

_____

_____

_____

_____

INFER

Re-read lines 89–102. Write down three words that describe Bittering's **character,** as revealed in these lines.

_____

_____

_____

_____

_____

_____

_____

_____

IDENTIFY

In the past, what thought allowed Bittering to cope with his life on Mars? Underline the sentence.

in your mind, a memory. It's quite natural. Imagination." He stopped. "You haven't been prowling up in those ruins, have you?"

"No, Papa." David looked at his shoes.

"See that you stay away from them. Pass the jam."

"Just the same," said little David, "I bet something happens."

Something happened that afternoon. Laura stumbled through the settlement, crying. She dashed blindly onto the porch.

80   "Mother, Father—the war, Earth!" she sobbed. "A radio flash just came. Atom bombs hit New York! All the space rockets blown up. No more rockets to Mars, ever!"

"Oh, Harry!" The mother held on to her husband and daughter.

"Are you sure, Laura?" asked the father quietly.

Laura wept. "We're stranded on Mars, forever and ever!"

For a long time there was only the sound of the wind in the late afternoon.

Alone, thought Bittering. _Only a thousand of us here. No_
90 _way back. No way. No way._ Sweat poured from his face and his hands and his body; he was drenched in the hotness of his fear. He wanted to strike Laura, cry, "No, you're lying! The rockets will come back!" Instead, he stroked Laura's head against him and said, "The rockets will get through someday."

"Father, what will we do?"

"Go about our business, of course. Raise crops and children. Wait. Keep things going until the war ends and the rockets come again."

The two boys stepped out onto the porch.

100   "Children," he said, sitting there, looking beyond them, "I've something to tell you."

"We know," they said.

In the following days, Bittering wandered often through the garden to stand alone in his fear. As long as the rockets had spun a silver web across space, he had been able to accept Mars. For he had always told himself: _Tomorrow, if I want, I can buy a ticket and go back to Earth._

But now: the web gone, the rockets lying in jigsaw heaps of molten girder[3] and unsnaked wire. Earth people left to the strangeness of Mars, the cinnamon dusts and wine airs, to be baked like gingerbread shapes in Martian summers, put into harvested storage by Martian winters. What would happen to him, the others? This was the moment Mars had waited for. Now it would eat them.

He got down on his knees in the flower bed, a spade in his nervous hands. *Work,* he thought, *work and forget.*

He glanced up from the garden to the Martian mountains. He thought of the proud old Martian names that had once been on those peaks. Earthmen, dropping from the sky, had gazed upon hills, rivers, Martian seas left nameless in spite of names. Once Martians had built cities, named cities; climbed mountains, named mountains; sailed seas, named seas. Mountains melted, seas drained, cities tumbled. In spite of this, the Earthmen had felt a silent guilt at putting new names to these ancient hills and valleys.

Nevertheless, man lives by symbol and label. The names were given.

Mr. Bittering felt very alone in his garden under the Martian sun, an anachronism bent here, planting Earth flowers in a wild soil.

Think. Keep thinking. Different things. Keep your mind free of Earth, the atom war, the lost rockets.

He perspired. He glanced about. No one watching. He removed his tie. *Pretty bold,* he thought. *First your coat off, now your tie.* He hung it neatly on a peach tree he had imported as a sapling from Massachusetts.

He returned to his philosophy of names and mountains. The Earthmen had changed names. Now there were Hormel Valleys, Roosevelt Seas, Ford Hills, Vanderbilt Plateaus, Rockefeller Rivers, on Mars. It wasn't right. The American settlers had shown wisdom, using old Indian prairie names: Wisconsin,

---

3. **molten girder:** A girder is a metal beam that helps to support a framework; *molten* means "melted."

IDENTIFY

Notice how Bradbury uses **figurative language,** comparisons that describe one thing in terms of something else. A **simile** compares two unlike things, using *like* or *as.* A **metaphor** says that one thing is another. It does not use *like* or *as.* Circle the only simile in lines 108–114. Then, choose the metaphor in this paragraph that you like best. Write it on the lines below.

_____

_____

_____

_____

_____

_____

_____

_____

_____

_____

_____

_____

WORDS TO OWN
anachronism
(ə·nak′rə·niz′əm) *n.:* something out of its proper time in history.

INTERPRET

Re-read lines 137–143. What does Bittering mean when he says "It wasn't right"? What kinds of names does he think Martian places should have?

INTERPRET

What do you think is happening to the peach blossoms and vegetables?

Minnesota, Idaho, Ohio, Utah, Milwaukee, Waukegan, Osseo. The old names, the old meanings.

Staring at the mountains wildly, he thought: *Are you up there? All the dead ones, you Martians? Well, here we are, alone, cut off! Come down, move us out! We're helpless!*

The wind blew a shower of peach blossoms.

He put out his sun-browned hand, gave a small cry. He touched the blossoms, picked them up. He turned them, he
150 touched them again and again. Then he shouted for his wife.

"Cora!"

She appeared at a window. He ran to her.

"Cora, these blossoms!"

She handled them.

"Do you see? They're different. They've changed! They're not peach blossoms any more!"

"Look all right to me," she said.

"They're not. They're *wrong*! I can't tell how. An extra petal, a leaf, something, the color, the smell!"
160 The children ran out in time to see their father hurrying about the garden, pulling up radishes, onions, and carrots from their beds.

"Cora, come look!"

They handled the onions, the radishes, the carrots among them.

"Do they look like carrots?"

"Yes . . . no." She hesitated. "I don't know."

"They're changed."

"Perhaps."
170 "You know they have! Onions but not onions, carrots but not carrots. Taste: the same but different. Smell: not like it used to be." He felt his heart pounding, and he was afraid. He dug his fingers into the earth. "Cora, what's happening? What is it? We've got to get away from this." He ran across the garden. Each tree felt his touch. "The roses. The roses. They're turning green!"

And they stood looking at the green roses.

And two days later Dan came running. "Come see the cow. I was milking her and I saw it. Come on!"

They stood in the shed and looked at their one cow.

180   It was growing a third horn.

And the lawn in front of their house very quietly and slowly was coloring itself like spring violets. Seed from Earth but growing up a soft purple.

"We must get away," said Bittering. "We'll eat this stuff and then we'll change—who knows to what? I can't let it happen. There's only one thing to do. Burn this food!"

"It's not poisoned."

"But it is. Subtly, very subtly. A little bit. A very little bit. We mustn't touch it."

190   He looked with dismay at their house. "Even the house. The wind's done something to it. The air's burned it. The fog at night. The boards, all warped out of shape. It's not an Earthman's house anymore."

"Oh, your imagination!"

He put on his coat and tie. "I'm going into town. We've got to do something now. I'll be back."

"Wait, Harry!" his wife cried.

But he was gone.

In town, on the shadowy step of the grocery store, the men sat
200   with their hands on their knees, conversing with great leisure and ease.

Mr. Bittering wanted to fire a pistol in the air.

What are you doing, you fools! he thought. *Sitting here! You've heard the news—we're stranded on this planet. Well, move! Aren't you frightened? Aren't you afraid? What are you going to do?*

"Hello, Harry," said everyone.

"Look," he said to them. "You did hear the news, the other day, didn't you?"

210   They nodded and laughed. "Sure. Sure, Harry."

"What are you going to do about it?"

"Do, Harry, do? What *can* we do?"

"Build a rocket, that's what!"

"A rocket, Harry? To go back to all that trouble? Oh, Harry!"

BUILD FLUENCY

Re-read the boxed passage aloud. When you read the words of the different characters, try to express how each one feels. What tone of voice will you choose for the narrator? Describe that tone on the lines below.

_____

_____

_____

INTERPRET

Re-read lines 184–198. How is Mars affecting the settlers and the things they brought from Earth?

_____

_____

_____

_____

_____

_____

_____

_____

_____

_____

_____

INFER

What **inference** can you make about how Bittering is different from the other men?

_____

_____

_____

_____

IDENTIFY

Underline the words in lines 222–225 that tell what Bittering seems to fear most.

_____

_____

_____

_____

_____

_____

IDENTIFY

What two changes does Bittering notice in how Sam looks?

_____

_____

_____

_____

_____

_____

"But you *must* want to go back. Have you noticed the peach blossoms, the onions, the grass?"

"Why, yes, Harry, seems we did," said one of the men.

"Doesn't it scare you?"

"Can't recall that it did much, Harry."

220 "Idiots!"

"Now, Harry."

Bittering wanted to cry. "You've got to work with me. If we stay here, we'll all change. The air. Don't you smell it? Something in the air. A Martian virus, maybe; some seed, or a pollen. Listen to me!"

They stared at him.

"Sam," he said to one of them.

"Yes, Harry?"

"Will you help me build a rocket?"

230 "Harry, I got a whole load of metal and some blueprints. You want to work in my metal shop on a rocket, you're welcome. I'll sell you that metal for five hundred dollars. You should be able to construct a right pretty rocket, if you work alone, in about thirty years."

Everyone laughed.

"Don't laugh."

Sam looked at him with quiet good humor.

"Sam," Bittering said. "Your eyes—"

"What about them, Harry?"

240 "Didn't they used to be gray?"

"Well, now, I don't remember."

"They were, weren't they?"

"Why do you ask, Harry?"

"Because now they're kind of yellow-colored."

"Is that so, Harry?" Sam said, casually.

"And you're taller and thinner—"

"You might be right, Harry."

"Sam, you shouldn't have yellow eyes."

"Harry, what color eyes have *you* got?" Sam said.

250 "My eyes? They're blue, of course."

INFER

Why does Bittering break the mirror? What does that action tell you about his mental state?

"Here you are, Harry." Sam handed him a pocket mirror. "Take a look at yourself."

Mr. Bittering hesitated and then raised the mirror to his face.

There were little, very dim flecks of new gold captured in the blue of his eyes.

"Now look what you've done," said Sam a moment later. "You've broken my mirror."

Harry Bittering moved into the metal shop and began to build the rocket. Men stood in the open door and talked and joked
260 without raising their voices. Once in a while they gave him a hand on lifting something. But mostly they just idled and watched him with their yellowing eyes.

"It's supper time, Harry," they said.

His wife appeared with his supper in a wicker basket.

"I won't touch it," he said. "I'll eat only food from our deep freezer. Food that came from Earth. Nothing from our garden."

His wife stood watching him. "You can't build a rocket."

"I worked in a shop once, when I was twenty. I know metal. Once I get it started, the others will help," he said, not looking
270 at her, laying out the blueprints.

"Harry, Harry," she said, helplessly.

"We've got to get away, Cora. We've *got* to!"

PREDICT

Do you think Bittering will succeed in building a rocket? Will the other men help him? What do you think is going to happen to the Bittering family?

The nights were full of wind that blew down the empty moon-lit sea meadows past the little white chess cities lying for their twelve-thousandth year in the shallows. In the Earthmen's settlement, the Bittering house shook with a feeling of change.

Lying abed, Mr. Bittering felt his bones shifted, shaped, melted like gold. His wife, lying beside him, was dark from many sunny afternoons. Dark she was, and golden-eyed, burnt
280 almost black by the sun, sleeping, and the children metallic in their beds, and the wind roaring forlorn and changing through the old peach trees, the violet grass, shaking out green rose petals.

The fear would not be stopped. It had his throat and heart. It dripped in a wetness of the arm and the temple and the trembling palm.

WORDS TO OWN
forlorn (fôr·lôrn') *adj:* hopeless.

INFER

Underline the strange word that Bittering speaks. What's your guess about what's happening to him?

_____

_____

_____

_____

RETELL

Pause at line 309. **Retell** what's happened to the humans on Mars since the rockets stopped coming from Earth.

_____

_____

_____

_____

_____

_____

_____

_____

_____

_____

_____

_____

_____

_____

A green star rose in the east.

A strange word emerged from Mr. Bittering's lips.

"*Iorrt. Iorrt.*" He repeated it.

It was a Martian word. He knew no Martian.

290   In the middle of the night he arose and dialed a call through to Simpson, the archaeologist.

"Simpson, what does the word *Iorrt* mean?"

"Why, that's the old Martian word for our planet Earth. Why?"

"No special reason."

The telephone slipped from his hand.

"Hello, hello, hello, hello," it kept saying while he sat gazing out at the green star. "Bittering? Harry, are you there?"

The days were full of metal sound. He laid the frame of the rocket with the reluctant help of three indifferent men. He grew
300   very tired in an hour or so and had to sit down.

"The altitude," laughed a man.

"Are you *eating*, Harry?" asked another.

"I'm eating," he said, angrily.

"From your deep freezer?"

"Yes!"

"You're getting thinner, Harry."

"I'm not!"

"And taller."

"Liar!"

310   **H**is wife took him aside a few days later.

"Harry, I've used up all the food in the deep freezer. There's nothing left. I'll have to make sandwiches using food grown on Mars."

He sat down heavily.

"You must eat," she said. "You're weak."

"Yes," he said.

He took a sandwich, opened it, looked at it, and began to nibble at it.

"And take the rest of the day off," she said. "It's hot. The
320   children want to swim in the canals and hike. Please come along."

"I can't waste time. This is a crisis!"

"Just for an hour," she urged. "A swim'll do you good."

He rose, sweating. "All right, all right. Leave me alone. I'll come."

"Good for you, Harry."

The sun was hot, the day quiet. There was only an immense staring burn upon the land. They moved along the canal, the father, the mother, the racing children in their swimsuits. They
330 stopped and ate meat sandwiches. He saw their skin baking brown. And he saw the yellow eyes of his wife and his children, their eyes that were never yellow before. A few tremblings shook him but were carried off in waves of pleasant heat as he lay in the sun. He was too tired to be afraid.

"Cora, how long have your eyes been yellow?"

She was bewildered. "Always, I guess."

"They didn't change from brown in the last three months?"

She bit her lips. "No. Why do you ask?"

"Never mind."

340 They sat there.

"The children's eyes," he said. "They're yellow, too."

"Sometimes growing children's eyes change color."

"Maybe *we're* children, too. At least to Mars. That's a thought." He laughed. "Think I'll swim."

They leaped into the canal water, and he let himself sink down and down to the bottom like a golden statue and lie there in green silence. All was water-quiet and deep, all was peace. He felt the steady, slow current drift him easily.

If I lie here long enough, he thought, *the water will work and*
350 *eat away my flesh until the bones show like coral. Just my skeleton left. And then the water can build on that skeleton— green things, deep-water things, red things, yellow things. Change. Change. Slow, deep, silent change. And isn't that what it is up* there?

He saw the sky submerged above him, the sun made Martian by atmosphere and time and space.

Up there, a big river, he thought, *a Martian river, all of us lying deep in it, in our pebble houses, in our sunken boulder*

INTERPRET

How do you know that Bittering feels less fearful of what might be happening to the humans on Mars? List three actions that show a change in his mental attitude.

_____
_____
_____
_____
_____
_____
_____
_____

INFER

Why does Bittering laugh (line 344)?

_____
_____
_____
_____
_____
_____
_____
_____

VISUALIZE

Read lines 345–361. Underline the details that help you picture Bittering's leap into the water, and the thoughts he has before he comes up. Write *P* over details that seem pleasant to you. Write *S* over details that seem scary or unpleasant. Would you say that this description, seen through Bittering's eyes, is mostly pleasant, or mostly unpleasant?

_____

_____

_____

_____

_____

_____

_____

_____

INFER

Why do you think Dan is so happy to have the name *Linnl*?

_____

_____

_____

_____

_____

_____

houses, like crayfish hidden, and the water washing away our
360 *old bodies and lengthening the bones and—*

He let himself drift up through the soft light.

Dan sat on the edge of the canal, regarding his father seriously.

"*Utha,*" he said.

"What?" asked his father.

The boy smiled. "You know. *Utha*'s the Martian word for 'father.'"

"Where did you learn it?"

"I don't know. Around. *Utha!*"

370 "What do you want?"

The boy hesitated. "I—I want to change my name."

"Change it?"

"Yes."

His mother swam over. "What's wrong with Dan for a name?"

Dan fidgeted. "The other day you called Dan, Dan, Dan. I didn't even hear. I said to myself, that's not my name. I've a new name I want to use."

Mr. Bittering held to the side of the canal, his body cold and his heart pounding slowly. "What is this new name?"

380 "Linnl. Isn't that a good name? Can I use it? Can't I, please?"

Mr. Bittering put his hand to his head. He thought of the silly rocket, himself working alone, himself alone even among his family, so alone.

He heard his wife say, "Why not?"

He heard himself say, "Yes, you can use it."

"Yaaa!" screamed the boy. "I'm Linnl, Linnl!"

Racing down the meadowlands, he danced and shouted.

Mr. Bittering looked at his wife. "Why did we do that?"

"I don't know," she said. "It just seemed like a good idea."

390 They walked into the hills. They strolled on old mosaic[4] paths, beside still-pumping fountains. The paths were covered with a thin film of cool water all summer long. You kept your bare feet cool all the day, splashing as in a creek, wading.

---

4. **mosaic** (mō·zā′ik): made of small pieces of colored glass, stone, and so on.

They came to a small deserted Martian villa with a good view of the valley. It was on top of a hill. Blue marble halls, large murals, a swimming pool. It was refreshing in this hot summertime. The Martians hadn't believed in large cities.

"How nice," said Mrs. Bittering, "if we could move up here to this villa for the summer."

400 "Come on," he said. "We're going back to town. There's work to be done on the rocket."

But as he worked that night, the thought of the cool blue marble villa entered his mind. As the hours passed, the rocket seemed less important.

In the flow of days and weeks, the rocket receded and dwindled. The old fever was gone. It frightened him to think he had let it slip this way. But somehow the heat, the air, the working conditions—

He heard the men murmuring on the porch of his metal shop.

410 "Everyone's going. You heard?"

"All going. That's right."

Bittering came out. "Going where?" He saw a couple of trucks, loaded with children and furniture, drive down the dusty street.

"Up to the villas," said the man.

"Yeah, Harry. I'm going. So is Sam. Aren't you, Sam?"

"That's right, Harry. What about you?"

"I've got work to do here."

"Work! You can finish that rocket in the autumn, when it's 420 cooler."

He took a breath. "I got the frame all set up."

"In the autumn is better." Their voices were lazy in the heat.

"Got to work," he said.

"Autumn," they reasoned. And they sounded so sensible, so right.

Autumn would be best, he thought. *Plenty of time, then.*

No! cried part of himself, deep down, put away, locked tight, suffocating. *No! No!*

"In the autumn," he said.

INTERPRET

Underline the details in lines 394–399 that give you some idea about how the Martians used to live. What do these details reveal about the Martian way of life?

IDENTIFY

Underline the words that tell you where the trucks loaded with people are going.

WORDS TO OWN
receded (ri·sē′id) *v.*: became more distant.
dwindled (dwin′dəld) *v.*: shrank.

INTERPRET

A **conflict** is going on inside Harry Bittering's mind and heart. What is on each side of the conflict? Which side wins out?

_____

_____

_____

INFER

Why are the humans using the Martian names for the canals and mountains that used to have the names of places on Earth?

_____

_____

_____

_____

PREDICT

Do you think the Bitterings will come back to get the furniture and encyclopedia they brought from Earth? What do you think will happen once they leave their cottage and move to a Martian villa in the mountains?

_____

_____

_____

_____

430   "Come on, Harry," they all said.

"Yes," he said, feeling his flesh melt in the hot liquid air. "Yes, in the autumn. I'll begin work again then."

"I got a villa near the Tirra Canal," said someone.

"You mean the Roosevelt Canal, don't you?"

"Tirra. The old Martian name."

"But on the map—"

"Forget the map. It's Tirra now. Now I found a place in the Pillan mountains—"

"You mean the Rockefeller range," said Bittering.

440   "I mean the Pillan mountains," said Sam.

"Yes," said Bittering, buried in the hot, swarming air. "The Pillan mountains."

Everyone worked at loading the truck in the hot, still afternoon of the next day.

Laura, Dan, and David carried packages. Or, as they preferred to be known, Ttil, Linnl, and Werr carried packages.

The furniture was abandoned in the little white cottage.

"It looked just fine in Boston," said the mother. "And here in the cottage. But up at the villa? No. We'll get it when we come

450 back in the autumn."

Bittering himself was quiet.

"I've some ideas on furniture for the villa," he said after a time. "Big, lazy furniture."

"What about your encyclopedia? You're taking it along, surely?"

Mr. Bittering glanced away. "I'll come and get it next week."

They turned to their daughter. "What about your New York dresses?"

The bewildered girl stared. "Why, I don't want them

460 anymore."

They shut off the gas, the water; they locked the doors and walked away. Father peered into the truck.

"Gosh, we're not taking much," he said. "Considering all we brought to Mars, this is only a handful!"

He started the truck.

Looking at the small white cottage for a long moment, he was filled with a desire to rush to it, touch it, say goodbye to it, for he felt as if he were going away on a long journey, leaving something to which he could never quite return, never

470 understand again.

Just then Sam and his family drove by in another truck.

"Hi, Bittering! Here we go!"

The truck swung down the ancient highway out of town. There were sixty others traveling the same direction. The town filled with a silent, heavy dust from their passage. The canal waters lay blue in the sun, and a quiet wind moved in the strange trees.

"Goodbye, town!" said Mr. Bittering.

"Goodbye, goodbye," said the family, waving to it.

480 They did not look back again.

Summer burned the canals dry. Summer moved like flame upon the meadows. In the empty Earth settlement, the painted houses flaked and peeled. Rubber tires upon which children had swung in backyards hung suspended like stopped clock pendulums[5] in the blazing air.

At the metal shop, the rocket frame began to rust.

In the quiet autumn Mr. Bittering stood, very dark now, very golden-eyed, upon the slope above his villa, looking at the valley.

490 "It's time to go back," said Cora.

"Yes, but we're not going," he said quietly. "There's nothing there anymore."

"Your books," she said. "Your fine clothes."

"Your *llles* and your fine *ior uele rre*," she said.

"The town's empty. No one's going back," he said. "There's no reason to, none at all."

The daughter wove tapestries and the sons played songs on ancient flutes and pipes, their laughter echoing in the marble villa.

---

5. **pendulums** (pĕn′dyŏō·ləmz): hanging weights that swing back and forth; used to regulate the movement of old-fashioned clocks.

INTERPRET

Re-read lines 473–480. Underline the detail that tells you how the Bittering family feels about the town they're leaving. Why is this detail important?

INFER

Re-read lines 481–499. Underline two details that show how Bittering has changed physically. What **inference** can you make about how happy the Bitterings are now, compared to the way they used to be?

INTERPRET

One important **conflict** in this story is between two ways of life: life in a town like many towns on Earth versus life on Mars. Which way of life does the narrator seem to prefer? Tell why you agree or disagree with the narrator.

_____

_____

_____

_____

_____

IDENTIFY

Underline the detail that tells why, five years later, a rocket comes to Mars. What do the rocket men find in the town? What do they find in the hills?

_____

_____

_____

_____

_____

_____

WORDS TO OWN
flimsy (flim′zē) *adj.*: poorly made.

500   Mr. Bittering gazed at the Earth settlement far away in the low valley. "Such odd, such ridiculous houses the Earth people built."

"They didn't know any better," his wife mused. "Such ugly people. I'm glad they've gone."

They both looked at each other, startled by all they had just finished saying. They laughed.

"Where did they go?" he wondered. He glanced at his wife. She was golden and slender as his daughter. She looked at him, and he seemed almost as young as their eldest son.

"I don't know," she said.

510   "We'll go back to town maybe next year, or the year after, or the year after that," he said, calmly. "Now—I'm warm. How about taking a swim?"

They turned their backs to the valley. Arm in arm they walked silently down a path of clear-running spring water.

Five years later a rocket fell out of the sky. It lay steaming in the valley. Men leaped out of it, shouting.

"We won the war on Earth! We're here to rescue you! Hey!"

But the American-built town of cottages, peach trees, and theaters was silent. They found a flimsy rocket frame rusting in

520 an empty shop.

The rocket men searched the hills. The captain established headquarters in an abandoned bar. His lieutenant came back to report.

"The town's empty, but we found native life in the hills, sir. Dark people. Yellow eyes. Martians. Very friendly. We talked a bit, not much. They learn English fast. I'm sure our relations will be most friendly with them, sir."

"Dark, eh?" mused the captain. "How many?"

"Six, eight hundred, I'd say, living in those marble ruins in

530 the hills, sir. Tall, healthy. Beautiful women."

"Did they tell you what became of the men and women who built this Earth settlement, Lieutenant?"

"They hadn't the foggiest notion of what happened to this town or its people."

"Strange. You think those Martians killed them?"

"They look surprisingly peaceful. Chances are a plague[6] did this town in, sir."

"Perhaps. I suppose this is one of those mysteries we'll never solve. One of those mysteries you read about."

540   The captain looked at the room, the dusty windows, the blue mountains rising beyond, the canals moving in the light, and he heard the soft wind in the air. He shivered. Then, recovering, he tapped a large fresh map he had thumbtacked to the top of an empty table.

"Lots to be done, Lieutenant." His voice droned on and quietly on as the sun sank behind the blue hills. "New settlements. Mining sites, minerals to be looked for. Bacteriological specimens taken. The work, all the work. And the old records were lost. We'll have a job of remapping to do,

550 renaming the mountains and rivers and such. Calls for a little imagination.

"What do you think of naming those mountains the Lincoln Mountains, this canal the Washington Canal, those hills—we can name those hills for you, Lieutenant. Diplomacy. And you, for a favor, might name a town for me. Polishing the apple. And why not make this the Einstein Valley, and further over . . . are you *listening*, Lieutenant?"

The lieutenant snapped his gaze from the blue color and the quiet mist of the hills far beyond the town.

560   "What? Oh, *yes,* sir!"

INFER

Re-read lines 552–560. Based on these lines, how is the captain's **character** different from the lieutenant's?

EVALUATE

How satisfying is the conclusion of this story? Give two reasons for your answer.

---

6. **plague:** deadly disease that spreads quickly.

"Sketch to Stretch"

Make a list of the words that describe the setting of "The Naming of Names." Use specific details from the story. Then, draw a sketch that represents how the story and its settings affected you. At the bottom of your sketch, explain briefly what you intended to show in your sketch.

Setting Words

Sketch

Explanation of My Sketch

_____

_____

_____

_____

_____

Vocabulary and Comprehension

A. Match words and definitions. Write the letter of the correct definition next to each word.

_____ **1.** interior   **a.** hopeless

_____ **2.** submerged   **b.** shrank

_____ **3.** amiss   **c.** sociable

_____ **4.** convivial   **d.** poorly made

_____ **5.** ceased   **e.** covered with liquid

_____ **6.** anachronism   **f.** withdrew

_____ **7.** forlorn   **g.** improper

_____ **8.** receded   **h.** inside

_____ **9.** dwindled   **i.** something out of its proper time in history

_____ **10.** flimsy   **j.** stopped

B. Choose three words from above. Use each word in a sentence.

1. _____

_____

2. _____

_____

3. _____

_____

C. Write **T** or **F** next to each statement to tell if it is true or false.

_____ **1.** The color of Harry Bittering's eyes changes from blue to gold.

_____ **2.** Martians name a mountain range after Abraham Lincoln.

_____ **3.** Dan Bittering changes his name to Linnl.

_____ **4.** The Bitterings finally make it back to Earth.

After Twenty Years

Make the Connection

What Should I Do Now?

Imagine that you write an advice column for an online magazine. One day you receive the following message. On the "screen" below, share your advice with "Confused."

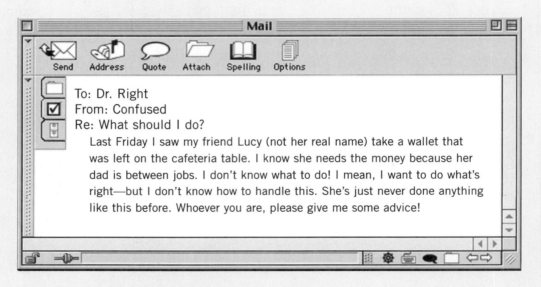

Mail

Send Address Quote Attach Spelling Options

To: Dr. Right
From: Confused
Re: What should I do?

Last Friday I saw my friend Lucy (not her real name) take a wallet that was left on the cafeteria table. I know she needs the money because her dad is between jobs. I don't know what to do! I mean, I want to do what's right—but I don't know how to handle this. She's just never done anything like this before. Whoever you are, please give me some advice!

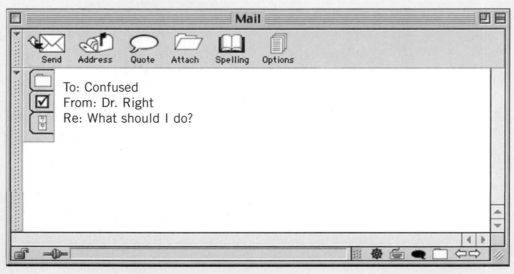

Mail

Send Address Quote Attach Spelling Options

To: Confused
From: Dr. Right
Re: What should I do?

After Twenty Years

O. Henry

VISUALIZE

Read the first two paragraphs. Underline the details that help you picture the **setting.**

INFER

You've been told a little about what the policeman and the man in the doorway look like. What **inferences,** or guesses, can you make about the policeman's **character,** and about the **character** of the man in the doorway?

WORDS TO OWN
habitual (hə·bich′oo·əl) *adj.:* customary.
intricate (in′tri·kit) *adj.:* complicated.

The policeman on the beat moved up the avenue impressively. The impressiveness was habitual and not for show, for spectators were few. The time was barely ten o'clock at night, but chilly gusts of wind with a taste of rain in them had well nigh depeopled the streets.

Trying doors as he went, twirling his club with many intricate and artful movements, turning now and then to cast his watchful eye down the pacific[1] thoroughfare, the officer,
10 with his stalwart form and slight swagger, made a fine picture of a guardian of the peace. The vicinity was one that kept early hours. Now and then you might see the lights of a cigar store or of an all-night lunch counter, but the majority of the doors belonged to business places that had long since been closed.

When about midway of a certain block, the policeman suddenly slowed his walk. In the doorway of a darkened hardware store a man leaned with an unlighted cigar in his mouth. As the policeman walked up to him, the man spoke up quickly.

"It's all right, officer," he said reassuringly. "I'm just waiting for a friend. It's an appointment made twenty years ago. Sounds
20 a little funny to you, doesn't it? Well, I'll explain if you'd like to make certain it's all straight. About that long ago there used to be a restaurant where this store stands—'Big Joe' Brady's restaurant."

"Until five years ago," said the policeman. "It was torn down then."

The man in the doorway struck a match and lit his cigar. The light showed a pale, square-jawed face with keen eyes and a little white scar near his right eyebrow. His scarf pin was a large diamond, oddly set.
30 "Twenty years ago tonight," said the man, "I dined here at 'Big Joe' Brady's with Jimmy Wells, my best chum and the finest chap in the world. He and I were raised here in New York, just like two brothers, together. I was eighteen and Jimmy was twenty. The next morning I was to start for the West to make my fortune. You couldn't have dragged Jimmy out of New York;

---

1. pacific: here, peaceful.

he thought it was the only place on earth. Well, we agreed that night that we would meet here again exactly twenty years from that date and time, no matter what our conditions might be or from what distance we might have to come. We figured that in
40   twenty years each of us ought to have our destiny worked out and our fortunes made, whatever they were going to be."

"It sounds pretty interesting," said the policeman. "Rather a long time between meets, though, it seems to me. Haven't you heard from your friend since you left?"

"Well, yes, for a time we corresponded," said the other. "But after a year or two we lost track of each other. You see, the West is a pretty big proposition, and I kept hustling around over it pretty lively. But I know Jimmy will meet me here if he's alive, for he always was the truest, staunchest old chap in the world.
50   He'll never forget. I came a thousand miles to stand in this door tonight, and it's worth it if my old partner turns up."

The waiting man pulled out a handsome watch, the lids of it set with small diamonds.

"Three minutes to ten," he announced. "It was exactly ten o'clock when we parted here at the restaurant door."

"Did pretty well out West, didn't you?" asked the policeman.

"You bet! I hope Jimmy has done half as well. He was a kind of plodder, though, good fellow as he was. I've had to compete with some of the sharpest wits going to get my pile.
60   A man gets in a groove in New York. It takes the West to put a razor edge on him."

The policeman twirled his club and took a step or two.

"I'll be on my way. Hope your friend comes around all right. Going to call time on him sharp?"

"I should say not!" said the other. "I'll give him half an hour at least. If Jimmy is alive on earth, he'll be here by that time. So long, officer."

"Good night, sir," said the policeman, passing on along his beat, trying doors as he went.
70   There was now a fine, cold drizzle falling, and the wind had risen from its uncertain puffs into a steady blow. The few foot passengers astir in that quarter hurried dismally and silently

IDENTIFY

Underline the words that tell about the agreement Jimmy Wells and the man in the doorway had made twenty years earlier. Re-read, starting at line 30. How old would Jimmy and the man in the doorway be when they met after twenty years?

INFER

Pause at line 61. What do these boasts suggest about how the man sees Jimmy? about how he sees himself?

WORDS TO OWN
dismally (diz′məl·ē) adv.: miserably.

along with coat collars turned high and pocketed hands. And in the door of the hardware store the man who had come a thousand miles to fill an appointment, uncertain almost to absurdity, with the friend of his youth, smoked his cigar and waited.

About twenty minutes he waited, and then a tall man in a long overcoat, with collar turned up to his ears, hurried across from the opposite side of the street. He went directly to the

80 waiting man.

"Is that you, Bob?" he asked, doubtfully.

"Is that you, Jimmy Wells?" cried the man in the door.

"Bless my heart!" exclaimed the new arrival, grasping both the other's hands with his own. "It's Bob, sure as fate. I was certain I'd find you here if you were still in existence. Well, well, well!—twenty years is a long time. The old restaurant's gone, Bob; I wish it had lasted, so we could have had another dinner there. How has the West treated you, old man?"

"Bully;[2] it has given me everything I asked it for. You've

90 changed lots, Jimmy. I never thought you were so tall by two or three inches."

"Oh, I grew a bit after I was twenty."

"Doing well in New York, Jimmy?"

"Moderately. I have a position in one of the city departments. Come on, Bob; we'll go around to a place I know of and have a good long talk about old times."

The two men started up the street, arm in arm. The man from the West, his <u>egotism</u> enlarged by success, was beginning to outline the history of his career. The other, submerged in his

100 overcoat, listened with interest.

At the corner stood a drugstore, brilliant with electric lights. When they came into this glare, each of them turned <u>simultaneously</u> to gaze upon the other's face.

The man from the West stopped suddenly and released his arm.

"You're not Jimmy Wells," he snapped. "Twenty years is a long time, but not long enough to change a man's nose from a Roman to a pug."

---

2. **bully:** informal term meaning "very well."

"It sometimes changes a good man into a bad one," said the 110 tall man. "You've been under arrest for ten minutes, 'Silky' Bob. Chicago thinks you may have dropped over our way and wires us she wants to have a chat with you. Going quietly, are you? That's sensible. Now, before we go to the station, here's a note I was asked to hand to you. You may read it here at the window. It's from Patrolman Wells."

The man from the West unfolded the little piece of paper handed him. His hand was steady when he began to read, but it trembled a little by the time he had finished. The note was rather short.

120   Bob: I was at the appointed place on time. When you struck the match to light your cigar, I saw it was the face of the man wanted in Chicago. Somehow I couldn't do it myself, so I went around and got a plainclothes man to do the job.

Jimmy

INTERPRET

Look back over the story and circle three clues **foreshadowing** that Bob might be a criminal. Put an F next to each circle.

EVALUATE

What is unexpected about the ending of the story? In your opinion, was it OK for Jimmy Wells to get his old friend Bob arrested? Tell why or why not.

_____
_____
_____
_____
_____
_____
_____
_____
_____
_____
_____
_____
_____
_____
_____
_____

Foreshadowing Chart

When you read a story, you often make predictions about what might happen next. Clever authors (like O. Henry) usually include clues—details that **foreshadow** a later event—to help readers make predictions.

   Now that you've read "After Twenty Years," go back and look for clues. Then, fill out the foreshadowing chart.

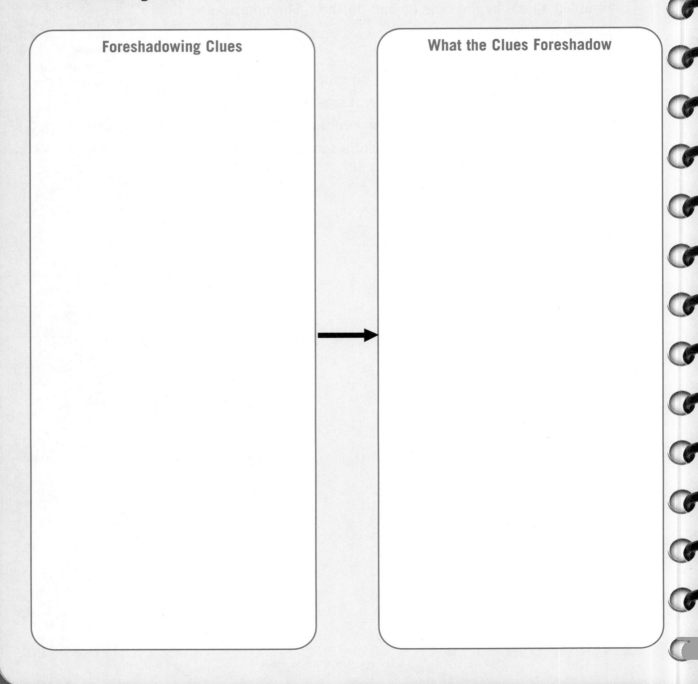

Foreshadowing Clues

What the Clues Foreshadow

Vocabulary and Comprehension

A. Match words and definitions. Write the letter of the correct definition next to each word.

_____ **1.** habitual

_____ **2.** intricate

_____ **3.** dismally

_____ **4.** egotism

_____ **5.** simultaneously

a. miserably; gloomily

b. at the same time

c. done or fixed by habit; customary

d. complicated; full of detail

e. conceit; talking about oneself too much

Word Bank
habitual
intricate
dismally
egotism
simultaneously

B. Choose three Word Bank words. Use each word in a sentence.

1. _____

_____

2. _____

_____

3. _____

_____

C. Write **T** or **F** next to each statement to tell if it is true or false.

_____ **1.** The night was chilly and the streets were empty.

_____ **2.** Jimmy and Bob had been writing to each other for twenty years.

_____ **3.** The two friends planned to meet at 10 P.M.

_____ **4.** Jimmy didn't want to leave New York.

_____ **5.** Bob didn't recognize Jimmy when he saw him.

A Mason-Dixon Memory

Make the Connection

"Hard Choices . . ."

How far would you go to do the right thing? Think of something you really care about. It could be a possession or an event you're looking forward to—anything you'd hate to give up. Can you imagine a situation in which doing the right thing might mean giving up the thing you want so much? For example, what if going to a party means you have to break a date with a friend who wasn't invited? Jot down your thoughts on how you might handle such a situation.

I'd go anyway because

_____

_____

_____

_____

_____

_____

I wouldn't go because

_____

_____

_____

_____

_____

_____

A Mason-Dixon
Memory

Clifton Davis

IDENTIFY

The **narrator** is the person telling the story. Circle the narrator's job at this event. On the lines below, tell why Dondré Green was attending this fund-raiser.

_____

_____

_____

_____

_____

_____

_____

_____

IDENTIFY

Re-read lines 19–30. Underline the game Dondré loves to play. Tell why the team had driven to another town.

_____

_____

_____

_____

WORDS TO OWN
civic (siv′ik) *adj.:* of a city or citizenship.
predominantly
(prē·däm′ə·nənt·lē) *adv.:* mainly.

Dondré Green glanced uneasily at the <u>civic</u> leaders and sports figures filling the hotel ballroom in Cleveland. They had come from across the nation to attend a fund-raiser for the National Minority College Golf Scholarship Foundation. I was the banquet's featured entertainer. Dondré, an eighteen-year-old high school senior from Monroe, Louisiana, was the evening's honored guest.

"Nervous?" I asked the handsome young man in his starched white shirt and rented tuxedo.

10 "A little," he whispered, grinning.

One month earlier, Dondré had been just one more black student attending a <u>predominantly</u> white Southern school. Although most of his friends and classmates were white, Dondré's race had never been an issue. Then, on April 17, 1991, Dondré's black skin provoked an incident that made nationwide news.

"Ladies and gentlemen," the emcee[1] said, "our special guest, Dondré Green."

As the audience stood applauding, Dondré walked to the
20 microphone and began his story. "I love golf," he said quietly. "For the past two years, I've been a member of the St. Frederick High School golf team. And though I was the only black member, I've always felt at home playing at the mostly white country clubs across Louisiana."

The audience leaned forward; even the waiters and busboys stopped to listen. As I listened, a memory buried in my heart since childhood began fighting its way to life.

"Our team had driven from Monroe," Dondré continued. "When we arrived at the Caldwell Parish Country Club in
30 Columbia, we walked to the putting green."

Dondré and his teammates were too absorbed to notice the conversation between a man and St. Frederick athletic director James Murphy. After disappearing into the clubhouse, Murphy returned to his players.

---

1. **emcee** (em′sē′): master of ceremonies.

"I want to see the seniors," he said. "On the double!" His face seemed strained as he gathered the four students, including Dondré.

"I don't know how to tell you this," he said, "but the Caldwell Parish Country Club is reserved for whites only."
40 Murphy paused and looked at Dondré. His teammates glanced at each other in disbelief. "I want you seniors to decide what our response should be," Murphy continued. "If we leave, we forfeit this tournament. If we stay, Dondré can't play."

As I listened, my own childhood memory from thirty-two years ago broke free.

In 1959 I was thirteen years old, a poor black kid living with my mother and stepfather in a small black ghetto on Long Island, New York. My mother worked nights in a hospital, and my stepfather drove a coal truck. Needless to say, our standard
50 of living was somewhat short of the American dream.

Nevertheless, when my eighth-grade teacher announced a graduation trip to Washington, D.C., it never crossed my mind that I would be left behind. Besides a complete tour of the nation's capital, we would visit Glen Echo Amusement Park in Maryland. In my imagination, Glen Echo was Disneyland, Knott's Berry Farm, and Magic Mountain rolled into one.

My heart beating wildly, I raced home to deliver the mimeographed letter describing the journey. But when my mother saw how much the trip would cost, she just shook her head. We
60 couldn't afford it.

After feeling sad for ten seconds, I decided to try to fund the trip myself. For the next eight weeks, I sold candy bars door-to-door, delivered newspapers, and mowed lawns. Three days before the deadline, I'd made just barely enough. I was going!

The day of the trip, trembling with excitement, I climbed onto the train. I was the only nonwhite in our section.

Our hotel was not far from the White House. My roommate was Frank Miller, the son of a businessman. Leaning together out of our window and dropping water balloons on passing
70 tourists quickly cemented our new friendship.

PREDICT

Underline the lines that tell you the choice the seniors have to make. What do you think they will decide to do?

_____

_____

_____

INFER

A **flashback** is a scene that breaks the normal time order of events to show a past event. Underline the details that suggest to you that the narrator is flashing back to an earlier time in his own life.

_____

_____

_____

_____

_____

_____

IDENTIFY

Re-read lines 46–64. Underline the details that show how determined the narrator is to go on the graduation trip.

_____

_____

VISUALIZE

Re-read lines 75–88. List three details that help you picture the Lincoln Memorial as described by the narrator.

_____

_____

_____

_____

_____

_____

_____

_____

_____

_____

_____

_____

_____

_____

_____

_____

IDENTIFY

Underline the details that tell what the Mason-Dixon line used to be, before the Civil War.

WORDS TO OWN

resolve (ri·zälv′) *v.*: decide; commit to an idea.

Every morning, almost a hundred of us loaded noisily onto our bus for another adventure. We sang our school fight song dozens of times—en route[2] to Arlington National Cemetery and even on an afternoon cruise down the Potomac River.

We visited the Lincoln Memorial twice, once in daylight, the second time at dusk. My classmates and I fell silent as we walked in the shadows of those thirty-six marble columns, one for every state in the Union that Lincoln labored to preserve. I stood next to Frank at the base of the nineteen-foot seated
80 statue. Spotlights made the white Georgian marble seem to glow. Together, we read those famous words from Lincoln's speech at Gettysburg, remembering the most bloody battle in the War Between the States: ". . . we here highly <u>resolve</u> that these dead shall not have died in vain—that this nation, under God, shall have a new birth of freedom. . . ."

As Frank motioned me into place to take my picture, I took one last look at Lincoln's face. He seemed alive and so terribly sad.

The next morning I understood a little better why he wasn't
90 smiling. "Clifton," a chaperone said, "could I see you for a moment?"

The other guys at my table, especially Frank, turned pale. We had been joking about the previous night's direct water-balloon hit on a fat lady and her poodle. It was a stupid, dangerous act, but luckily nobody got hurt. We were celebrating our escape from punishment when the chaperone asked to see me.

"Clifton," she began, "do you know about the Mason-Dixon line?"

"No," I said, wondering what this had to do with drenching
100 fat ladies.

"Before the Civil War," she explained, "the Mason-Dixon line was originally the boundary between Maryland and Pennsylvania—the dividing line between the slave and free states." Having escaped one disaster, I could feel another brewing. I noticed that her eyes were damp and her hands shaking.

_____

2. en route (en rōot′): on the way.

"Today," she continued, "the Mason-Dixon line is a kind of invisible border between the North and the South. When you cross that invisible line out of Washington, D.C., into Maryland, things change."

110 There was an <u>ominous</u> drift to this conversation, but I wasn't following it. Why did she look and sound so nervous?

"Glen Echo Amusement Park is in Maryland," she said at last, "and the management doesn't allow Negroes inside." She stared at me in silence.

I was still grinning and nodding when the meaning finally sank in. "You mean I can't go to the park," I stuttered, "because I'm a Negro?"

She nodded slowly. "I'm sorry, Clifton," she said, taking my hand. "You'll have to stay in the hotel tonight. Why don't you
120 and I watch a movie on television?"

I walked to the elevators feeling confusion, disbelief, anger, and a deep sadness. "What happened, Clifton?" Frank said when I got back to the room. "Did the fat lady tell on us?"

Without saying a word, I walked over to my bed, lay down, and began to cry. Frank was stunned into silence. Junior-high boys didn't cry, at least not in front of each other.

It wasn't just missing the class adventure that made me feel so sad. For the first time in my life, I was learning what it felt like to be a "nigger." Of course there was discrimination in the
130 North, but the color of my skin had never officially kept me out of a coffee shop, a church—or an amusement park.

"Clifton," Frank whispered, "what is the matter?"

"They won't let me go to Glen Echo Park tonight," I sobbed.

"Because of the water balloon?" he asked.

"No," I answered, "because I'm a Negro."

"Well, that's a relief!" Frank said, and then he laughed, obviously relieved to have escaped punishment for our caper with the balloons. "I thought it was serious!"

Wiping away the tears with my sleeve, I stared at him. "It
140 *is* serious. They don't let Negroes into the park. I can't go with you!" I shouted. "That's pretty serious to me."

IDENTIFY

Circle the details that tell what the Mason-Dixon line was at the time of this **flashback**.

_____

_____

INTERPRET

What does the Mason-Dixon line have to do with Clifton's trip to the amusement park?

_____
_____
_____
_____
_____
_____
_____
_____
_____
_____
_____

WORDS TO OWN
ominous (ăm′ə·nəs) *adj.:* warning of something bad.

INFER

Why does Clifton almost sock Frank in the jaw? Underline Frank's words that stop him.

_____

_____

_____

INFER

What was more important to the boys than the trip to the park?

_____

_____

_____

IDENTIFY

Underline the detail in lines 159–163 that tells you that the narrator is changing from the past (his own story) to the present (Dondré Green's story).

_____

_____

IDENTIFY

What choice did Dondré's teammates make? Underline the details that tell about their choice. Then, circle the details that tell how the people of Louisiana backed up that choice.

I was about to wipe the silly grin off Frank's face with a blow to his jaw when I heard him say, "Then I won't go either."

For an instant we just froze. Then Frank grinned. I will never forget that moment. Frank was just a kid. He wanted to go to that amusement park as much as I did, but there was something even more important than the class night out. Still, he didn't explain or expand.

The next thing I knew, the room was filled with kids
150 listening to Frank. "They don't allow Negroes in the park," he said, "so I'm staying with Clifton."

"Me too," a second boy said.

"Those jerks," a third muttered. "I'm with you, Clifton." My heart began to race. Suddenly, I was not alone. A pint-sized revolution had been born. The "water-balloon brigade," eleven white boys from Long Island, had made its decision: "We won't go." And as I sat on my bed in the center of it all, I felt grateful. But above all, I was filled with pride.

Dondré Green's story brought that childhood memory back to
160 life. His golfing teammates, like my childhood friends, had an important decision to make. Standing by their friend would cost them dearly. But when it came time to decide, no one hesitated. "Let's get out of here," one of them whispered.

"They just turned and walked toward the van," Dondré told us. "They didn't debate it. And the younger players joined us without looking back."

Dondré was astounded by the response of his friends—and the people of Louisiana. The whole state was outraged and tried to make it right. The Louisiana House of Representatives
170 proclaimed a Dondré Green Day and passed legislation permitting lawsuits for damages, attorneys' fees, and court costs against any private facility that invites a team, then bars any member because of race.

As Dondré concluded, his eyes glistened with tears. "I love my coach and my teammates for sticking by me," he said. "It goes to show that there are always good people who will not

give in to bigotry. The kind of love they showed me that day will conquer hatred every time."

Suddenly, the banquet crowd was standing, applauding
180 Dondré Green.

My friends, too, had shown that kind of love. As we sat in the hotel, a chaperone came in waving an envelope. "Boys!" he shouted. "I've just bought thirteen tickets to the Senators-Tigers game. Anybody want to go?"

The room erupted in cheers. Not one of us had ever been to a professional baseball game in a real baseball park.

On the way to the stadium, we grew silent as our driver paused before the Lincoln Memorial. For one long moment, I stared through the marble pillars at Mr. Lincoln, bathed in that
190 warm yellow light. There was still no smile and no sign of hope in his sad and tired eyes.

". . . we here highly resolve . . . that this nation, under God, shall have a new birth of freedom. . . ."

In his words and in his life, Lincoln had made it clear that freedom is not free. Every time the color of a person's skin keeps him out of an amusement park or off a country-club fairway, the war for freedom begins again. Sometimes the battle is fought with fists and guns, but more often the most effective weapon is a simple act of love and courage.

200 Whenever I hear those words from Lincoln's speech at Gettysburg, I remember my eleven white friends, and I feel hope once again. I like to imagine that when we paused that night at the foot of his great monument, Mr. Lincoln smiled at last. As Dondré said, "The kind of love they showed me that day will conquer hatred every time."

INFER

Write your best guess as to what *bigotry* (line 177) means. Use Dondré's story to help you make the guess. Then, look up the word and write its dictionary definition.

_____

_____

_____

BUILD FLUENCY

Read the boxed lines aloud. Try to capture the narrator's tone of voice as he reads the words from Lincoln's Gettysburg Address, and tells how important they are.

INTERPRET

Why does the narrator imagine that Lincoln's statue smiles?

_____

_____

_____

_____

_____

_____

_____

WORDS TO OWN
erupted (ē·rup′tid) v.: exploded.

Comparison Chart

In "A Mason-Dixon Memory," Clifton Davis describes two experiences with discrimination. To see how the experiences are alike, fill in the chart below.

	Experience	Friends' Response
Dondré Green	Member of: Segregated place: Coach Murphy's decision:	What friends say and do: Green's reaction to friends:
Clifton Davis	Member of: Segregated place: Chaperone's decision:	What friends say and do: Davis's reaction to friends:

Vocabulary and Comprehension

A. Match words and definitions. Write the letter of the correct definition next to each word.

_____ **1.** erupted

_____ **2.** predominately

_____ **3.** civic

_____ **4.** resolve

_____ **5.** ominous

a. of a city

b. threatening

c. mainly

d. to decide

e. burst forth

> **Word Bank**
> erupted
> predominately
> civic
> resolve
> ominous

B. Choose two words from above. Use each word in a sentence.

1. _____

_____

2. _____

_____

C. Answer each question below.

1. Why was Clifton so upset when he wasn't allowed in the amusement park?

_____

_____

2. What do Clifton's friends do when they learn he is not allowed in the amusement park?

_____

_____

3. What did Dondré Green's teammates decide to do when the Caldwell Parish Country Club would not let Dondré play?

_____

_____

Bargain

Make the Connection

Justice or Revenge?

What do the words *justice* and *revenge* mean to you? On the protest sign at the left, write down three words that you think of when you hear the word *justice*. Then, somewhere on the sign, draw a picture or a symbol (such as a flag or a balance scale) that stands for what justice means to you. On the protest sign at the right, do the same thing—write three words and draw a symbol—for the word *revenge*.

JUSTICE!

REVENGE!

BARGAIN

A. B. Guthrie

IDENTIFY

When a story is told by a character in the story, we say it is told from the **first-person point of view.** Circle the pronoun in the first sentence that indicates that one of the characters is telling this story.

_____

_____

_____

INFER

Underline the name that Slade calls Mr. Baumer. Based on this name, what **inferences** can you make about Baumer? What inferences can you make about Slade's **character?**

_____

_____

_____

_____

_____

_____

_____

_____

_____

IDENTIFY

Underline what Slade does to Baumer's bill. Circle what Slade does to Baumer.

Mr. Baumer and I had closed the Moon Dance Mercantile Company and were walking to the post office, and he had a bunch of bills in his hand ready to mail. There wasn't anyone or anything much on the street because it was suppertime. A buckboard[1] and a saddle horse were tied at Hirsches' rack, and a rancher in a wagon rattled for home ahead of us, the sound of his going fading out as he prodded his team. Freighter[2] Slade stood alone in front of the Moon Dance Saloon, maybe wondering whether to have one more before going to supper.

10 People said he could hold a lot without showing it except in being ornerier[3] even than usual.

Mr. Baumer didn't see him until he was almost on him, and then he stopped and fingered through the bills until he found the right one. He stepped up to Slade and held it out.

Slade said, "What's this, Dutchie?"

Mr. Baumer had to tilt his head up to talk to him. "You know vat it is."

Slade just said, "Yeah?" You never could tell from his face what went on inside his skull. He had dark skin and shallow

20 cheeks and a thick-growing moustache that fell over the corners of his mouth.

"It is a bill," Mr. Baumer said. "I tell you before, it is a bill. For twenty-vun dollars and fifty cents."

"You know what I do with bills, don't you, Dutchie?" Slade asked.

Mr. Baumer didn't answer the question. He said, "For merchandise."

Slade took the envelope from Mr. Baumer's hand and squeezed it up in his fist and let it drop on the plank sidewalk.

30 Not saying anything, he reached down and took Mr. Baumer's nose between the knuckles of his fingers and twisted it up into his eyes. That was all. That was all at the time. Slade half turned and slouched to the door of the bar and let himself in. Some men were laughing in there.

---

1. **buckboard** _n._: open carriage.
2. **freighter** _n. used as adj._: here, person who transports goods.
3. **ornerier** (ôr′nər·ē·ər) _adj._: dialect for "meaner and more stubborn."

Mr. Baumer stooped and picked up the bill and put it on top of the rest and smoothed it out for mailing. When he straightened up, I could see tears in his eyes from having his nose screwed around.

He didn't say anything to me, and I didn't say anything to
40 him, being so much younger and feeling embarrassed for him. He went into the post office and slipped the bills in the slot, and we walked on home together. At the last, at the crossing where I had to leave him, he remembered to say, "Better study, Al. Is good to know to read and write and figure." I guess he felt he had to push me a little, my father being dead.

I said, "Sure. See you after school tomorrow"—which he knew I would anyway. I had been working in the store for him during the summer and after classes ever since pneumonia took my dad off.

50 Three of us worked there regularly: Mr. Baumer, of course, and me and Colly Coleman, who knew enough to drive the delivery wagon but wasn't much help around the store except for carrying orders out to the rigs[4] at the hitchpost and handling heavy things like the whiskey barrel at the back of the store which Mr. Baumer sold quarts and gallons out of.

The store carried quite a bit of stuff—sugar and flour and dried fruits and canned goods and such on one side and yard goods and coats and caps and aprons and the like of that on the other, besides kerosene and bran and buckets and linoleum
60 and pitchforks in the storehouse at the rear—but it wasn't a big store like Hirsch Brothers up the street. Never would be, people guessed, going on to say, with a sort of slow respect, that it would have gone under long ago if Mr. Baumer hadn't been half mule and half beaver. He had started the store just two years before and, the way things were, worked himself close to death.

He was at the high desk at the end of the grocery counter when I came in the next afternoon. He had an eyeshade on and black sateen protectors on his forearms, and his pencil was in his hand instead of behind his ear and his glasses were roosted

---

4. **rigs** *n.:* carriages with their horses.

PREDICT

Pause here at line 39. Think how you would feel if you were treated this way. How do you think Baumer will react to Slade's treatment? What do you predict will happen?

_____

_____

_____

_____

_____

_____

_____

IDENTIFY

Pause at line 50. Underline the details that give you important information about the **narrator,** the person who tells the story. What advice does Baumer give the narrator? Using your own words, write that advice on the lines below.

_____

_____

_____

IDENTIFY

Circle and number fourteen items listed in lines 56–65 that Baumer's store sells. Underline the details that tell the community's opinion of the shopkeeper.

INFER

Underline the feature that makes Baumer's face memorable. Why do you think the author mentions this feature?

_____

_____

_____

_____

_____

_____

_____

INTERPRET

Re-read lines 93–103. Underline the lines that tell why Baumer believes that Slade hates him. Do you agree with Baumer that Slade hates him especially, or with Al, who says that Slade "hates everybody"? Give a reason for your answer.

_____

_____

_____

_____

_____

_____

70 on the nose that Slade had twisted. He didn't hear me open and close the door or hear my feet as I walked back to him, and I saw he wasn't doing anything with the pencil but holding it over paper. I stood and studied him for a minute, seeing a small, stooped man with a little paunch bulging through his unbuttoned vest. He was a man you wouldn't remember from meeting once. There was nothing in his looks to set itself in your mind unless maybe it was his chin, which was a small pink hill in the gentle plain of his face.

While I watched him, he lifted his hand and felt carefully of
80 his nose. Then he saw me. His eyes had that kind of mistiness that seems to go with age or illness, though he wasn't really old or sick, either. He brought his hand down quickly and picked up the pencil, but he saw I still was looking at the nose, and finally he sighed and said, "That Slade."

Just the sound of the name brought Slade to my eye. I saw him slouched in front of the bar, and I saw him and his string[5] coming down the grade from the buttes,[6] the wheel horses held snug and the rest lined out pretty, and then the string leveling off and Slade's whip lifting hair from a horse that wasn't up in
90 the collar.[7] I had heard it said that Slade could make a horse scream with that whip. Slade's name wasn't Freighter, of course. Our town had nicknamed him that because that was what he was.

"I don't think it's any good to send him a bill, Mr. Baumer," I said. "He can't even read."

"He could pay yet."

"He don't pay anybody," I said.

"I think he hate me," Mr. Baumer went on. "That is the thing. He hate me for coming not from this country. I come here, sixteen years old, and learn to read and write, and I make
100 a business, and so I think he hate me."

"He hates everybody."

Mr. Baumer shook his head. "But not to pinch the nose. Not to call Dutchie."

---

5. **string** _n._: here, a group of horses.
6. **buttes** (byo͞ots) _n._: steep, flat-topped hills that stand alone on a plain.
7. **up in the collar**: pulling as hard as the other horses.

The side door squeaked open, but it was only Colly Coleman coming in from a trip, so I said, "Excuse me, Mr. Baumer, but you shouldn't have trusted him in the first place."

"I know," he answered, looking at me with his misty eyes. "A man make mistakes. I think some do not trust him, so he will pay me because I do. And I do not know him well then.
110 He only came back to town three, four months ago, from being away since before I go into business."

"People who knew him before could have told you," I said.

"A man make mistakes," he explained again.

"It's not my business, Mr. Baumer, but I would forget the bill."

His eyes rested on my face for a long minute, as if they didn't see me but the problem itself. He said, "It is not twenty-vun dollars and fifty cents now, Al. It is not that anymore."

"What is it?"

He took a little time to answer. Then he brought his two
120 hands up as if to help him shape the words. "It is the thing. You see, it is the thing."

I wasn't quite sure what he meant.

He took his pencil from behind the ear where he had put it and studied the point of it. "That Slade. He steal whiskey and call it evaporation. He sneak things from his load. A thief, he is. And too big for me."

I said, "I got no time for him, Mr. Baumer, but I guess there never was a freighter didn't steal whiskey. That's what I hear."

It was true, too. From the railroad to Moon Dance was fifty
130 miles and a little better—a two-day haul in good weather, heck knew how long in bad. Any freight string bound home with a load had to lie out at least one night. When a freighter had his stock tended to and maybe a little fire going against the dark, he'd tackle a barrel of whiskey or of grain alcohol if he had one aboard consigned to Hirsch Brothers or Mr. Baumer's or the Moon Dance Saloon or the Gold Leaf Bar. He'd drive a hoop out of place, bore a little hole with a nail or bit and draw off what he wanted. Then he'd plug the hole with a whittled peg and pound the hoop back. That was evaporation. Nobody complained much. With
140 freighters you generally took what they gave you, within reason.

BUILD FLUENCY

Read the boxed **dialogue,** or conversation, between Baumer and Al aloud. Practice until you can read it smoothly. Pay attention to the punctuation so you'll know when to pause at commas and when to stop at the end of sentences. Try to express the feelings and ideas of the characters.

INFER

What do you think Baumer means by "the thing" (lines 120–121)?

_____

_____

_____

_____

_____

_____

_____

_____

_____

_____

IDENTIFY

Underline the details in lines 129–140 that tell you what Slade usually steals from the load and how he steals it.

INFER

Why doesn't Al tell you what Baumer is thinking (lines 143–146)? What do you think Baumer might be thinking about?

"Moore steals it, too," I told Mr. Baumer. Moore was Mr. Baumer's freighter.

"Yah," he said, and that was all, but I stood there for a minute, thinking there might be something more. I could see thought swimming in his eyes, above that little hill of chin. Then a customer came in, and I had to go wait on him.

Nothing happened for a month, nothing between Mr. Baumer and Slade, that is, but fall drew on toward winter and the first flight of ducks headed south and Mr. Baumer hired Miss Lizzie 150 Webb to help with the just-beginning Christmas trade and here it was, the first week in October, and he and I walked up the street again with the monthly bills. He always sent them out. I guess he had to. A bigger store, like Hirsches', would wait on the ranchers until their beef or wool went to market.

Up to a point things looked and happened almost the same as they had before, so much the same that I had the crazy feeling I was going through that time again. There was a wagon and a rig tied up at Hirsches' rack and a saddle horse standing hipshot[8] in front of the harness shop. A few more people were 160 on the street now, not many, and lamps had been lit against the shortened day.

It was dark enough that I didn't make out Slade right away. He was just a figure that came out of the yellow wash of light from the Moon Dance Saloon and stood on the boardwalk and with his head made the little motion of spitting. Then I recognized the lean, raw shape of him and the muscles flowing down into the sloped shoulders, and in the settling darkness I filled the picture in—the dark skin and the flat cheeks and the peevish eyes and the moustache growing rank.

170 There was Slade and here was Mr. Baumer with his bills and here I was, just as before, just like in the second go-round of a bad dream. I felt like turning back, being embarrassed and half scared by trouble even when it wasn't mine. Please, I said to myself, don't stop, Mr. Baumer! Don't bite off anything! Please, shortsighted the way you are, don't catch sight of him at

---

8. **hipshot** *adj.:* with one hip lower than the other.

all! I held up and stepped around behind Mr. Baumer and came up on the outside so as to be between him and Slade, where maybe I'd cut off his view.

But it wasn't any use. All along I think I knew it was no use, 180 not the praying or the walking between or anything. The act had to play itself out.

Mr. Baumer looked across the front of me and saw Slade and hesitated in his step and came to a stop. Then in his slow, business way, his chin held firm against his mouth, he began fingering through the bills, squinting to make out the names. Slade had turned and was watching him, munching on a cud of tobacco like a bull waiting.

"You look, Al," Mr. Baumer said without lifting his face from the bills. "I cannot see so good."

190 So I looked, and while I was looking, Slade must have moved. The next I knew, Mr. Baumer was staggering ahead, the envelopes spilling out of his hands. There had been a thump, the clap of a heavy hand swung hard on his back.

Slade said, "Haryu, Dutchie?"

Mr. Baumer caught his balance and turned around, the bills he had trampled shining white between them and at Slade's feet the hat that Mr. Baumer had stumbled out from under.

Slade picked up the hat and scuffed through the bills and held it out. "Cold to be goin' without a skypiece," he said.

200 Mr. Baumer hadn't spoken a word. The lampshine from inside the bar caught his eyes, and in them, it seemed to me, a light came and went as anger and the uselessness of it took turns in his head.

Two men had come up on us and stood watching. One of them was Angus McDonald, who owned the Ranchers' Bank, and the other was Dr. King. He had his bag in his hand.

Two others were drifting up, but I didn't have time to tell who. The light came in Mr. Baumer's eyes, and he took a step ahead and swung. I could have hit harder myself. The fist landed on 210 Slade's cheek without hardly so much as jogging his head, but it let the devil loose in the man. I didn't know he could move

PREDICT

Al believes that something is going to happen. What do you think is going to happen?

_____

_____

_____

_____

_____

_____

RETELL

Go back to line 170, and re-read to line 203. Tell what has happened up to this point in this new conflict between Baumer and Slade.

_____

_____

_____

_____

_____

_____

_____

_____

_____

INFER

What does the fight tell you about the **character** of each man—Baumer and Slade?

_____

_____

_____

_____

INTERPRET

Underline the reason Slade gives for fighting Baumer. How truthful is he? (Review lines 190–197 if you've forgotten how the fight started.)

_____

_____

_____

IDENTIFY

Why does Slade call Baumer "Dutch penny pincher"? A person who **stereotypes** unfairly and illogically suggests or claims that all members of a group are the same. Explain what this stereotyping of Baumer reveals about Slade.

_____

_____

_____

_____

_____

so fast. He slid in like a practiced fighter and let Mr. Baumer have it full in the face.

Mr. Baumer slammed over on his back, but he wasn't out. He started lifting himself. Slade leaped ahead and brought a boot heel down on the hand he was lifting himself by. I heard meat and bone under that heel and saw Mr. Baumer fall back and try to roll away.

Things had happened so fast that not until then did anyone
220 have a chance to get between them. Now Mr. McDonald pushed at Slade's chest, saying, "That's enough, Freighter. That's enough, now," and Dr. King lined up, too, and another man I didn't know, and I took a place, and we formed a kind of screen between them. Dr. King turned and bent to look at Mr. Baumer.

"Fool hit me first," Slade said.

"That's enough," Mr. McDonald told him again while Slade looked at all of us as if he'd spit on us for a nickel. Mr. McDonald went on, using a half-friendly tone, and I knew it was because he didn't want to take Slade on any more than the rest of us did.
230 "You go on home and sleep it off, Freighter. That's the ticket."

Slade just snorted.

From behind us, Dr. King said, "I think you've broken this man's hand."

"Lucky for him I didn't kill him," Slade answered. "Dutch penny pincher!" He fingered the chew out of his mouth. "Maybe he'll know enough to leave me alone now."

Dr. King had Mr. Baumer on his feet. "I'll take him to the office," he said.

Blood was draining from Mr. Baumer's nose and rounding
240 the curve of his lip and dripping from the sides of his chin. He held his hurt right hand in the other. But the thing was that he didn't look beaten even then, not the way a man who has given up looks beaten. Maybe that was why Slade said, with a show of that fierce anger, "You stay away from me! Hear? Stay clear away, or you'll get more of the same!"

Dr. King led Mr. Baumer away, Slade went back into the bar, and the other men walked off, talking about the fight. I got down and picked up the bills, because I knew Mr. Baumer

would want me to, and mailed them at the post office, dirty as
250 they were. It made me sorer, someway, that Slade's bill was one
of the few that wasn't marked up. The cleanness of it seemed
to say that there was no getting the best of him.

Mr. Baumer had his hand in a sling the next day and wasn't
much good at waiting on the trade. I had to hustle all afternoon
and so didn't have a chance to talk to him even if he had
wanted to talk. Mostly he stood at his desk, and once, passing
it, I saw he was practicing writing with his left hand. His nose
and the edges of the cheeks around it were swollen some.

At closing time I said, "Look, Mr. Baumer, I can lay out of
260 school a few days until you kind of get straightened out here."

"No," he answered as if to wave the subject away. "I get
somebody else. You go to school. Is good to learn."

I had a half notion to say that learning hadn't helped him
with Slade. Instead, I blurted out that I would have the law
on Slade.

"The law?" he asked.

"The sheriff or somebody."

"No, Al," he said. "You would not."

I asked why.

270 "The law, it is not for plain fights," he said. "Shooting?
Robbing? Yes, the law come quick. The plain fights, they are
too many. They not count enough."

He was right. I said, "Well, I'd do something anyhow."

"Yes," he answered with a slow nod of his head.
"Something you vould do, Al." He didn't tell me what.

Within a couple of days he got another man to clerk for
him—it was Ed Hempel, who was always finding and losing
jobs—and we made out. Mr. Baumer took his hand from the
sling in a couple or three weeks, but with the tape on it, it still
280 wasn't any use to him. From what you could see of the fingers
below the tape, it looked as if it never would be.

He spent most of his time at the high desk, sending me or
Ed out on the errands he used to run, like posting and getting
the mail. Sometimes I wondered if that was because he was
afraid of meeting Slade. He could just as well have gone

IDENTIFY

In lines 253–258, underline
the sentences that suggest
that Baumer is not easily
discouraged by pain or
hardship.

EVALUATE

Baumer tells Al that the
law is not for "plain fights."
Tell why you think that
statement was true or not
true back in the 1800s.
Then, tell why you think
it's true or not true today.

IDENTIFY

In lines 289–300, underline a surprising plot development. Circle Slade's first response to Baumer's offer. What causes him to change his mind?

_____

_____

_____

_____

PREDICT

The deal is made between Slade and Baumer. Why do you think Baumer wants Slade to work for him? How do you think this employee-employer relationship will work out?

_____

_____

_____

_____

_____

_____

_____

_____

_____

_____

himself. He wasted a lot of hours just looking at nothing, though I will have to say he worked hard at learning to write left-handed.

Then, a month and a half before Christmas, he hired Slade
290 to haul his freight for him.

Ed Hempel told me about the deal when I showed up for work. "Yessir," he said, resting his foot on a crate in the storeroom where we were supposed to be working. "I tell you he's throwed in with Slade. Told me this morning to go out and locate him if I could and bring him in. Slade was at the saloon, o' course, and says to the devil with Dutchie, but I told him this was honest-to-God business, like Baumer had told me to, and there was a quart of whiskey right there in the store for him if he'd come and get it. He was out of money, I reckon, because
300 the quart fetched him."

"What'd they say?" I asked him.

"Search me. There was two or three people in the store and Baumer told me to wait on 'em, and he and Slade palavered[9] back by the desk."

"How do you know they made a deal?"

Ed spread his hands out. "'Bout noon, Moore came in with his string, and I heard Baumer say he was makin' a change. Moore didn't like it too good, either."

It was a hard thing to believe, but there one day was Slade
310 with a pile of stuff for the Moon Dance Mercantile Company, and that was proof enough with something left for boot.

Mr. Baumer never opened the subject up with me, though I gave him plenty of chances. And I didn't feel like asking. He didn't talk much these days but went around absent-minded, feeling now and then of the fingers that curled yellow and stiff out of the bandage like the toes on the leg of a dead chicken. Even on our walks home he kept his thoughts to himself.

I felt different about him now and was sore inside. Not that I blamed him exactly. A hundred and thirty-five pounds
320 wasn't much to throw against two hundred. And who could

---

9. **palavered** (pə·lav′ərd) _v._: talked; met to discuss something.

tell what Slade would do on a bellyful of whiskey? He had promised Mr. Baumer more of the same, hadn't he? But I didn't feel good. I couldn't look up to Mr. Baumer like I used to and still wanted to. I didn't have the beginning of an answer when men cracked jokes or shook their heads in sympathy with Mr. Baumer, saying Slade had made him come to time.

Slade hauled in a load for the store, and another, and Christmas time was drawing on and trade heavy, and the winter that had started early and then pulled back came on again. There was a blizzard and then a still cold and another blizzard and afterwards a sunshine that was iceshine on the drifted snow. I was glad to be busy, selling overshoes and sheep-lined coats and mitts and socks as thick as saddle blankets and Christmas candy out of buckets and hickory nuts and the fresh oranges that the people in our town never saw except when Santa Claus was coming.

One afternoon, when I lit out from class, the thermometer on the school porch read forty-two degrees below. But you didn't have to look at it to know how cold the weather was. Your nose and fingers and toes and ears and the bones inside you told you. The snow cried when you stepped on it.

I got to the store and took my things off and scuffed my hands at the stove for a minute so's to get life enough in them to tie a parcel. Mr. Baumer—he was always polite to me—said, "Hello, Al. Not so much to do today. Too cold for customers." He shuddered a little, as if he hadn't got the chill off even yet, and rubbed his broken hand with the good one. "Ve need Christmas goods," he said, looking out the window to the furrows that wheels had made in the snow-banked street, and I knew he was thinking of Slade's string, inbound from the railroad, and the time it might take even Slade to travel those hard miles.

Slade never made it at all.

Less than an hour later our old freighter, Moore, came in, his beard white and stiff with frost. He didn't speak at first but looked around and clumped to the stove and took off his heavy mitts, holding his news inside him.

Then he said, not pleasantly, "Your new man's dead, Baumer."

330

340

350

IDENTIFY

Underline details that reveal what the narrator is feeling in lines 322–326. What do you think it means when the men say Slade had made Baumer "come to time"?

_____

_____

_____

VISUALIZE

Re-read lines 330–341. Circle five details that help you picture winter in this frontier town.

_____

_____

PREDICT

Pause at line 357. What do you think caused Slade's death?

_____

_____

_____

_____

_____

_____

INTERPRET

Underline the words that give Moore's opinion of why Slade died. Circle Baumer's reaction.

_____

_____

_____

INFER

Does Baumer's reaction to news of Slade's death seem strange to you? Tell why or why not.

_____

_____

_____

_____

_____

_____

_____

_____

_____

_____

_____

"My new man?" Mr. Baumer said.

"Who do you think? Slade. He's dead."

360   All Mr. Baumer could say was "Dead!"

"Froze to death, I figger," Moore told him, while Colly Coleman and Ed Hempel and Miss Lizzie and I and a couple of customers stepped closer.

"Not Slade," Mr. Baumer said. "He know too much to freeze."

"Maybe so, but he sure's froze now. I got him in the wagon."

We stood looking at one another and at Moore. Moore was enjoying his news, enjoying feeding it out bit by bit so's to hold the stage. "Heart might've give out, for all I know."

The side door swung open, letting in a cloud of cold and
370 three men who stood, like us, waiting on Moore. I moved a little and looked through the window and saw Slade's freight outfit tied outside with more men around it. Two of them were on a wheel of one of the wagons, looking inside.

"Had a extra man, so I brought your stuff in," Moore went on. "Figgered you'd be glad to pay for it."

"Not Slade," Mr. Baumer said again.

"You can take a look at him."

Mr. Baumer answered no.

"Someone's takin' word to Connor to bring his hearse.
380 Anyhow, I told 'em to. I carted old Slade this far. Connor can have him now."

Moore pulled on his mitts. "Found him there by the Deep Creek crossin', doubled up in the snow an' his fire out." He moved toward the door. "I'll see to the horses, but your stuff'll have to set there. I got more'n enough work to do at Hirsches'."

Mr. Baumer just nodded.

I put on my coat and went out and waited my turn and climbed on a wagon wheel and looked inside, and there was Slade piled on some bags of bran. Maybe because of being frozen,
390 his face was whiter than I ever saw it, whiter and deader, too, though it never had been lively. Only the moustache seemed still alive, sprouting thick like greasewood from alkali.[10] Slade

---

10. **greasewood from alkali:** Greasewood is a thorny desert plant. Alkali is dry, salty soil that might look white and chalky, like Slade's face.

was doubled up all right, as if he had died and stiffened leaning forward in a chair.

I got down from the wheel, and Colly and then Ed climbed up. Moore was unhitching, tossing off his pieces of information while he did so. Pretty soon Mr. Connor came up with his old hearse, and he and Moore tumbled Slade into it, and the team, which was as old as the hearse, made off, the tires squeaking
400 in the snow. The people trailed on away with it, their breaths leaving little ribbons of mist in the air. It was beginning to get dark.

Mr. Baumer came out of the side door of the store, bundled up, and called to Colly and Ed and me. "We unload," he said. "Already is late. Al, better you get a couple lanterns now." We did a fast job, setting the stuff out of the wagons onto the platform and then carrying it or rolling it on the one truck that the store owned and stowing it inside according to where Mr. Baumer's good hand pointed.
410 A barrel was one of the last things to go in. I edged it up and Colly nosed the truck under it, and then I let it fall back. "Mr. Baumer," I said, "we'll never sell all this, will we?"

"Yah," he answered. "Sure we sell it. I get it cheap. A bargain, Al, so I buy it."

I looked at the barrel head again. There in big letters I saw "Wood Alcohol—Deadly Poison."

"Hurry now," Mr. Baumer said. "Is late." For a flash and no longer I saw through the mist in his eyes, saw, you might say, that hilly chin repeated there. "Then ve go home, Al. Is
420 good to know to read."

INTERPRET

Underline the words that Al finds written on the barrel he unloads. What do you remember about Slade's reading ability? What do you think Baumer means when he says the wood alcohol is a "bargain" (line 413)?

_____

_____

_____

INTERPRET

What really caused Slade's death? Who is responsible for his death? Was Slade's death a matter of justice or revenge? Give two or three reasons to support your opinion.

_____

_____

_____

_____

_____

_____

_____

_____

_____

_____

_____

Plot Diagram

Keeping track of the major elements of the plot will help you **retell** the story. Fill out the plot diagram below after you read "Bargain."

Basic Situation and Conflict:

Complications (problems, events):

Climax (crisis, big event):

Resolution:

Vocabulary and Comprehension

A. Remember that some words have more than one meaning. In "Bargain," *rank* is used to describe Slade's moustache. *Rank* can also mean a person's place in the military, like the rank of a general. When you are unsure which meaning of a **multiple-meaning word** is intended, use the words, phrases, and sentences around the word to help you figure out its meaning.

- In "Bargain," a wagon "rattled for home." Find three different meanings of *rattle* in a dictionary, and write a sentence showing each meaning.

1. _____

_____

2. _____

_____

3. _____

_____

B. Answer each question below.

1. Describe the narrator of the story.

_____

_____

2. Why does Mr. Baumer hire Slade?

_____

_____

3. What do you think of the way the story ends? Was Baumer right to take justice into his own hands? Explain.

_____

_____

Amigo Brothers

Make the Connection

Fighters—Together

In this story two best friends must fight each other in a boxing ring. The winner of the fight will get the prize both of them want more than anything. If you've ever done it, you know how tough it is to compete against a good friend in a contest or sport. In the graphic organizer below, list some rules that might make the competition easier for two best friends who are both competing for the same prize.

Rules for Competing Against a Friend

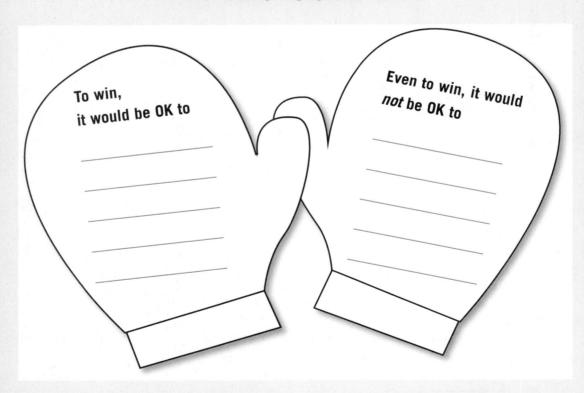

To win,
it would be OK to

_____

_____

_____

_____

Even to win, it would
not be OK to

_____

_____

_____

_____

Amigo Brothers

Piri Thomas

Background

This story is about two friends (**amigos** in Spanish) living on the Lower East Side of New York City. Many boys from the Lower East Side have dreamed of building a better life by winning the New York Golden Gloves, a tournament started in 1927 by Paul Gallico, a newspaper writer. This tournament marks an amateur's entry into the world of big-time boxing.

IDENTIFY

Underline the names of the two **main characters.** Circle three details that tell how *similar,* or alike, they are. How are they different?

_____

_____

_____

_____

INTERPRET

Underline the details that describe each youngster's fighting style. What does the author mean when he says Antonio is "the better boxer" while Felix is "the better slugger"?

_____

_____

_____

_____

_____

_____

_____

WORDS TO OWN

tenement (ten′ə·mənt) *n. used as adj.:* apartment.
bouts (bouts) *n.:* matches; contests.
elimination (ē·lim′ə·nā′shən) *n. used as adj.:* removal from competition.

Antonio Cruz and Felix Vargas were both seventeen years old. They were so together in friendship that they felt themselves to be brothers. They had known each other since childhood, growing up on the Lower East Side of Manhattan in the same <u>tenement</u> building on Fifth Street between Avenue A and Avenue B.

Antonio was fair, lean, and lanky, while Felix was dark, short, and husky. Antonio's hair was always falling over his eyes, while Felix wore his black hair in a natural Afro style.

10   Each youngster had a dream of someday becoming lightweight champion of the world. Every chance they had, the boys worked out, sometimes at the Boys' Club on 10th Street and Avenue A and sometimes at the pro's gym on 14th Street. Early morning sunrises would find them running along the East River Drive, wrapped in sweat shirts, short towels around their necks, and handkerchiefs Apache style around their foreheads.

While some youngsters were into street negatives, Antonio and Felix slept, ate, rapped, and dreamt positive. Between them, they had a collection of *Fight* magazines second to none, plus a

20   scrapbook filled with torn tickets to every boxing match they had ever attended, and some clippings of their own. If asked a question about any given fighter, they would immediately zip out from their memory banks divisions, weights, records of fights, knockouts, technical knockouts, and draws or losses.

Each had fought many <u>bouts</u> representing their community and had won two gold-plated medals plus a silver and bronze medallion. The difference was in their style. Antonio's lean form and long reach made him the better boxer, while Felix's short and muscular frame made him the better slugger.

30   Whenever they had met in the ring for sparring sessions,[1] it had always been hot and heavy.

Now, after a series of <u>elimination</u> bouts, they had been informed that they were to meet each other in the division finals that were scheduled for the seventh of August, two weeks

---

1. **sparring sessions:** practice matches in which boxers use light punches.

away—the winner to represent the Boys' Club in the Golden Gloves Championship Tournament.

The two boys continued to run together along the East River Drive. But even when joking with each other, they both sensed a wall rising between them.

40   One morning less than a week before their bout, they met as usual for their daily workout. They fooled around with a few jabs at the air, slapped skin, and then took off, running lightly along the dirty East River's edge.

Antonio glanced at Felix, who kept his eyes purposely straight ahead, pausing from time to time to do some fancy leg work while throwing one-twos followed by uppercuts to an imaginary jaw. Antonio then beat the air with a <u>barrage</u> of body blows and short devastating lefts with an overhead jaw-breaking right.

50   After a mile or so, Felix puffed and said, "Let's stop a while, bro. I think we both got something to say to each other."

Antonio nodded. It was not natural to be acting as though nothing unusual was happening when two ace-boon buddies were going to be blasting each other within a few short days.

They rested their elbows on the railing separating them from the river. Antonio wiped his face with his short towel. The sunrise was now creating day.

Felix leaned heavily on the river's railing and stared across to the shores of Brooklyn. Finally, he broke the silence.

60   "Man. I don't know how to come out with it."

Antonio helped. "It's about our fight, right?"

"Yeah, right." Felix's eyes squinted at the rising orange sun.

"I've been thinking about it too, panin.[2] In fact, since we found out it was going to be me and you, I've been awake at night, pulling punches on you, trying not to hurt you."

"Same here. It ain't natural not to think about the fight. I mean, we both are cheverote[3] fighters and we both want to win. But only one of us can win. There ain't no draws in the eliminations."

---

2. **panin** (pä·nēn′) *n.*: Puerto Rican Spanish slang for "pal" or "buddy."
3. **cheverote** (chev′er·ôt′te) *adj.*: Puerto Rican Spanish slang for "good" or "fine."

INTERPRET

What does it mean that "they both sensed a wall rising between them" (lines 38–39)? What is the wall?

_____

_____

_____

_____

IDENTIFY

Underline phrases that indicate that Antonio and Felix are feeling tense.

_____

_____

PREDICT

Pause at line 69. How do you think Antonio and Felix will solve the problem they have about fighting each other?

_____

_____

_____

_____

_____

_____

WORDS TO OWN
barrage (bə·räzh′) *n.*: heavy attack.

RETELL

Re-read lines 70–92. Then, **retell** what the friends decide about how they will fight and how they will prepare for the fight.

70   Felix tapped Antonio gently on the shoulder. "I don't mean to sound like I'm bragging, bro. But I wanna win, fair and square."

Antonio nodded quietly. "Yeah. We both know that in the ring the better man wins. Friend or no friend, brother or no . . ."

Felix finished it for him. "Brother. Tony, let's promise something right here. OK?"

"If it's fair, hermano,⁴ I'm for it." Antonio admired the courage of a tugboat pulling a barge five times its welterweight size.

"It's fair, Tony. When we get into the ring, it's gotta be like

80   we never met. We gotta be like two heavy strangers that want the same thing and only one can have it. You understand, don't cha?"

"Sí, I know." Tony smiled. "No pulling punches. We go all the way."

"Yeah, that's right. Listen, Tony. Don't you think it's a good idea if we don't see each other until the day of the fight? I'm going to stay with my Aunt Lucy in the Bronx. I can use Gleason's Gym for working out. My manager says he got some sparring partners with more or less your style."

90   Tony scratched his nose <u>pensively</u>. "Yeah, it would be better for our heads." He held out his hand, palm upward. "Deal?"

"Deal." Felix lightly slapped open skin.

"Ready for some more running?" Tony asked lamely.

"Naw, bro. Let's cut it here. You go on. I kinda like to get things together in my head."

"You ain't worried, are you?" Tony asked.

"No way, man." Felix laughed out loud. "I got too much smarts for that. I just think it's cooler if we split right here. After the fight, we can get it together again like nothing ever

100   happened."

The amigo brothers were not ashamed to hug each other tightly.

WORDS TO OWN

pensively (pen′siv·lē) *adv.:* thoughtfully.

---

4. **hermano** (er·mä′nô) *n.:* Spanish for "brother."

"Guess you're right. Watch yourself, Felix. I hear there's some pretty heavy dudes up in the Bronx. Suavecito,[5] OK?"

"OK. You watch yourself too, sabe?"[6]

Tony jogged away. Felix watched his friend disappear from view, throwing rights and lefts. Both fighters had a lot of psyching up to do before the big fight.

The days in training passed much too slowly. Although they
110 kept out of each other's way, they were aware of each other's progress via the ghetto grapevine.

The evening before the big fight, Tony made his way to the roof of his tenement. In the quiet early dark, he peered over the ledge. Six stories below, the lights of the city blinked and the sounds of cars mingled with the curses and the laughter of children in the street. He tried not to think of Felix, feeling he had succeeded in psyching his mind. But only in the ring would he really know. To spare Felix hurt, he would have to knock him out, early and quick.

120 Up in the South Bronx, Felix decided to take in a movie in an effort to keep Antonio's face away from his fists. The flick was *The Champion* with Kirk Douglas, the third time Felix was seeing it.

The champion was getting beaten, his face being pounded into raw, wet hamburger. His eyes were cut, jagged, bleeding, one eye swollen, the other almost shut. He was saved only by the sound of the bell.

Felix became the champ and Tony the challenger.

The movie audience was going out of its head, roaring in
130 blood lust at the butchery going on. The champ hunched his shoulders, grunting and sniffing red blood back into his broken nose. The challenger, confident that he had the championship in the bag, threw a left. The champ countered with a dynamite right that exploded into the challenger's brains.

Felix's right arm felt the shock. Antonio's face, superimposed on the screen, was shattered and split apart by the awesome

---

5. **suavecito** (swä′vä·sē′tồ) *adj.:* Puerto Rican Spanish slang for "be cool."
6. **sabe** (sä′bā) *v.:* Spanish for "you know."

INTERPRET

Conflict is a struggle between opposing characters or forces. In this story, the fight is an example of **external conflict.** One friend is supposed to knock the other one out. The friends also struggle with **internal conflict,** a fight that takes place inside a character's mind. What internal conflict do they have?

_____

_____

_____

_____

_____

_____

INFER

In line 116, the night before the fight, why does Tony try not to think of Felix?

_____

_____

_____

_____

_____

_____

INTERPRET

How does watching the movie help Felix prepare for the fight?

_____

_____

_____

_____

_____

_____

_____

INTERPRET

How would you describe Antonio's **conflict** in lines 156–167? What does he fear will happen to his friendship with Felix?

_____

_____

_____

_____

_____

_____

_____

_____

_____

WORDS TO OWN

torrent (tôr′ənt) _n._: flood.

force of the killer blow. Felix saw himself in the ring, blasting Antonio against the ropes. The champ had to be forcibly restrained. The challenger was allowed to crumble slowly to the
140 canvas, a broken bloody mess.

When Felix finally left the theater, he had figured out how to psych himself for tomorrow's fight. It was Felix the Champion vs. Antonio the Challenger.

He walked up some dark streets, deserted except for small pockets of wary-looking kids wearing gang colors. Despite the fact that he was Puerto Rican like them, they eyed him as a stranger to their turf. Felix did a fast shuffle, bobbing and weaving, while letting loose a <u>torrent</u> of blows that would demolish whatever got in its way. It seemed to impress the
150 brothers, who went about their own business.

Finding no takers, Felix decided to split to his aunt's. Walking the streets had not relaxed him; neither had the fight flick. All it had done was to stir him up. He let himself quietly into his Aunt Lucy's apartment and went straight to bed, falling into a fitful sleep with sounds of the gong for Round One.

Antonio was passing some heavy time on his rooftop. How would the fight tomorrow affect his relationship with Felix? After all, fighting was like any other profession. Friendship had nothing to do with it. A gnawing doubt crept in. He cut
160 negative thinking real quick by doing some speedy fancy dance steps, bobbing and weaving like mercury. The night air was blurred with perpetual motions of left hooks and right crosses. Felix, his amigo brother, was not going to be Felix at all in the ring. Just an opponent with another face. Antonio went to sleep, hearing the opening bell for the first round. Like his friend in the South Bronx, he prayed for victory via a quick clean knockout in the first round.

Large posters plastered all over the walls of local shops announced the fight between Antonio Cruz and Felix Vargas
170 as the main bout.

The fight had created great interest in the neighborhood. Antonio and Felix were well liked and respected. Each had his own loyal following. Betting fever was high and ranged from a bottle of Coke to cold hard cash on the line.

Antonio's fans bet with unbridled faith in his boxing skills. On the other side, Felix's admirers bet on his dynamite-packed fists.

Felix had returned to his apartment early in the morning of August 7th and stayed there, hoping to avoid seeing Antonio.
180 He turned the radio on to salsa[7] music sounds and then tried to read while waiting for word from his manager.

The fight was scheduled to take place in Tompkins Square Park. It had been decided that the gymnasium of the Boys' Club was not large enough to hold all the people who were sure to attend. In Tompkins Square Park, everyone who wanted could view the fight, whether from ringside or window fire escapes or tenement rooftops.

The morning of the fight Tompkins Square was a beehive of activity with numerous workers setting up the ring, the seats,
190 and the guest speakers' stand. The scheduled bouts began shortly after noon and the park had begun filling up even earlier.

The local junior high school across from Tompkins Square Park served as the dressing room for all the fighters. Each was given a separate classroom with desk tops, covered with mats, serving as resting tables. Antonio thought he caught a glimpse of Felix waving to him from a room at the far end of the corridor. He waved back just in case it had been him.

The fighters changed from their street clothes into fighting
200 gear. Antonio wore white trunks, black socks, and black shoes. Felix wore sky-blue trunks, red socks, and white boxing shoes. They had dressing gowns to match their fighting trunks with their names neatly stitched on the back.

The loudspeakers blared into the open windows of the school. There were speeches by dignitaries, community leaders, and great boxers of yesteryear. Some were well prepared; some improvised on the spot. They all carried the same message of

PREDICT

Who do you think will win the fight? Will Antonio and Felix still be friends after the fight? Tell what you think will happen.

IDENTIFY

Circle the details in lines 182–205 that help to build **suspense.**

---

7. **salsa** (säl′sə) *n.:* Latin American dance music, usually played at fast tempos.

great pleasure and honor at being part of such a historic event. This great day was in the tradition of champions emerging from the streets of the Lower East Side.

Interwoven with the speeches were the sounds of the other boxing events. After the sixth bout, Felix was much relieved when his trainer, Charlie, said, "Time change. Quick knockout. This is it. We're on."

Waiting time was over. Felix was escorted from the classroom by a dozen fans in white T-shirts with the word FELIX across their fronts.

Antonio was escorted down a different stairwell and guided through a roped-off path.

As the two climbed into the ring, the crowd exploded with a roar. Antonio and Felix both bowed gracefully and then raised their arms in acknowledgment.

Antonio tried to be cool, but even as the roar was in its first birth, he turned slowly to meet Felix's eyes looking directly into his. Felix nodded his head and Antonio responded. And both as one, just as quickly, turned away to face his own corner.

Bong—bong—bong. The roar turned to stillness.

"Ladies and Gentlemen, Señores y Señoras."

The announcer spoke slowly, pleased at his bilingual efforts.

"Now the moment we have all been waiting for—the main event between two fine young Puerto Rican fighters, products of our Lower East Side."

"Loisaida,"[8] called out a member of the audience.

"In this corner, weighing 134 pounds, Felix Vargas. And in this corner, weighing 133 pounds, Antonio Cruz. The winner will represent the Boys' Club in the tournament of champions, the Golden Gloves. There will be no draw. May the best man win."

The cheering of the crowd shook the window panes of the old buildings surrounding Tompkins Square Park. At the center of the ring, the referee was giving instructions to the youngsters.

---

8. **Loisaida** (loi·sī′dä): Puerto Rican English dialect for "Lower East Side."

BUILD FLUENCY

Go back and re-read this boxed passage. Re-read it again aloud. This time, pretend you are the announcer, and later the referee. Use a tone of voice that will get the attention of the crowd and help build suspense.

WORDS TO OWN
interwoven (in′tər·wō′vən) v. used as adj.: closely connected.

"Keep your punches up. No low blows. No punching on the back of the head. Keep your heads up. Understand? Let's have a clean fight. Now shake hands and come out fighting."

Both youngsters touched gloves and nodded. They turned and danced quickly to their corners. Their head towels and dressing gowns were lifted neatly from their shoulders by their trainers' nimble fingers. Antonio crossed himself. Felix did the same.

250

BONG! BONG! ROUND ONE. Felix and Antonio turned and faced each other squarely in a fighting pose. Felix wasted no time. He came in fast, head low, half-hunched toward his right shoulder, and lashed out with a straight left. He missed a right cross as Antonio slipped the punch and countered with one-two-three lefts that snapped Felix's head back, sending a mild shock coursing through him. If Felix had any small doubt about their friendship affecting their fight, it was being neatly dispelled.

260

Antonio danced, a joy to behold. His left hand was like a piston pumping jabs one right after another with seeming ease. Felix bobbed and weaved and never stopped boring in. He knew that at long range he was at a disadvantage. Antonio had too much reach on him. Only by coming in close could Felix hope to achieve the dreamed-of knockout.

Antonio knew the dynamite that was stored in his amigo brother's fist. He ducked a short right and missed a left hook. Felix trapped him against the ropes just long enough to pour some punishing rights and lefts to Antonio's hard midsection.

270 Antonio slipped away from Felix, crashing two lefts to his head, which set Felix's right ear to ringing.

Bong! Both amigos froze a punch well on its way, sending up a roar of approval for good sportsmanship.

Felix walked briskly back to his corner. His right ear had not stopped ringing. Antonio gracefully danced his way toward his stool none the worse, except for glowing glove burns showing angry red against the whiteness of his midribs.

VISUALIZE

Re-read the description of the first round in lines 251–273. Notice the details that help you see, hear, and even feel what's happening in the ring. Circle five of the details that help you picture the fight.

INFER

Who do you think is winning the fight so far? Tell why you think so.

WORDS TO OWN
dispelled (di·speld′) *v.:* driven away.

"Watch that right, Tony." His trainer talked into his ear. "Remember Felix always goes to the body. He'll want you to 280 drop your hands for his overhand left or right. Got it?"

Antonio nodded, spraying water out between his teeth. He felt better as his sore midsection was being firmly rubbed.

Felix's corner was also busy.

"You gotta get in there, fella." Felix's trainer poured water over his curly Afro locks. "Get in there or he's gonna chop you up from way back."

Bong! Bong! Round two. Felix was off his stool and rushed Antonio like a bull, sending a hard right to his head. Beads of water exploded from Antonio's long hair.

290 Antonio, hurt, sent back a blurring barrage of lefts and rights that only meant pain to Felix, who returned with a short left to the head followed by a looping right to the body. Antonio countered with his own flurry, forcing Felix to give ground. But not for long.

Felix bobbed and weaved, bobbed and weaved, occasionally punching his two gloves together.

Antonio waited for the rush that was sure to come. Felix closed in and feinted with his left shoulder and threw a right instead. Lights suddenly exploded inside Felix's head as 300 Antonio slipped the blow and hit him with a pistonlike left, catching him flush on the point of his chin.

Bedlam broke loose as Felix's legs momentarily buckled. He fought off a series of rights and lefts and came back with a strong right that taught Antonio respect.

Antonio danced in carefully. He knew Felix had the habit of playing possum when hurt, to sucker an opponent within reach of the powerful bombs he carried in each fist.

A right to the head slowed Antonio's pretty dancing. He answered with his own left at Felix's right eye that began 310 puffing up within three seconds.

Antonio, a bit too eager, moved in too close, and Felix had him entangled into a rip-roaring, punching toe-to-toe slugfest that brought the whole Tompkins Square Park screaming to its feet.

VISUALIZE

Circle five details in lines 297–301 that use boxing terms to help you picture the fast action.

INFER

The author states that Felix had the habit of "playing possum when hurt." Underline the lines that explain what he means. Then, explain what he means using your own words.

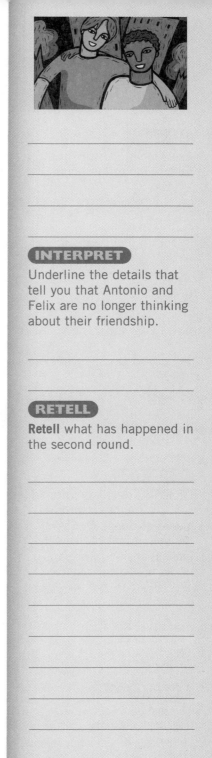

Rights to the body. Lefts to the head. Neither fighter was giving an inch. Suddenly a short right caught Antonio squarely on the chin. His long legs turned to jelly and his arms flailed out desperately. Felix, grunting like a bull, threw wild punches from every direction. Antonio, groggy, bobbed and weaved,
320 <u>evading</u> most of the blows. Suddenly his head cleared. His left flashed out hard and straight, catching Felix on the bridge of his nose.

Felix lashed back with a haymaker, right off the ghetto streets. At the same instant, his eye caught another left hook from Antonio. Felix swung out, trying to clear the pain. Only the <u>frenzied</u> screaming of those along ringside let him know that he had dropped Antonio. Fighting off the growing haze, Antonio struggled to his feet, got up, ducked, and threw a smashing right that dropped Felix flat on his back.

330 Felix got up as fast as he could in his own corner, groggy but still game. He didn't even hear the count. In a fog, he heard the roaring of the crowd, who seemed to have gone insane. His head cleared to hear the bell sound at the end of the round. He was glad. His trainer sat him down on the stool.

In his corner, Antonio was doing what all fighters do when they are hurt. They sit and smile at everyone.

The referee signaled the ring doctor to check the fighters out. He did so and then gave his OK. The cold-water sponges brought clarity to both amigo brothers. They were rubbed until
340 their circulation ran free.

Bong! Round three—the final round. Up to now it had been tic-tac-toe, pretty much even. But everyone knew there could be no draw and that this round would decide the winner.

This time, to Felix's surprise, it was Antonio who came out fast, charging across the ring. Felix braced himself but couldn't ward off the barrage of punches. Antonio drove Felix hard against the ropes.

The crowd ate it up. Thus far the two had fought with mucho corazón.[9] Felix tapped his gloves and commenced his

---

9. **mucho corazón** (moo'chô côr·ä·sôn'): Spanish for "a lot of heart."

INTERPRET

Underline the details that tell you that Antonio and Felix are no longer thinking about their friendship.

RETELL

Retell what has happened in the second round.

WORDS TO OWN
evading (ē·vād'iŋ) *v. used as adj:* avoiding.
frenzied (fren'zēd) *adj.:* wild.

RETELL

Retell what happens in the final round of the fight.

_____

_____

_____

_____

_____

_____

_____

_____

IDENTIFY

Underline details that build suspense right up to the **climax** of the story. Circle the action that resolves the **internal conflict,** when you find out whether Antonio and Felix can still be friends.

_____

_____

INTERPRET

The last sentence refers to both fighters as "champions." In what way are they both champions?

_____

_____

_____

_____

350 attack anew. Antonio, throwing boxer's caution to the winds, jumped in to meet him.

Both pounded away. Neither gave an inch and neither fell to the canvas. Felix's left eye was tightly closed. Claret-red blood poured from Antonio's nose. They fought toe-to-toe.

The sounds of their blows were loud in contrast to the silence of a crowd gone completely mute. The referee was stunned by their savagery.

Bong! Bong! Bong! The bell sounded over and over again. Felix and Antonio were past hearing. Their blows continued to
360 pound on each other like hailstones.

Finally the referee and the two trainers pried Felix and Antonio apart. Cold water was poured over them to bring them back to their senses.

They looked around and then rushed toward each other. A cry of alarm surged through Tompkins Square Park. Was this a fight to the death instead of a boxing match?

The fear soon gave way to wave upon wave of cheering as the two amigos embraced.

No matter what the decision, they knew they would always
370 be champions to each other.

BONG! BONG! BONG! "Ladies and Gentlemen. Señores and Señoras. The winner and representative to the Golden Gloves Tournament of Champions is . . ."

The announcer turned to point to the winner and found himself alone. Arm in arm the champions had already left the ring.

Comparison and Contrast

Finding Similarities and Differences

Piri Thomas begins his story by contrasting the two best friends: "Antonio was fair, lean, and lanky, while Felix was dark, short, and husky." A **comparison** points out similarities between things; a **contrast** points out differences. Go back over the story, and use a **Venn diagram** to help you identify the ways in which Felix and Antonio are alike and different. Write their likenesses in the part where the circles overlap.

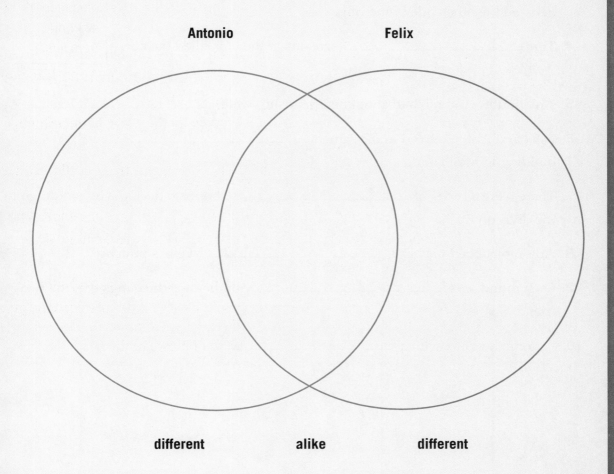

Antonio   Felix

different   alike   different

Vocabulary

A. Complete each sentence with a word from the Word Bank.

Word Bank
tenement
bouts
elimination
barrage
pensively
torrent
interwoven
dispelled
evading
frenzied

1. Both Antonio and Felix fought many _____ with other young boxers.

2. Antonio gazed _____ at his best friend, whom he was about to face in the boxing ring.

3. Antonio felt a _____ of emotion when he saw Felix on the other side of the ring.

4. The _____ screams of the fans filled the air.

5. Any doubts Antonio had about his friendship were _____.

6. Felix and Antonio lived in the same _____ building in Manhattan.

7. There were a series of _____ bouts to decide who would go to the division finals.

8. Antonio bobbed his head, _____ Felix's punches.

9. Each round was _____ with the mixed feelings that the two friends shared.

10. Antonio hit Felix with a _____ of blows to the head.

Comprehension

B. Write **T** or **F** next to each statement to tell if it is true or false.

_____ **1.** Antonio and Felix are best friends.

_____ **2.** They live in the same apartment building.

_____ **3.** Antonio does not want to represent the Boys' Club in the Golden Gloves Championship Tournament.

_____ **4.** The boys agree they will not hurt each other in the ring.

_____ **5.** The fight is held in Tompkins Square Park because it is bigger than the Boys' Club.

_____ **6.** Felix drops out of the match.

C. Answer the question below using complete sentences.

How did you react to the way the story ends? Were you disappointed not to find out who won? Did you find this story true to life? How realistic is it for two friends to fight and still stay friends? Give reasons for your opinions.

_____

_____

_____

_____

_____

_____

_____

_____

_____

_____

The Highwayman

Make the Connection

Sketch a Story

A highwayman, an eighteenth-century outlaw, rides along a moonlit road to a country inn. This highwayman is the main character in a **narrative poem**, a poem that tells a story. **Conflict** is basic to the plot of every story, so you know that this daring young man is going to meet some obstacle or problem along the way. Here's your chance to **predict** what will happen. (Maybe you'll like the events you predict better than the actual events in the poem!)

On the road below, draw the highwayman on his horse. In the space to the right of the moon, draw the inn. At the window of the inn, draw what you think the highwayman seeks. Then, on the road, draw what you think will come between the highwayman and his goal. Don't worry about how well you draw. The important thing is to show what you think the highwayman might be seeking and what will get in his way. Use labels and arrows if you think you need them.

The Highwayman

Alfred Noyes

VISUALIZE

Stop at line 6. Underline the words that help you picture the **setting**. In a word or two, describe the mood the setting creates.

_____

_____

_____

IDENTIFY

A **narrative poem**, like any other narrative, contains a setting, characters, conflict, and plot. Circle the **major characters** in this narrative so far.

INFER

What does the description of Tim (lines 19–23) reveal about his **character**?

_____

_____

_____

_____

INFER

What person-to-person **conflict** might be suggested here? Who is on each side of the conflict?

_____

_____

_____

_____

_____

Part 1

The wind was a torrent of darkness among the gusty trees,
The moon was a ghostly galleon[1] tossed upon cloudy seas,
The road was a ribbon of moonlight over the purple moor,
And the highwayman came riding——
5   Riding——riding——
The highwayman came riding, up to the old inn door.

He'd a French cocked hat on his forehead, a bunch of lace
     at his chin,
A coat of the claret[2] velvet, and breeches of brown doeskin.
They fitted with never a wrinkle. His boots were up to
     the thigh.
10   And he rode with a jeweled twinkle,
          His pistol butts a-twinkle,
His rapier hilt[3] a-twinkle, under the jeweled sky.

Over the cobbles he clattered and clashed in the dark
     inn yard.
And he tapped with his whip on the shutters, but all was
     locked and barred.
He whistled a tune to the window, and who should be
15   waiting there
But the landlord's black-eyed daughter,
          Bess, the landlord's daughter,
Plaiting[4] a dark red love knot into her long black hair.

And dark in the dark old inn yard a stable wicket[5] creaked
Where Tim the ostler[6] listened. His face was white and
20   peaked.
His eyes were hollows of madness, his hair like moldy hay,
But he loved the landlord's daughter,

---

1. **galleon:** large sailing ship.
2. **claret** (klar′it): purplish red, like claret wine.
3. **rapier** (rā′pē·ər) **hilt:** sword handle.
4. **plaiting:** braiding.
5. **wicket:** small door or gate.
6. **ostler** (äs′lər): person who takes care of horses; groom.

The landlord's red-lipped daughter,
Dumb as a dog he listened, and he heard the robber say——

25 "One kiss, my bonny sweetheart, I'm after a prize tonight,
But I shall be back with the yellow gold before the morning
      light;
Yet, if they press me sharply, and harry[7] me through
      the day,
Then look for me by moonlight,
      Watch for me by moonlight,
I'll come to thee by moonlight, though hell should bar
30   the way."

He rose upright in the stirrups. He scarce could reach
      her hand,
But she loosened her hair in the casement.[8] His face burnt
      like a brand
As the black cascade of perfume came tumbling over
      his breast;
And he kissed its waves in the moonlight,
35   (Oh, sweet black waves in the moonlight!)
Then he tugged at his rein in the moonlight, and galloped
      away to the west.

Part 2
He did not come in the dawning. He did not come at
      noon;
And out of the tawny sunset, before the rise of the moon,
When the road was a gypsy's ribbon, looping the
      purple moor,
40 A redcoat troop came marching——
      Marching——marching——
King George's men came marching, up to the old inn door.

---

7. **harry:** harass or push along.
8. **casement:** window that opens outward on hinges.

IDENTIFY
Underline the promise that the highwayman makes to the landlord's daughter. When does he say he will return?

_____
_____
_____
_____

INFER
What is your impression of the highwayman's **character**? Find and circle words or passages in Part 1 that back up your reaction to him.

_____
_____
_____
_____
_____

PREDICT
What do you think will happen if the highwayman returns while the soldiers are still there?

_____
_____
_____
_____
_____

INFER

Who is the dead man referred to in line 51? Why does the narrator call him a dead man?

_____

_____

_____

_____

_____

_____

_____

RETELL

Pause at line 67. **Retell** what has happened since the highwayman left the landlord's daughter (line 37).

_____

_____

_____

_____

_____

_____

_____

_____

_____

_____

_____

They said no word to the landlord. They drank his ale
    instead.
But they gagged his daughter, and bound her, to the foot of
    her narrow bed.
Two of them knelt at her casement, with muskets at
45   their side!
There was death at every window;
    And hell at one dark window;
For Bess could see, through her casement, the road that _he_
    would ride.

They had tied her up to attention, with many a
    sniggering jest;
They had bound a musket beside her, with the muzzle
50   beneath her breast!
"Now, keep good watch!" and they kissed her. She heard
    the dead man say——
Look for me by moonlight;
Watch for me by moonlight;
I'll come to thee by moonlight, though hell should bar
    the way!

She twisted her hands behind her; but all the knots
55   held good!
She writhed her hands till her fingers were wet with sweat
    or blood!
They stretched and strained in the darkness, and the hours
    crawled by like years,
Till, now, on the stroke of midnight,
    Cold, on the stroke of midnight,
The tip of one finger touched it! The trigger at least
60   was hers!

The tip of one finger touched it; she strove no more for
    the rest!
Up, she stood up to attention, with the muzzle beneath
    her breast.

She would not risk their hearing; she would not strive again;
For the road lay bare in the moonlight;

65   Blank and bare in the moonlight;
And the blood of her veins, in the moonlight, throbbed to
     her love's refrain.

Tlot-tlot; tlot-tlot! Had they heard it? The horse hoofs
     ringing clear;
Tlot-tlot, tlot-tlot, in the distance? Were they deaf that they
     did not hear?
Down the ribbon of moonlight, over the brow of the hill,

70   The highwayman came riding,
          Riding, riding!
The redcoats looked to their priming![9] She stood up, straight
     and still.

Tlot-tlot, in the frosty silence! *Tlot-tlot,* in the echoing night!
Nearer he came and nearer. Her face was like a light!
Her eyes grew wide for a moment; she drew one last deep

75   breath,
Then her fingers moved in the moonlight,
          Her musket shattered the moonlight,
Shattered her breast in the moonlight and warned him——
     with her death.

He turned. He spurred to the west; he did not know who
     stood
Bowed, with her head o'er the musket, drenched with her

80   own blood!
Not till the dawn he heard it, his face grew gray to hear
How Bess, the landlord's daughter,
          The landlord's black-eyed daughter,
Had watched for her love in the moonlight, and died in the
     darkness there.

---

9. priming: explosive for firing a gun.

INTERPRET

Underline the words and phrases repeated in lines 68–71. Why do you think these words, and so many other words and phrases, are repeated in this poem?

_____

_____

_____

_____

EVALUATE

Bess's action is the **climax,** the most suspenseful moment in the plot where the conflict is decided one way or the other. Why do you think Bess pulls the trigger? Do you think she was right or wrong to do what she did? What other action, if any, could she have taken?

_____

_____

_____

_____

INFER

Why does the highwayman return to the inn even though he knows he might die?

_____

BUILD FLUENCY

After you've read lines 91–101, practice re-reading them until you can read smoothly and with expression. Decide how to read each line—loudly, softly, quickly, slowly, with rising excitement, with sorrow, and so on. Look for ways to capture the powerful rhythm with your voice.

INTERPRET

Why do you think the poet included lines 91–101? What different feeling would you have about the poem if it ended at line 90?

_____

_____

_____

_____

EVALUATE

How do you like the way the poem ends? Give a reason for your answer. If you could write a new ending for this poem, what would it be?

_____

_____

_____

_____

_____

_____

Back, he spurred like a madman, shouting a curse to
    the sky,
85
With the white road smoking behind him and his rapier
    brandished high.
Blood-red were his spurs in the golden noon; wine-red was
    his velvet coat;
When they shot him down on the highway,
    Down like a dog on the highway,
And he lay in his blood on the highway, with the bunch of
90   lace at his throat.

> *And still of a winter's night, they say, when the wind is in*
>   *the trees,*
> *When the moon is a ghostly galleon tossed upon*
>   *cloudy seas,*
> *When the road is a ribbon of moonlight over the*
>   *purple moor,*
> *A highwayman comes riding——*
> 95   *Riding——riding——*
> *A highwayman comes riding, up to the old inn door.*
>
> *Over the cobbles he clatters and clangs in the dark inn yard;*
> *He taps with his whip on the shutters, but all is locked*
>   *and barred.*
> *He whistles a tune to the window, and who should be*
>   *waiting there*
> 100 *But the landlord's black-eyed daughter,*
>   *Bess, the landlord's daughter,*
> *Plaiting a dark red love knot into her long black hair.*

Theme Web

"The Highwayman" is a **narrative poem** that tells a story about love, betrayal, and death. Complete the theme web below to help you analyze its theme. Fill in the side boxes first. Then tell what you learned about "The Highwayman" by filling in the center box.

What I learned about Bess:

_____
_____
_____
_____

What Bess's actions show about life:

_____
_____
_____

Theme

This poem showed me that:

_____
_____
_____
_____
_____
_____
_____

What I learned about the Highwayman:

_____
_____
_____
_____

What the Highwayman's actions show about life:

_____
_____
_____

What I learned about Tim and the troops:

_____
_____
_____
_____

What Tim's actions show about life:

_____
_____
_____

What I learned from the setting:

_____
_____
_____
_____

What the setting contributes to the story:

_____
_____
_____

Annabel Lee

Make the Connection

By the Sea

"Annabel Lee" is a love poem written after the poet's young wife died of tuberculosis. She was laid to rest in New York, near the Hudson River, in a sepulcher (sep′əl·kər), a burial vault that stands above ground.

Poe's poem reads like a sad fairy tale set in a kingdom by the sea. When Poe looked at the sea, he recalled his beautiful wife and her sad death. Think about the sea as you have known it, either through your experience or through reading. In the waves below, write five to ten words and phrases that come into your mind when you focus on that word *sea*. A few words have been done for you. If you can't connect those words to your feelings about the sea, cross them out and add different ones.

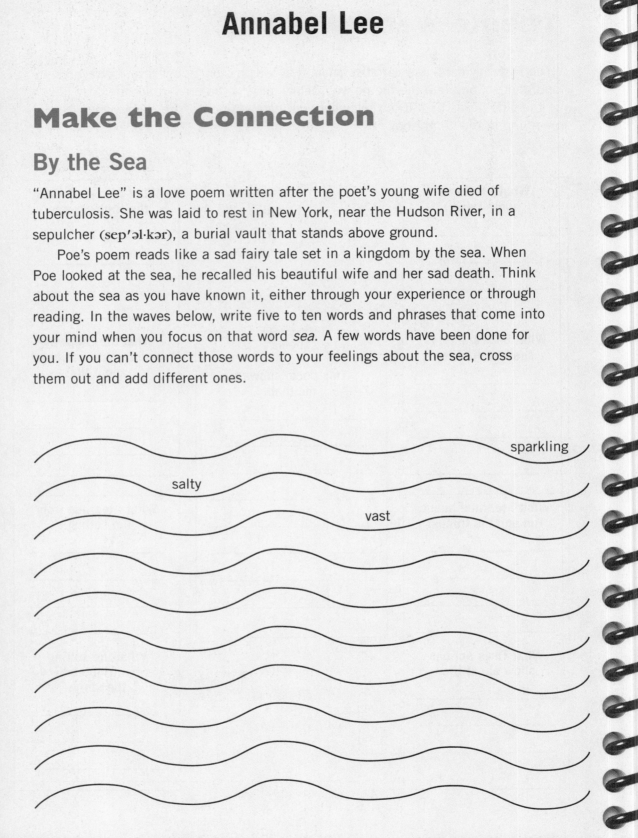

sparkling

salty

vast

Annabel Lee

Edgar Allan Poe

IDENTIFY

Underline the words that tell when and where the events in this poem take place (its **setting**). Circle the name of the person who lived there.

_____

_____

INTERPRET

Pause at line 12. Circle the word in the first two stanzas that is repeated most. Why do you think these words are repeated?

_____

_____

_____

It was many and many a year ago,
    In a kingdom by the sea,
That a maiden there lived whom you may know
    By the name of Annabel Lee;
5 And this maiden she lived with no other thought
    Than to love and be loved by me.

I was a child and *she* was a child,
    In this kingdom by the sea:
But we loved with a love that was more than love—
10   I and my Annabel Lee—
With a love that the wingèd seraphs[1] of heaven
    Coveted[2] her and me.

---

1. **seraphs** (ser'əfs): angels.
2. **coveted**: envied.

INFER

Circle the details in lines 25–26 that suggest the cause of Annabel Lee's death.

RETELL

Pause at line 33. **Retell** what the speaker is saying in lines 21–33.

_____

_____

_____

_____

_____

INTERPRET

How does the speaker feel about Annabel Lee? Even though she is dead, what still endures for him?

BUILD FLUENCY

Re-read the poem. Underline words that deepen the mood of the poem, words that are repeated with haunting regularity. Then, read the poem aloud, listening to the repeated words and phrases. Write one word that sums up Poe's feelings about the sea. Write another word that you think describes the overall feeling that Poe achieves in this poem.

_____

_____

And this was the reason that, long ago,
    In this kingdom by the sea,
15 A wind blew out of a cloud, chilling
    My beautiful Annabel Lee;
So that her highborn kinsmen came
    And bore her away from me,
To shut her up in a sepulcher
20   In this kingdom by the sea.

The angels, not half so happy in heaven,
    Went envying her and me—
Yes!—that was the reason (as all men know,
    In this kingdom by the sea)
25 That the wind came out of the cloud by night,
    Chilling and killing my Annabel Lee.
But our love it was stronger by far than the love
    Of those who were older than we—
    Of many far wiser than we—
30 And neither the angels in heaven above,
    Nor the demons down under the sea,
Can ever dissever[3] my soul from the soul
    Of the beautiful Annabel Lee—

For the moon never beams, without bringing me dreams
35   Of the beautiful Annabel Lee;
And the stars never rise, but I feel the bright eyes
    Of the beautiful Annabel Lee;
And so, all the night-tide, I lie down by the side
Of my darling—my darling—my life and my bride,
40   In the sepulcher there by the sea,
    In her tomb by the sounding sea.

---

3. **dissever** (di·sev′ər): separate.

Theme Chart

A **theme** is an idea or a message about life revealed in a work of literature. Although themes usually are not stated directly, you can make **inferences** about the theme by thinking about the details in the selection.

   After you read "Annabel Lee," fill out the theme chart below with four important details from the poem. Then think about these details, and write a statement that expresses your understanding of the theme of the poem.

Detail

Detail

Detail

Detail

↓

Theme

When the Earth Shakes

Make the Connection

The Power of Knowledge

A Richter scale measures the power of an earthquake. If you were to measure your knowledge of earthquakes on a scale of 1–10, with 10 being the highest, what number would you give yourself?

Start at 1 on the Knowledge Scale below. On each line beside a number, write one fact that you already know about earthquakes. Then, draw an arrow to the number that matches the number of facts you know. After you finish reading "When the Earth Shakes," add some of the new facts you've learned. See if you can reach a power of 10 on the Knowledge Scale. Then, draw another arrow to the new number of facts you know.

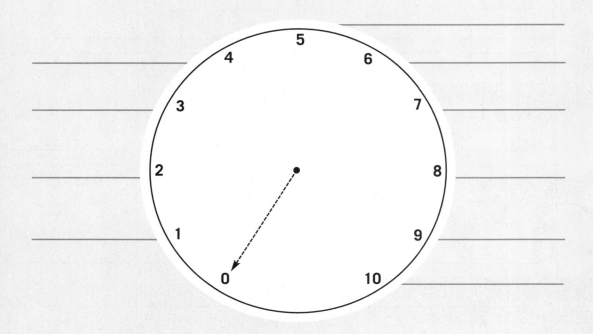

WHEN THE EARTH SHAKES

from Earthquakes: New Scientific Ideas
About How and Why the Earth Shakes

Patricia Lauber

IDENTIFY

Underline the details that tell when and where this true story takes place.

PREDICT

Pause at line 8. What do you think is going to follow this description of a calm, quiet afternoon?

_____

_____

_____

_____

VISUALIZE

Circle the details that help you picture what is happening in lines 11–32.

_____

_____

_____

_____

_____

_____

_____

WORDS TO OWN

churning (chʉrn′iŋ) v.: shaking violently, like milk shaken into butter in a churn.
bluff (bluf) n.: steep cliff.
buckled (buk′əld) v.: collapsed.

It was late afternoon, March 27, 1964. Above Alaska the sky was the color of lead, and in some places a light snow fell. Anchorage, the biggest city, lay quiet, for this gray day was both Good Friday and the eve of Passover.

Schools were empty. Many shops and offices had closed early, and at 5:30 most people were home. Outside, the air was raw, the sky dark. Inside, lights glowed, furnaces hummed, and pots simmered on stoves.

Then it happened. Suddenly the familiar and the cozy
10 vanished. In their place came the strange and the fearful.

At Turnagain, on the edge of Anchorage, people first heard a deep rumble, like the sound of thunder. Next, their houses began to shake. They rushed to their doors, looked out, and thought the world was coming to an end. The earth at their feet was <u>churning</u> and crumbling and sinking away. It was cracking into huge, tilted blocks.

Neighbor helped neighbor to escape. Behind them trees fell. Houses were ripped in two or upended.

Turnagain was built on high ground, on a <u>bluff</u> overlooking
20 the water. The violent shaking triggered a landslide. The front of the bluff slid away, carrying houses and garages with it.

In downtown Anchorage, big buildings creaked and groaned. Their floors rose and fell in waves.

Automobiles bounced like rubber balls. Great chunks of buildings crashed to the street. A movie theater dropped thirty feet into a hole that opened beneath it. A flower shop snapped in two.

Anchorage was not alone in this nightmare. As it shook and cracked and jolted, so did much of Alaska. Buildings trembled
30 and fell. Land tore open. Highways <u>buckled</u>. Railroad tracks were twisted into curls of steel. Snowcapped mountains shuddered, and ice and rock swept down their slopes.

Alaska had been struck by a mighty earthquake that hit without warning. At 5:35 P.M. all was well. By 5:38 half of Alaska seemed to be in the grip of an angry giant. The earth shook with terrible violence.

All along the coast, port towns suffered great damage. One reason was the kind of land on which they stood.

Much of Alaska's coast is rugged, rocky land that stands high above the water. The port towns were built in the low-lying places. But here the ground was not very solid. Also, it sloped down steeply to the ocean floor. When the earthquake shook such land, the soil began to slide. Whole waterfronts vanished in underwater landslides.

That was one of the things that happened at Seward.

Seward was both a port and the end of a rail line. The rail line brought in oil, which was stored in tanks before being shipped. When the earthquake hit, the tanks broke and the oil caught fire.

Flames roared along the waterfront. Just then a great landslide took place. The entire waterfront slid into the bay. The slide caused water to surge away from the land. Burning oil was carried into the bay and then swept back. Fiery water flooded inland. Tugs, fishing boats, and a tanker were washed ashore by the great surge of water. Docks and small-boat harbors were destroyed by fire and wave. For hours that night the bay was ablaze with burning material.

By then, the earthquake had long since ended. The earth was still twitching, and it would go on doing so for weeks. But the earthquake itself was over. In fact, it had lasted only about five minutes.

During that time, the earthquake did great damage. Scientists who studied it reported some astounding effects. Among other things, the quake changed the very face of Alaska.

In the Gulf of Alaska the ocean floor rose. So did land along the coast. All in all, a region the size of Maine was lifted three to eight feet. Inland, another big region sank. Part of an island rose thirty-eight feet. When the quake ended, the town of Valdez was ten feet higher than it had been before.

A whole peninsula moved. Carrying along its mountains and lakes, Kenai Peninsula moved sideways as much as sixty feet and sank seven feet or more.

IDENTIFY

Port towns were built on low-lying places where the ground was not solid. How did the earthquake affect these port towns? Circle two effects mentioned in lines 39–49.

IDENTIFY

Circle what was brought to Seward on the rail line. In lines 50–61, underline what happened in Seward when the earthquake hit.

IDENTIFY

In lines 62–72, the author describes the effects of the earthquake on "the very face of Alaska." List three of those effects below.

IDENTIFY

Re-read lines 85–89. Circle the sentence that contains the **main idea** that is developed in this six-paragraph passage.

IDENTIFY

Re-read lines 85–94. Both paragraphs state the same important idea in two different ways. Circle the sentence that contains that idea in each of the two paragraphs. Then, restate it below in your own words.

_____

_____

_____

_____

INTERPRET

In lines 95–101, the author uses two **similes,** comparisons of two unlike things using comparing words such as *like* or *as.* Underline the two similes in the text. Then, fill in the blanks below:

The _____, the _____, and the _____ are

arranged like _____

_____ .

The crust of the earth is

like the _____

_____ .

There were other changes. Near Valdez a huge wave reached 220 feet above sea level and clawed at the earth. A piece of land 4,000 feet long and 600 feet wide fell into the sea.

Water in Kenai Lake sloshed back and forth. It moved with such force that its water and ice peeled the bark off trees along the shore.

A mountain split apart. One side of it plunged downward, 80 flying over a ridge like a skier taking a jump. The flying mountain spread into a carpet of rocks a mile long and two miles wide. The carpet traveled without touching the ground. Finally it landed on a glacier. Scientists later found it there and figured out what had happened.

The 1964 Alaska earthquake was one of the strongest ever recorded. It was one of the mightiest earthquakes known to man. But it took place for the same reason that all earthquakes do. It took place because rock within the earth suddenly shifted.

90 An earthquake can be strong, as Alaska's was in 1964. Or it can be slight. It can be so slight that no person feels it, though instruments record it. But big or small, an earthquake is just what its name says it is—a shaking of the earth. The earth shakes when rock within it suddenly shifts.

The earth is mostly made of rock. Beneath its soil and oceans, it is a big ball of rock. The ball has three main regions: the core, the mantle, and the crust. They are arranged like the layers of an onion. The core is at the center of the earth. The mantle surrounds the core. The crust surrounds the mantle.

100 Like the crust on a loaf of bread, the earth's crust is a thin outside covering. It is made of two main kinds of rock.

One is a fairly light rock. Its most familiar form is granite, and that is what it is often called. The upper part of the continents is made of this granitelike rock. It is usually about twenty-five miles thick. The continental crust does not end at the water's edge. It reaches out under the sea in what is called a continental shelf. Where the shelf ends, the oceanic crust begins.

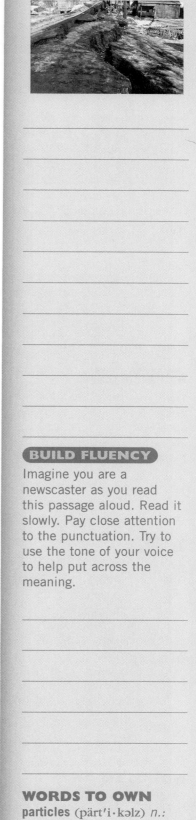

The crust under the oceans is a different kind of rock. It is
much more dense. That is, the rock <u>particles</u> are packed more
closely together. The most familiar form of this rock is the dark,
heavy kind called basalt. The crust under the oceans is about
five miles thick.

The inside of the earth is very hot. And so the crust grows
hotter as it goes deeper. Oil wells drilled deep into the crust
reach rock hot enough to boil water. When volcanoes erupt,
molten rock spills out of them. The rock may have a
temperature of two thousand degrees Fahrenheit. This molten
rock has come from the lower crust or upper mantle.

The mantle is about 1,800 miles thick. It is made of rock,
but this is not rock as we know it. The rock is under very great
pressure, deep within the earth. It is also very hot. The heat
and pressure make the rock behave in ways that are strange
to us.

Sometimes rock of the mantle behaves like a very gummy
liquid. It can flow like thick tar.

But it also behaves like a solid. It can suddenly shift or
snap. When it does, an earthquake takes place. Earthquakes
also occur when rock of the crust suddenly shifts or breaks.

Rock shifts or breaks for the same reason that anything else
does: because it has been put under great strain. If you take a
ruler and bend it, you are putting it under strain. If you bend,
or strain, it too much, it will break.

There are forces within the earth that bend, squeeze, and
twist the rock of the crust and the upper mantle. As a result,
the rock is put under great strain. That is, a large amount of
energy is stored in it as strain. When the strain becomes too
great, the rock suddenly gives way and the stored-up energy is
released.

Something like this happens if you shoot a bow and arrow.
As you pull, the bow and string are bent and forced out of
shape. Energy from your muscles is stored in them as strain.
When you let go, the bow and string snap back into shape, and
the stored-up energy is released. It speeds the arrow through
the air.

110

120

130

140

several **examples**—the ruler, the bow and arrow, and the ten people lined up—to explain earthquakes? Which of those three examples do you find clearest and easiest to understand? Why?

_____

_____

_____

INTERPRET

The author uses the stick example to try to make clear several facts about earthquakes. Write one of those facts below.

_____

_____

INFER

Re-read lines 167–177. Underline the sentence that includes the **main idea** for these four paragraphs. Circle three places where earthquake waves travel. What place where earthquake waves travel causes _no_ damage at all?

_____

_____

WORDS TO OWN
observatories
(əb·zʉrv′ə·tôr′ēz) _n.:_ buildings equipped to collect and study scientific information.

Energy released from rock takes the form of waves. A wave is a kind of giant push. It is a push that passes from one rock particle to the next, much as a push can pass through a line of people. Imagine ten people lined up, each with his hands on
150 the person ahead. If the last person in line is given a sharp push, the push will be felt all through the line. The people stay in place, but the push passes through them.

That is how earthquake waves travel through the inside of the earth. The pushes pass from one rock particle to the next.

You can feel what happens if you snap a stick between your hands. As you slowly bend it, energy is stored as strain. Finally the strain becomes too great. The stick snaps. All the stored-up energy is released. And you feel a sharp stinging. Stored-up energy has changed to waves that are passing through the
160 wood. One wood particle pushes the next. When the pushes reach your hands, you feel them as a sting.

Meanwhile, the broken ends of the stick are vibrating. That is, they are very quickly moving back and forth. They set air waves in motion. Particles of air push other particles. Waves, or pushes, pass through the air. These movements are the source of the sound you hear when the stick snaps.

When an earthquake takes place, waves travel out from the shifting rock in all directions.

Some waves travel through the air. They account for the
170 rumbling sounds that may accompany an earthquake.

Some waves travel deep in the earth. They are seldom felt by people. But instruments in earthquake observatories record them. Earthquake waves that pass through the earth are recorded thousands of miles away.

Some waves travel along the earth's surface. Surface waves are the ones that do the damage—the ones that shake buildings, tear up roads, and cause landslides.

They are not, however, the only cause of earthquake damage. There can be another kind, and it is a kind that comes
180 from the sea.

Multiple-Effects Chart

A single event may have more than one effect. Fill in the charts below with details from the selection to show the multiple effects that happen because of each cause.

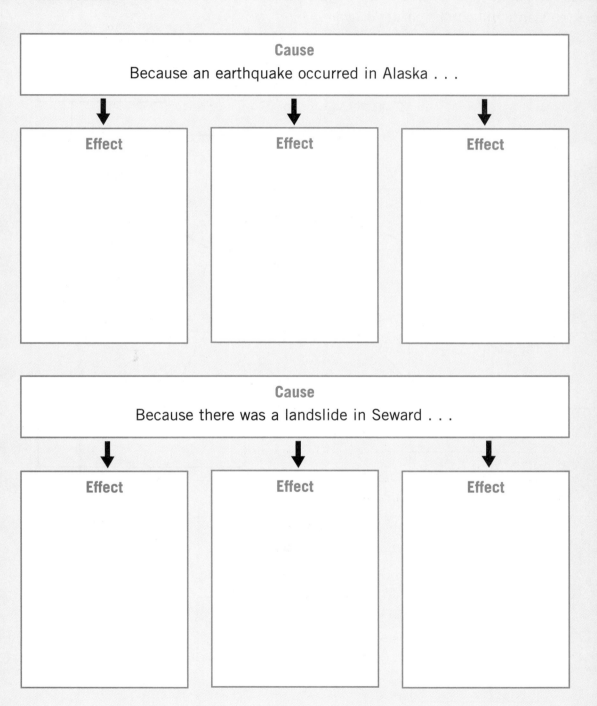

Cause
Because an earthquake occurred in Alaska . . .

Effect	Effect	Effect

Cause
Because there was a landslide in Seward . . .

Effect	Effect	Effect

Cluster Diagram

A **cluster diagram** is a useful way to organize important ideas and details. In the cluster diagram below, collect the information you learned about the earth's three main regions as you read "When the Earth Shakes." You might want to review lines 95–129 of the selection before you start to fill out the cluster diagram.

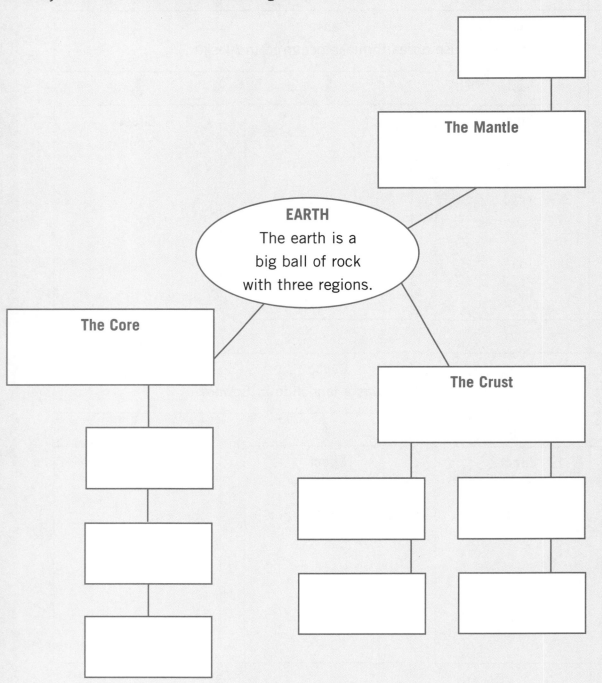

Vocabulary and Comprehension

A. Complete each sentence with a word from the Word Bank.

Word Bank
churning
bluff
buckled
particles
observatories

1. When the earthquake hit, clouds of dust _____ covered many towns and cities.

2. Houses built on a _____ in the town of Turnagain fell into the sea during a landslide.

3. Bridges twisted, _____, and collapsed after an earthquake in Los Angeles.

4. The earth at their feet was _____ and crumbling and sinking away.

5. Special buildings with instruments for recording earthquakes are called earthquake _____ .

B. Write **T** or **F** next to each statement to tell if it is true or false.

_____ **1.** The 1964 Alaska earthquake was one of the strongest ever recorded.

_____ **2.** An earthquake wave travels from one rock particle to another.

_____ **3.** An earthquake is always strong and causes a lot of damage.

_____ **4.** The earth is mostly made of rock.

_____ **5.** Scientific instruments can record only those earthquakes felt by humans.

_____ **6.** Earthquakes can affect the ocean floor.

_____ **7.** The earth shakes when rock within it suddenly shifts.

Echo and Narcissus

Make the Connection

Dear Me

Mirror, mirror on the wall
Who's the fairest of us all?
The evil queen in the story of Snow White would accept only one answer to that question. In this myth, you'll meet another character who's obsessed with good looks. How important is looking good? What could happen to a person who takes too much pride in looking good? Completing the four sentences below may help you think about what beauty is—and the effects it can have.

Beauty is _____
_____
_____ .

In my opinion, the most beautiful person is _____
because _____
_____ .

Vain, self-centered people often _____
_____
_____ .

If I were outstandingly good-looking, I _____
_____
_____ .

Roger Lancelyn Green

Echo and Narcissus

IDENTIFY

Pause at line 5. Underline two words that describe Echo. Circle the words that tell who Hera was.

IDENTIFY

Underline the details that tell why Hera becomes angry with Echo.

INFER

Underline the punishment that Hera gives Echo. What does this punishment reveal about Hera's character? What other **inferences** have you made so far about Hera's character?

_____

_____

_____

_____

_____

_____

INFER

Pause at line 34. Describe Narcissus in your own words.

_____

_____

_____

_____

WORDS TO OWN
detain (dē·tān') v.: hold back; delay.

Up on the wild, lonely mountains of Greece lived the Oreades,[1] the nymphs or fairies of the hills, and among them one of the most beautiful was called Echo. She was one of the most talkative, too, and once she talked too much and angered Hera, wife of Zeus, king of the gods.

When Zeus grew tired of the golden halls of Mount Olympus, the home of the immortal gods, he would come down to earth and wander with the nymphs on the mountains. Hera, however, was jealous and often came to see what he was doing.
10 It seemed strange at first that she always met Echo, and that Echo kept her listening for hours on end to her stories and her gossip.

But at last Hera realized that Echo was doing this on purpose to <u>detain</u> her while Zeus went quietly back to Olympus as if he had never really been away.

"So nothing can stop you talking?" exclaimed Hera. "Well, Echo, I do not intend to spoil your pleasure. But from this day on, you shall be able only to repeat what other people say—and never speak unless someone else speaks first."
20 Hera returned to Olympus, well pleased with the punishment she had made for Echo, leaving the poor nymph to weep sadly among the rocks on the mountainside and speak only the words which her sisters and their friends shouted happily to one another.

She grew used to her strange fate after a while, but then a new misfortune befell her.

There was a beautiful youth called Narcissus,[2] who was the son of a nymph and the god of a nearby river. He grew up in the plain of Thebes[3] until he was sixteen years old and then
30 began to hunt on the mountains toward the north where Echo and her sister Oreades lived.

As he wandered through the woods and valleys, many a nymph looked upon him and loved him. But Narcissus laughed at them scornfully, for he loved only himself.

---

1. **Oreades** (ô'rē·ad'ēz).
2. **Narcissus** (när·sis'əs).
3. **Thebes** (thēbz).

Farther up the mountains Echo saw him. And at once her lonely heart was filled with love for the beautiful youth, so that nothing else in the world mattered but to win him.

Now she wished indeed that she could speak to him words of love. But the curse which Hera had placed upon her tied her
40 tongue, and she could only follow wherever he went, hiding behind trees and rocks, and feasting her eyes vainly upon him.

One day Narcissus wandered farther up the mountain than usual, and all his friends, the other Theban youths, were left far behind. Only Echo followed him, still hiding among the rocks, her heart heavy with unspoken love.

Presently Narcissus realized that he was lost, and hoping to be heard by his companions, or perhaps by some mountain shepherd, he called out loudly:

"Is there anybody here?"
50 "Here!" cried Echo.

Narcissus stood still in amazement, looking all around in vain. Then he shouted, even more loudly:

"Whoever you are, come to me!"

"Come to me!" cried Echo eagerly.

Still no one was visible, so Narcissus called again:

"Why are you avoiding me?"

Echo repeated his words, but with a sob in her breath, and Narcissus called once more:

"Come here, I say, and let us meet!"
60 "Let us meet!" cried Echo, her heart leaping with joy as she spoke the happiest words that had left her lips since the curse of Hera had fallen on her. And to make good her words, she came running out from behind the rocks and tried to clasp her arms about him.

But Narcissus flung the beautiful nymph away from him in scorn.

"Away with these embraces!" he cried angrily, his voice full of cruel contempt. "I would die before I would have you touch me!"
70 "I would have you touch me!" repeated poor Echo.

PREDICT

What do you think will happen when Echo and Narcissus meet?

_____

_____

_____

_____

_____

_____

_____

_____

_____

BUILD FLUENCY

After you've read lines 49–64, practice reading this boxed passage aloud. Use different voices that fit the two characters and the narration.

WORDS TO OWN

vainly (vān′lē) adv.: uselessly.
What other meaning for the adjective vain could be applied to Narcissus?

_____

_____

INTERPRET

In your opinion, if Echo could speak normally, would Narcissus's opinion of her change? Explain why or why not.

_____

_____

_____

_____

_____

_____

_____

INFER

Underline the words that tell who Aphrodite is.

IDENTIFY

Re-read lines 83–87. Circle the details that tell why Aphrodite decides to punish Narcissus. Circle the details that tell how she's going to punish him.

INFER

What has happened to Narcissus?

_____

_____

_____

WORDS TO OWN
unrequited (un'ri·kwīt'id) v.
used as adj.: not returned.
parched (pärcht) adj.: hot
and dry.

"Never will I let you kiss me!"

"Kiss me! Kiss me!" murmured Echo, sinking down among the rocks, as Narcissus cast her violently from him and sped down the hillside.

"One touch of those lips would kill me!" he called back furiously over his shoulder.

"Kill me!" begged Echo.

And Aphrodite,[4] the goddess of love, heard her and was kind to her, for she had been a true lover. Quietly and
80 painlessly, Echo pined away and died. But her voice lived on, lingering among the rocks and answering faintly whenever Narcissus or another called.

"He shall not go unpunished for this cruelty," said Aphrodite. "By scorning poor Echo like this, he scorns love itself. And scorning love, he insults me. He is altogether eaten up with self-love . . . Well, he shall love himself and no one else, and yet shall die of unrequited love!"

It was not long before Aphrodite made good her threat, and in a very strange way. One day, tired after hunting, Narcissus
90 came to a still, clear pool of water away up the mountainside, not far from where he had scorned Echo and left her to die of a broken heart.

With a cry of satisfaction, for the day was hot and cloudless, and he was parched with thirst, Narcissus flung himself down beside the pool and leaned forward to dip his face in the cool water.

What was his surprise to see a beautiful face looking up at him through the still waters of the pool. The moment he saw, he loved—and love was a madness upon him so that he could
100 think of nothing else.

"Beautiful water nymph!" he cried. "I love you! Be mine!"

Desperately he plunged his arms into the water—but the face vanished and he touched only the pebbles at the bottom

---

4. Aphrodite (af'rə·dīt'ē).

of the pool. Drawing out his arms, he gazed <u>intently</u> down and, as the water grew still again, saw once more the face of his beloved.

Poor Narcissus did not know that he was seeing his own reflection, for Aphrodite hid this knowledge from him—and perhaps this was the first time that a pool of water had reflected the face of anyone gazing into it.

Narcissus seemed enchanted by what he saw. He could not leave the pool, but lay by its side day after day looking at the only face in the world which he loved—and could not win— and pining just as Echo had pined.

Slowly Narcissus faded away, and at last his heart broke.

"Woe is me for I loved in vain!" he cried.

"I loved in vain!" sobbed the voice of Echo among the rocks.

"Farewell, my love, farewell," were his last words, and Echo's voice broke and its whisper shivered into silence: "My love . . . farewell!"

So Narcissus died, and the earth covered his bones. But with the spring, a plant pushed its green leaves through the earth where he lay. As the sun shone on it, a bud opened and a new flower blossomed for the first time—a white circle of petals round a yellow center. The flowers grew and spread, waving in the gentle breeze which whispered among them like Echo herself come to kiss the blossoms of the first Narcissus flowers.

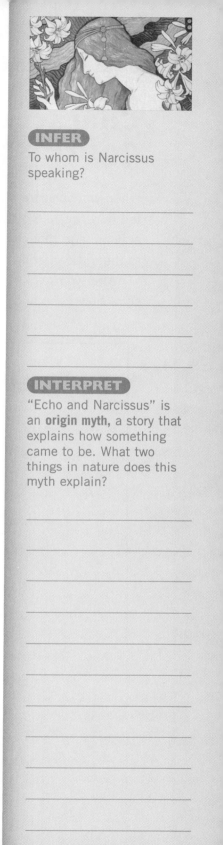

INFER
To whom is Narcissus speaking?

_____
_____
_____
_____
_____
_____

INTERPRET
"Echo and Narcissus" is an **origin myth,** a story that explains how something came to be. What two things in nature does this myth explain?

_____
_____
_____
_____
_____
_____
_____
_____
_____
_____

WORDS TO OWN
intently (in·tent′lē) *adv.:* with great concentration.

Character Comparison-and-Contrast Chart

When you **compare** characters, you tell how they are alike. When you **contrast** them, you tell how they are different. You can compare and contrast characters' words, looks, actions, and thoughts. You can also compare and contrast the way other people respond to them. Comparing and contrasting deepens your understanding of a character.

After you read "Echo and Narcissus," fill out this chart. Find details in the story that show how Echo and Narcissus are alike and different.

What is Echo like?	What is Narcissus like?	How are Echo and Narcissus similar?
Echo . . .	Narcissus . . .	Both . . .

Vocabulary and Comprehension

A. The names of characters from mythology are at the core of quite a few modern English words. For example, our word *echo* is derived from the name of the nymph. Answer the following questions about words related to mythological characters. Use a dictionary if you need help.

1. What kind of personality flaws does a *narcissistic* person have?

   _____

2. *Jove* is another name for Jupiter. What kind of person is *jovial*?

   _____

3. Pluto's name in ancient Greek meant "the rich one." What kind of person do you suppose a *plutocrat* is?

   _____

4. What name of a common breakfast food is derived from *Ceres,* the name of the goddess of agriculture?

   _____

B. Answer the following questions.

1. Why does Hera decide to visit the earth?

   _____

   _____

2. What is Narcissus's problem? Why does he scorn the nymphs?

   _____

   _____

3. What happens to Echo after Narcissus runs away from her?

   _____

   _____

The Flight of Icarus

Make the Connection

Wings or Wheels?

Long before airplanes were invented, some people dreamed of flying. They imagined themselves climbing, dipping, and floating, as free as birds in the sky. But not everyone wishes for wings. For whatever reason, some people have always had a fear of flying. They'd just as soon travel on wheels, safely on the ground. On and around the graphics below, use symbols, sketches, and words to describe your feelings about flying through the air and traveling on the ground.

The Flight of Icarus

Sally Benson

Cast of Characters

King Minos (mī′näs′) tyrant of Crete, enemy of Athens.

Theseus (thē′sē·əs) hero from Athens held captive by Minos. Daedalus helped him escape from the labyrinth on Crete.

Daedalus (ded′′l·əs) great Athenian architect who built the labyrinth on Crete.

Icarus (ik′ə·rəs) Daedalus's young son.

IDENTIFY

Underline the names of the two people who are the main characters opposing each other in the **conflict** described here. Circle the name of the son of one of these characters. On what kind of landform are the father and son imprisoned?

_____

_____

VISUALIZE

Re-read lines 13–22. Underline the words that help you picture the process of making the wings. Number each step, placing the number above each step described.

PREDICT

Do you think the wings will work? Will Daedalus and Icarus manage to escape? Tell what you think will happen.

_____

_____

_____

_____

_____

_____

_____

_____

When Theseus escaped from the labyrinth, King Minos flew into a rage with its builder, Daedalus, and ordered him shut up in a high tower that faced the lonely sea. In time, with the help of his young son, Icarus, Daedalus managed to escape from the tower, only to find himself a prisoner on the island. Several times he tried by bribery to stow away on one of the vessels sailing from Crete, but King Minos kept strict watch over them, and no ships were allowed to sail without being carefully searched.

10 Daedalus was an ingenious artist and was not discouraged by his failures. "Minos may control the land and sea," he said, "but he does not control the air. I will try that way."

He called his son, Icarus, to him and told the boy to gather up all the feathers he could find on the rocky shore. As thousands of gulls soared over the island, Icarus soon collected a huge pile of feathers. Daedalus then melted some wax and made a skeleton in the shape of a bird's wing. The smallest feathers he pressed into the soft wax and the large ones he tied on with thread. Icarus played about on the beach happily while his father

20 worked, chasing the feathers that blew away in the strong wind that swept the island and sometimes taking bits of the wax and working it into strange shapes with his fingers.

It was fun making the wings. The sun shone on the bright feathers; the breezes ruffled them. When they were finished, Daedalus fastened them to his shoulders and found himself lifted upwards, where he hung poised in the air. Filled with excitement, he made another pair for his son. They were smaller than his own, but strong and beautiful.

Finally, one clear, wind-swept morning, the wings were

30 finished, and Daedalus fastened them to Icarus's shoulders and taught him how to fly. He bade him watch the movements of the birds, how they soared and glided overhead. He pointed out the slow, graceful sweep of their wings as they beat the air steadily, without fluttering. Soon Icarus was sure that he, too, could fly and, raising his arms up and down, skirted over the white sand and even out over the waves, letting his feet

touch the snowy foam as the water thundered and broke over the sharp rocks. Daedalus watched him proudly but with misgivings.

40 He called Icarus to his side and, putting his arm round the boy's shoulders, said, "Icarus, my son, we are about to make our flight. No human being has ever traveled through the air before, and I want you to listen carefully to my instructions. Keep at a moderate height, for if you fly too low, the fog and spray will clog your wings, and if you fly too high, the heat will melt the wax that holds them together. Keep near me and you will be safe."

He kissed Icarus and fastened the wings more securely to his son's shoulders. Icarus, standing in the bright sun,
the shining wings drooping gracefully from his shoulders, his
50 golden hair wet with spray, and his eyes bright and dark with excitement, looked like a lovely bird. Daedalus's eyes filled with tears, and turning away, he soared into the sky, calling to Icarus to follow. From time to time, he looked back to see that the boy was safe and to note how he managed his wings in his flight. As they flew across the land to test their prowess before setting out across the dark wild sea, plowmen below stopped their work and shepherds gazed in wonder, thinking Daedalus and Icarus were gods.

Father and son flew over Samos and Delos, which lay on
60 their left, and Lebinthus,[1] which lay on their right. Icarus, beating his wings in joy, felt the thrill of the cool wind on his face and the clear air above and below him. He flew higher and higher up into the blue sky until he reached the clouds. His father saw him and called out in alarm. He tried to follow him, but he was heavier and his wings would not carry him. Up and up Icarus soared, through the soft, moist clouds and out again toward the glorious sun. He was bewitched by a sense of freedom and beat his wings frantically so that they would carry him higher and higher to heaven itself. The blazing sun beat
70 down on the wings and softened the wax. Small feathers fell from the wings and floated softly down, warning Icarus to stay

---

1. **Samos** (sā′mäs), **Delos** (dē′läs), **and Lebinthus** (lə·bin′thəs): Greek islands in the Aegean Sea.

INFER

As Icarus practices flying (lines 34–38), which of his actions might give Daedalus some cause for worry?

_____

IDENTIFY

Underline the instructions that Daedalus gives Icarus.

_____

BUILD FLUENCY

Read Daedalus's advice to his son aloud, pretending you are a parent. Use the tone of voice that a parent might use when advising a young son about such an important matter.

INFER

Underline the **simile** in lines 47–58. A simile is a comparison of two unlike things using a comparing word such as *like* or *as*. Why do Daedalus's eyes fill with tears? How old do you think Icarus is? Tell why you think so.

_____

_____

_____

_____

_____

INFER

Why does the narrator call Icarus "the enchanted boy"? What do you think *enchanted* means in the context of this paragraph?

_____

_____

_____

RETELL

Go back to line 59. **Retell** what happens to Icarus.

_____

_____

_____

_____

INTERPRET

Based on the details in this myth, and also on your prior knowledge of parents and young people, do you think that Daedalus should have been able to predict what Icarus would do? What could he have said or done that might have saved Icarus?

_____

_____

_____

_____

_____

_____

his flight and glide to earth. But the enchanted boy did not notice them until the sun became so hot that the largest feathers dropped off and he began to sink. Frantically he fluttered his arms, but no feathers remained to hold the air. He cried out to his father, but his voice was submerged in the blue waters of the sea, which has forever after been called by his name.

Daedalus, crazed by anxiety, called back to him, "Icarus! Icarus, my son, where are you?" At last he saw the feathers
80 floating from the sky, and soon his son plunged through the clouds into the sea. Daedalus hurried to save him, but it was too late. He gathered the boy in his arms and flew to land, the tips of his wings dragging in the water from the double burden they bore. Weeping bitterly, he buried his small son and called the land Icaria in his memory.

Then, with a flutter of wings, he once more took to the air, but the joy of his flight was gone and his victory over the air was bitter to him. He arrived safely in Sicily, where he built a temple to Apollo and hung up his wings as an offering to the
90 god, and in the wings he pressed a few bright feathers he had found floating on the water where Icarus fell. And he mourned for the birdlike son who had thrown caution to the winds in the exaltation of his freedom from the earth.

Story Map

The elements of a story or myth can be charted in a **story map** like the one below. Use the first five boxes to outline the main parts of the **plot** of "The Flight of Icarus." Then, review the information you've written, and try to state the myth's **theme,** or message. Think about what Icarus attempts to do, what he ignores, and what happens to him as a result.

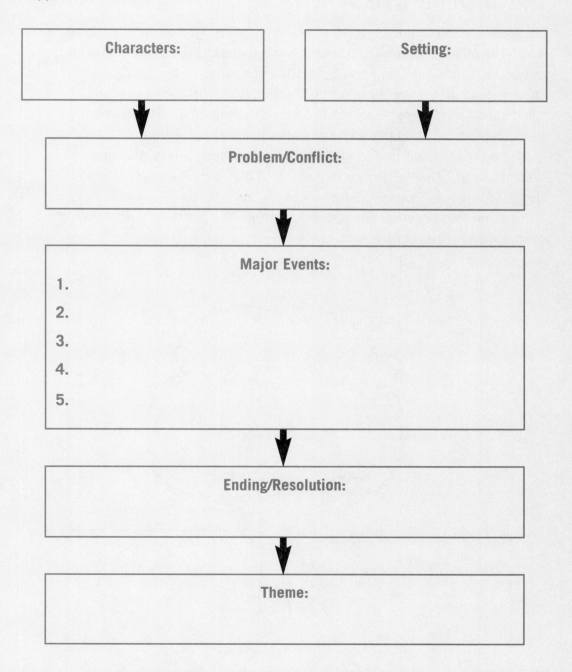

Characters:

Setting:

Problem/Conflict:

Major Events:

1.

2.

3.

4.

5.

Ending/Resolution:

Theme:

Aschenputtel

Make the Connection

The Wishing Tree

Did you know that there are more than nine hundred versions of the Cinderella story? The oldest one goes back more than a thousand years to China. The version of "Cinderella" we know best is the one retold in the 1600s by Charles Perrault, a French writer. "Aschenputtel" is the German version of "Cinderella." The name *Aschenputtel* means "Cinder-fool." That's what her mean stepsisters called the young girl whose wishes came true.

As you read, you'll find some differences between "Cinderella" and "Aschenputtel." One difference is that a bird flies out of a magic tree and brings Aschenputtel whatever she wishes for.

Imagine that you have a magic wishing tree. You get three wishes. Write down a wish on each of the lines below.

Aschenputtel

Jakob and
Wilhelm Grimm

IDENTIFY

Underline the three characters introduced in the first two paragraphs. Circle the words "she felt her end drawing near." In your own words, explain what that means.

_____

_____

_____

_____

INFER

Write down three words that describe the maiden's character.

_____

_____

_____

INFER

Underline the words from the text that describe the cruel treatment the maiden gets from her stepsisters. Why do you think they treat her so badly?

_____

_____

_____

_____

_____

_____

WORDS TO OWN
pious (pī′əs) *adj.:* deeply religious.
expired (ek·spīrd′) *v.:* died; breathed out for the last time.

There was once a rich man whose wife lay sick, and when she felt her end drawing near, she called to her only daughter to come near her bed and said,

"Dear child, be pious and good, and God will always take care of you, and I will look down upon you from heaven and will be with you."

And then she closed her eyes and expired. The maiden went every day to her mother's grave and wept and was always pious and good. When the winter came, the snow covered

10 the grave with a white covering, and when the sun came in the early spring and melted it away, the man took to himself another wife.

The new wife brought two daughters home with her and they were beautiful and fair in appearance but at heart were wicked and ugly. And then began very evil times for the poor stepdaughter.

"Is the stupid creature to sit in the same room with us?" said they. "Those who eat food must earn it. Out with the kitchen maid!"

20 They took away her pretty dresses and put on her an old gray kirtle[1] and gave her wooden shoes to wear.

"Just look now at the proud princess, how she is decked out!" cried they, laughing, and then they sent her into the kitchen. There she was obliged to do heavy work from morning to night, get up early in the morning, draw water, make the fires, cook, and wash. Besides that, the sisters did their utmost to torment her—mocking her and strewing peas and lentils among the ashes and setting her to pick them up. In the evenings, when she was quite tired out with her hard day's

30 work, she had no bed to lie on but was obliged to rest on the hearth among the cinders. And as she always looked dusty and dirty, they named her Aschenputtel.

It happened one day that the father went to the fair, and he asked his two stepdaughters what he should bring back for them.

---

1. **kirtle:** old-fashioned word for "dress."

"Fine clothes!" said one.

"Pearls and jewels!" said the other.

"But what will you have, Aschenputtel?" said he.

"The first twig, Father, that strikes against your hat on the way home; this is what I should like you to bring me."

40 So he bought for the two stepdaughters fine clothes, pearls, and jewels, and on his way back, as he rode through a green lane, a hazel twig struck against his hat; and he broke it off and carried it home with him. And when he reached home, he gave to the stepdaughters what they had wished for, and to Aschenputtel he gave the hazel twig. She thanked him and went to her mother's grave, and planted this twig there, weeping so bitterly that the tears fell upon it and watered it, and it flourished and became a fine tree. Aschenputtel went to see it three times a day and wept and prayed, and each time a
50 white bird rose up from the tree, and, if she uttered any wish, the bird brought her whatever she had wished for.

Now it came to pass that the king ordained a festival that should last for three days and to which all the beautiful young women of that country were bidden so that the king's son might choose a bride from among them. When the two stepdaughters heard that they too were bidden to appear, they felt very pleased, and they called Aschenputtel and said,

"Comb our hair, brush our shoes, and make our buckles fast, we are going to the wedding feast at the king's castle."

60 Aschenputtel, when she heard this, could not help crying, for she too would have liked to go to the dance, and she begged her stepmother to allow her.

"What, you Aschenputtel!" said she. "In all your dust and dirt, you want to go to the festival! You that have no dress and no shoes! You want to dance!"

But since she persisted in asking, at last the stepmother said,

"I have scattered a dish full of lentils in the ashes, and if you can pick them all up again in two hours, you may go with us."

70 Then the maiden went to the back door that led into the garden and called out,

BUILD FLUENCY

Re-read the boxed passage once for practice. Then, re-read it to bring out the different characters of Aschenputtel and her stepmother. When you read the description of the birds, try to imitate the happy sounds they make as they help Aschenputtel.

_____

_____

_____

PREDICT

What do you think will happen to the two dishfuls of lentils? Why do you think the stepmother doesn't seem to have any idea about what's going to happen?

_____

_____

_____

_____

_____

_____

_____

_____

_____

O gentle doves, O turtledoves,
And all the birds that be,
The lentils that in ashes lie
Come and pick up for me!
    The good must be put in the dish,
    The bad you may eat if you wish.

80 Then there came to the kitchen window two white doves, and after them some turtledoves, and at last a crowd of all the birds under heaven, chirping and fluttering, and they alighted among the ashes; and the doves nodded with their heads and began to pick, peck, pick, peck, and then all the others began to pick, peck, pick, peck and put all the good grains into the dish. Before an hour was over, all was done, and they flew away. Then the maiden brought the dish to her stepmother, feeling joyful and thinking that now she should go to the feast; but the stepmother said,

"No, Aschenputtel, you have no proper clothes, and you do not know how to dance, and you would be laughed at!"

90 And when Aschenputtel cried for disappointment, she added,

"If you can pick two dishfuls of lentils out of the ashes, nice and clean, you shall go with us," thinking to herself, "for that is not possible." When she had strewed two dishfuls of lentils among the ashes, the maiden went through the back door into the garden and cried,

O gentle doves, O turtledoves,
And all the birds that be,
The lentils that in ashes lie
100 Come and pick up for me!
    The good must be put in the dish,
    The bad you may eat if you wish.

So there came to the kitchen window two white doves, and then some turtledoves, and at last a crowd of all the other birds under heaven, chirping and fluttering, and they alighted among

the ashes, and the doves nodded with their heads and began to pick, peck, pick, peck, and then all the others began to pick, peck, pick, peck and put all the good grains into the dish. And before half an hour was over, it was all done, and they flew
110 away. Then the maiden took the dishes to the stepmother, feeling joyful and thinking that now she should go with them to the feast. But her stepmother said, "All this is of no good to you; you cannot come with us, for you have no proper clothes and cannot dance; you would put us to shame."

Then she turned her back on poor Aschenputtel and made haste to set out with her two proud daughters.

And as there was no one left in the house, Aschenputtel went to her mother's grave, under the hazel bush, and cried,

> Little tree, little tree, shake over me,
> 120 That silver and gold may come down
> and cover me.

Then the bird threw down a dress of gold and silver and a pair of slippers embroidered with silk and silver. And in all haste she put on the dress and went to the festival. But her stepmother and sisters did not know her and thought she must be a foreign princess, she looked so beautiful in her golden dress.

Of Aschenputtel they never thought at all and supposed that she was sitting at home, picking the lentils out of the ashes.
130 The King's son came to meet her and took her by the hand and danced with her, and he refused to stand up with anyone else so that he might not be obliged to let go her hand; and when anyone came to claim it, he answered,

"She is my partner."

And when the evening came, she wanted to go home, but the prince said he would go with her to take care of her, for he wanted to see where the beautiful maiden lived. But she escaped him and jumped up into the pigeon house. Then the prince waited until her father came along, and told him that the
140 strange maiden had jumped into the pigeon house. The father

INTERPRET

The number three is a **motif,** a repeated element in storytelling. In European folklore, three is a charmed number. Events often happen in threes. For instance, in line 49, Aschenputtel visits her mother's grave three times a day. Notice here that the stepmother refuses Aschenputtel's request three times. As you continue reading the story, look for and circle more things that happen in threes. How does expecting events to repeat three times build **suspense**?

_____

_____

_____

IDENTIFY

Underline the words that tell Aschenputtel's first wish. Circle the words that tell how the wish is granted (lines 117–127).

INFER

Underline the words that the prince says when others try to dance with Aschenputtel. What **inference** about the prince's feelings can you draw from this statement?

_____

_____

_____

PREDICT

Pause at line 157. What do you predict will happen when Aschenputtel goes to the hazel bush a second time?

_____

_____

_____

_____

RETELL

Stop when you get to line 180, and **retell** what has happened in the story since Aschenputtel got her first wish. What is the only difference between what happens the first time and what happens the second time?

_____

_____

_____

_____

_____

_____

_____

_____

_____

_____

thought to himself, "It cannot surely be Aschenputtel" and called for axes and hatchets and had the pigeon house cut down, but there was no one in it. And when they entered the house, there sat Aschenputtel in her dirty clothes among the cinders, and a little oil lamp burnt dimly in the chimney; for Aschenputtel had been very quick and had jumped out of the pigeon house again and had run to the hazel bush; and there she had taken off her beautiful dress and had laid it on the grave, and the bird had carried it away again, and then she 150 had put on her little gray kirtle again and had sat down in the kitchen among the cinders.

The next day, when the festival began anew, and the parents and stepsisters had gone to it, Aschenputtel went to the hazel bush and cried,

> Little tree, little tree, shake over me,
> That silver and gold may come down
> and cover me.

Then the bird cast down a still more splendid dress than on the day before. And when she appeared in it among the guests, 160 everyone was astonished at her beauty. The prince had been waiting until she came, and he took her hand and danced with her alone. And when anyone else came to invite her, he said,

"She is my partner."

And when the evening came, she wanted to go home, and the prince followed her, for he wanted to see to what house she belonged; but she broke away from him and ran into the garden at the back of the house. There stood a fine large tree, bearing splendid pears; she leapt as lightly as a squirrel among the branches, and the prince did not know what had become of 170 her. So he waited until her father came along, and then he told him that the strange maiden had rushed from him, and that he thought she had gone up into the pear tree. The father thought to himself,

"It cannot surely be Aschenputtel" and called for an axe and felled the tree, but there was no one in it. And when they went

into the kitchen, there sat Aschenputtel among the cinders, as usual, for she had got down the other side of the tree and had taken back her beautiful clothes to the bird on the hazel bush and had put on her old gray kirtle again.

180   On the third day, when the parents and the stepchildren had set off, Aschenputtel went again to her mother's grave and said to the tree,

> Little tree, little tree, shake over me,
> That silver and gold may come down
>   and cover me.

Then the bird cast down a dress the likes of which had never been seen for splendor and brilliancy, and slippers that were of gold.

And when she appeared in this dress at the feast, nobody
190 knew what to say for wonderment. The prince danced with her alone, and if anyone else asked her, he answered,

"She is my partner."

And when it was evening, Aschenputtel wanted to go home, and the prince was about to go with her when she ran past him so quickly that he could not follow her. But he had laid a plan and had caused all the steps to be spread with pitch,[2] so that as she rushed down them, her left shoe remained sticking in it. The prince picked it up and saw that it was of gold and very small and slender. The next morning he went to the father and
200 told him that none should be his bride save the one whose foot the golden shoe should fit. Then the two sisters were very glad, because they had pretty feet. The eldest went to her room to try on the shoe, and her mother stood by. But she could not get her great toe into it, for the shoe was too small; then her mother handed her a knife, and said,

"Cut the toe off, for when you are queen, you will never have to go on foot." So the girl cut her toe off, squeezed her foot into the shoe, concealed the pain, and went down to the

---

2. **pitch:** here, black, sticky tar.

INTERPRET

Why is this set of events happening for a third time? Why do you think Aschenputtel doesn't let the prince find out who she is on the *first* day of the festival? Give two reasons.

_____

_____

_____

EVALUATE

What do you think of the prince's plan? What's good about it? What could cause problems? What better plan can you suggest?

_____

_____

_____

INTERPRET

Underline the details that tell how the stepmother hopes to fool the prince. What do these details reveal about the **characters** of the stepmother and stepsisters?

_____

_____

_____

INFER

The birds in this story are far from ordinary. Underline the places where the prince hears the pigeons. What new ability do the birds reveal here? Why do you think they are so determined to help Aschenputtel?

_____

_____

_____

_____

_____

_____

_____

_____

_____

_____

_____

_____

_____

_____

_____

_____

WORDS TO OWN
stunted (stunt′id) _v. used as adj.:_ not properly grown.

prince. Then he took her with him on his horse as his bride and
210 rode off. They had to pass by the grave, and there sat the two
pigeons on the hazel bush and cried,

> There they go, there they go!
> There is blood on her shoe;
> The shoe is too small,
> —Not the right bride at all!

Then the prince looked at her shoe and saw the blood
flowing. And he turned his horse round and took the false bride
home again, saying she was not the right one and that the other
sister must try on the shoe. So she went into her room to do so
220 and got her toes comfortably in, but her heel was too large.
Then her mother handed her the knife, saying, "Cut a piece off
your heel; when you are queen, you will never have to go on
foot."

So the girl cut a piece off her heel and thrust her foot into
the shoe, concealed the pain, and went down to the prince,
who took his bride before him on his horse and rode off. When
they passed by the hazel bush, the two pigeons sat there and
cried,

> There they go, there they go!
230 > There is blood on her shoe;
> The shoe is too small,
> —Not the right bride at all!

Then the prince looked at her foot and saw how the blood
was flowing from the shoe and staining the white stocking. And
he turned his horse round and brought the false bride home
again.

"This is not the right one," said he. "Have you no other
daughter?"

"No," said the man, "only my dead wife left behind her a
240 little <u>stunted</u> Aschenputtel; it is impossible that she can be the

bride." But the King's son ordered her to be sent for, but the mother said,

"Oh, no! She is much too dirty; I could not let her be seen."

But he would have her fetched, and so Aschenputtel had to appear.

First she washed her face and hands quite clean and went in and curtseyed to the prince, who held out to her the golden shoe. Then she sat down on a stool, drew her foot out of the heavy wooden shoe, and slipped it into the golden one, which
250 fitted it perfectly. And when she stood up and the prince looked in her face, he knew again the beautiful maiden that had danced with him, and he cried,

"This is the right bride!"

The stepmother and the two sisters were thunderstruck and grew pale with anger, but the prince put Aschenputtel before him on his horse and rode off. And as they passed the hazel bush, the two white pigeons cried,

There they go, there they go!
No blood on her shoe;
260   The shoe's not too small,
The right bride is she after all.

And when they had thus cried, they came flying after and perched on Aschenputtel's shoulders, one on the right, the other on the left, and so remained.

And when her wedding with the prince was appointed to be held, the false sisters came, hoping to curry favor[3] and to take part in the festivities. So as the bridal procession went to the church, the eldest walked on the right side and the younger on the left, and the pigeons picked out an eye of each of them.
270 And as they returned, the elder was on the left side and the younger on the right, and the pigeons picked out the other eye of each of them. And so they were condemned for the rest of their days because of their wickedness and falsehood.

---

3. **curry favor:** try to win approval by flattering and fawning.

INTERPRET

What do the father's comments in lines 239–241 reveal about his character? Do you think he has changed since the beginning of the story, or has he always been like this? If you think he has changed, tell what may have changed him.

_____

_____

_____

_____

_____

INTERPRET

How do the pigeons' cries illustrate the **motif** of "threes" in this story?

_____

_____

_____

EVALUATE

How do you feel about the conclusion of this story? Underline the sentence that suggests one of the story's main ideas or messages.

_____

_____

_____

_____

Story Map

Long stories and novels are more likely to have plot complications than short stories. Fill out the story map below after you read "Aschenputtel" to be sure you understand the plot events.

Main Characters	Descriptions

Conflict

_____

_____

_____

What Happens?

Complication: _____

Complication: _____

Complication: _____

Complication: _____

Climax

_____

_____

Resolution

_____

_____

Vocabulary and Comprehension

A. Use a dictionary or a thesaurus to find a **synonym** for each Word to Own below. Next, write a sentence or two using context clues that make the meaning of the synonym clear.

EXAMPLE: pitch: _sticky tar_   _Her shoe got stuck in the sticky tar. It wouldn't come out even when she pulled on it._

Words to Own	Synonyms	Sentences
1. pious		
2. expired		
3. ordained		
4. persisted		
5. stunted		

B. Answer the following questions.

1. Why does Aschenputtel ask her father for a twig?

2. How does Aschenputtel's stepmother try to prevent her from going to the festival?

3. What magical event allows Aschenputtel to attend the festival?

4. How does the prince find out that Aschenputtel should be his bride?

PART 2   READING INFORMATIONAL MATERIALS

"Look, Mom, No Cavities"

The Main Idea

The **main idea** of a text is the most important idea, the one the writer wants you to remember. Sometimes a writer will state the main idea directly. Most of the time, it's up to you to figure out the main idea. You have to think about all the details in the text and make an **inference,** or educated guess, about its main idea.

Here are some strategies for figuring out the main idea:

- Look at the **title.** Does it tell you what the text is going to focus on? Sometimes the title doesn't point to the central idea at all. Instead, it is a "grabber"—it wants to grab your attention. (This article has a grabber for a title.)
- Look for a **sentence that seems to state a key idea** in general terms. Sometimes these statements come first or last in a text.
- If you can't find a key sentence that clearly states the main idea, go back over the text, and find its major details. Ask yourself: **What do all these details tell me?**

How good are you at recognizing a main idea? Get some practice by completing the chart below. First, read the sentences about the two topics. Then, decide which sentences are main ideas and which are supporting details, and put a check mark in the appropriate box.

Main Idea or Supporting Detail?

Topic 1: How to maintain a healthy diet	Main Idea	Supporting Detail
Some physicians recommend having a salad twice a week.		
Fruits and vegetables are part of a nutritious diet.		
You've probably heard the old saying, "An apple a day keeps the doctor away."		
Topic 2: Computers in the classroom		
Students would save time by conducting their research on the World Wide Web.		
Computerized texts would allow students to leave those heavy textbooks at home.		
There are numerous benefits to having a computer at every student's desk.		

"LOOK, MOM, NO CAVITIES"

Flo Ota De Lange

IDENTIFY

Re-read the first two paragraphs. Underline the **main idea** of the article. Then, circle the details in the second paragraph that support the main idea.

IDENTIFY

Pause at line 19. What do you think is the **main idea** in the third paragraph?

_____

_____

_____

INTERPRET

Rename "Look, Mom, No Cavities" with a title that points to the article's **main idea.**

_____

_____

WORDS TO OWN

species (spē′shēz) *n.:* in biology, a naturally existing population of similar organisms that usually breed only among themselves.

ligaments (lig′ə·mənts) *n.:* in anatomy, bands of tough tissue that connect bones and hold organs in place.

adaptation (ad′əp·tā′shən) *n.:* in biology, a change in structure, function, or form that improves an animal's or a plant's chances of survival.

prey (prā) *n.:* animal hunted or killed for food by another animal.

Snakes are believed to have evolved from reptiles with legs and to have been on earth for 95 million years. There are now about 2,700 species of snakes. The cobra, native to South Asia, Australia, and Africa, is one of these species. A king cobra can grow to some eighteen feet in length, making it the longest of the poisonous snakes. The cobra has many unusual features.

Like all other snakes, cobras are carnivorous. As a cobra grows bigger on its flesh-eating diet, it outgrows its skin and so must shed it four to six times a year. That may be one

10 reason why a cobra's eyes are lidless. Imagine a cobra trying to shed its skin if it had eyelids. Ouch! That's also why a cobra's eyes never seem to change expression, why they appear to have such an intense, fixed stare.

A cobra comes equipped with loose folds of skin on its neck that expand into that famous hood. A cobra spreads its hood by spreading its neck ribs, much as you would open an umbrella. This makes it look bigger and more frightening but does not make it more dangerous—cobras are always dangerous.

Unlike your jaw, which opens and closes by means of a set

20 of interlocking bones known as the temporal-mandibular joint, a cobra's jaw bones are connected only by ligaments, permitting them to disconnect. The top jaw can open almost flat against its forehead, while the bottom jaw drops almost straight down. It's this adaptation that allows a cobra to swallow prey bigger than its head. A dentist would never have to tell a cobra to open wider. This is so for three reasons: First, a cobra can spread its jaws like a pair of entry doors. Second, a cobra most likely never gets cavities. Third, a cobra must gulp its victims whole—an experience most dentists would like to avoid.

Main-Idea Chart

The **main idea** of an informative article is the most important point the writer makes about the topic, or subject. In a well written article, the main idea is supported by details.

After you read "Look, Mom, No Cavities," fill out this chart. First record the supporting details that the article provides about cobras. Then think about these details, and write a statement that expresses the main idea.

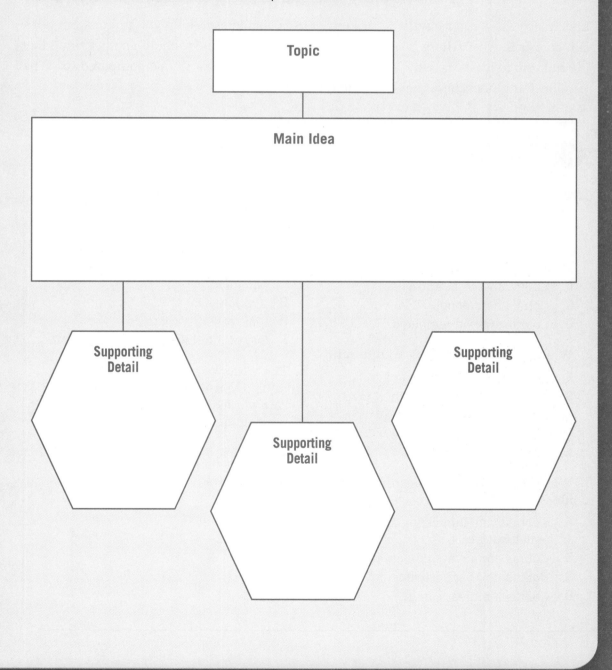

Topic

Main Idea

Supporting Detail

Supporting Detail

Supporting Detail

Reading Check

1. How long can a king cobra be? If you had to help someone visualize its length, what would you compare it with? _____

2. Why can a cobra swallow an object larger than its head? _____

_____

3. Which paragraph explains the **title?** _____

4. Like many good science writers, this writer uses analogies to help you understand difficult concepts. An **analogy** (ə·nal′ə·jē) is a comparison of one thing to another thing that is similar in at least one way. What familiar thing is the cobra's hood compared to? What familiar thing does the writer compare the cobra's jaw to?

_____

Test Practice

Circle the correct answer.

1. Which of the following is a **fact**—a statement that can be proved true?

   A Cobras are disgusting.
   B Cobras live in South Asia.
   C Cobras hate people.
   D Cobras are bad-tempered.

2. Which of the following is an **opinion?**

   F There are 2,700 species of snakes.
   G Cobras can disconnect their jaws.
   H Cobras are more interesting than pythons.
   J Cobras have hoods.

3. Which sentence *best* states the **main idea** of this article?

   A Cobras have interesting and unusual features.
   B Cobras are always dangerous.
   C Cobras never get cavities.
   D Cobras are meat eaters.

4. The writer uses a **context clue** to help you figure out what a temporal-mandibular joint is. Which word or words in paragraph 4 define *temporal-mandibular joint?*

   F ligaments
   G top jaw
   H pair of entry doors
   J set of interlocking bones

5. The writer uses another **context clue** to help you figure out what the word carnivorous means. Which word or words in paragraph 2 help you understand *carnivorous?*

   A flesh-eating
   B outgrows
   C skin
   D none of these

Vocabulary: Words to Own

Words from Latin

Doctors and other scientists used to study Latin because much of the vocabulary of science (including the vocabulary words from "Look, Mom, No Cavities") is derived from Latin.

1. Match the letter of the vocabulary word in the left column with the Latin word it comes from in the right column.

	Word Bank
	species
	ligaments
	adaptation
	prey

    a. species   _____ *adaptare* (to fit)

    b. ligaments   _____ *ligare* (to tie)

    c. adaptation   _____ *prehendere* (to seize)

    d. prey   _____ *specere* (to see)

2. How is the meaning of the Latin word reflected in the meaning of the English word?

    species _____

    ligaments _____

    adaptation _____

    prey _____

3. Below, write down which Latin word each English word comes from. Then, write how the Latin word is reflected in the meaning of each word.

    spectacles _____ ligature _____

    prehensile _____ adapter _____

4. Fill out the chart by writing in the third column an English word derived from the Latin word in the first column.

Latin Word	English Meaning	English Word
credere	to believe	
ignire	to light	
jus	law	
locus	place	
pedis	of the foot	

India's History

Textbooks are a good source of information. **Textbooks** have particular features that help readers locate information and review what they have learned. Textbooks also offer photographs and artwork that can lead you to even further investigations of a subject.

The next few pages contain excerpts from a geography textbook called *People, Places, and Change*. See how well you understand the structure of a textbook.

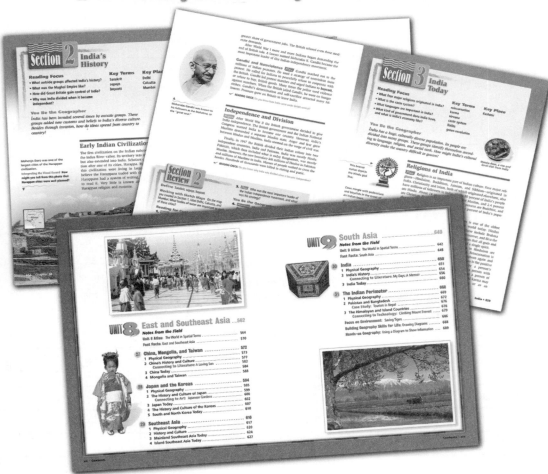

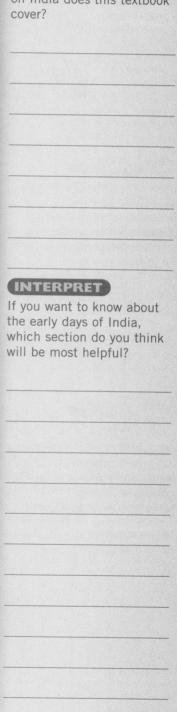

South Asia 640

Notes from the Field

Contents

INTERPRET

History and science books often sum up the focus of each chapter. Look at the **Reading Focus** list. If you want information on India under British rule, will you find it here?

_____

_____

INTERPRET

Illustrations have **captions,** text that explains the subject of the illustration. Circle the caption for the photo that runs across the bottom of the page.

_____

_____

_____

INTERPRET

Note the **inset,** which is a very small map showing where the subject of the photo is located. Usually a star or a circle indicates the exact location. Find and circle the city of Mohenjo Daro. Is it in present-day Pakistan or India?

_____

_____

_____

_____

Section 2 India's History

Reading Focus

- What outside groups affected India's history?
- What was the Mughal Empire like?
- How did Great Britain gain control of India?
- Why was India divided when it became independent?

Key Terms
Sanskrit
sepoys
boycott

Key Places
Delhi
Calcutta
Mumbai

Coat of arms of the
East India Company

You Be the Geographer

India has been invaded several times by outside groups. These groups added new customs and beliefs to India's diverse culture. Besides through invasion, how do ideas spread from country to country?

Early Indian Civilizations

The first civilization on the Indian subcontinent was centered around the Indus River valley. Its territory was mainly in present-day Pakistan but also extended into India. Scholars call this the Harappan civilization after one of its cities, Harappa. By about 2500 B.C. the people of this civilization were living in large, well-planned cities. Scholars believe the Harappans traded with the peoples of Mesopotamia. The Harappans had a system of writing, but scholars have not been able to read it. Very little is known about Harappan religion and customs.

Mohenjo Daro was one of the largest cities of the Harappan civilization.

Interpreting the Visual Record How might you tell from this photo that Harappan cities were well planned? ▼

The Taj Mahal is one of the most famous buildings in the world.

The British

Movement During the 1700s and 1800s the British slowly took control of India. At first this was done by the English East India Company. This company won rights to trade in the Mughal Empire in the 1600s. The East India Company first took control of small trading posts. Later the British gained more Indian territory.

Company Rule As the Mughal Empire grew weaker, the English East India Company expanded its political power. The company also built up its own military force. This army was made up mostly of **sepoys**, Indian troops commanded by British officers. The British used the strategy of backing one Indian ruler against another in exchange for cooperation. By the mid-1800s the company controlled more than half of India. The rest was divided into small states ruled by local princes.

The British changed the Indian economy to benefit British industry. India produced raw materials, including cotton, indigo—a natural dye—and jute. These materials were then shipped to Britain for use in British factories. Spices, sugar, tea, and wheat were also grown in India for export. Railroads were built to ship the raw materials to Calcutta, Bombay (now Mumbai), and other port cities. India also became a market for British manufactured goods. Indians, who had woven cotton cloth for centuries, were now forced to buy British cloth.

In September 1857, British and loyal Sikh troops stormed the gate of Delhi, defended by rebel sepoys. Bloody fighting continued until late 1858.

Interpreting the Visual Record
How did the Indian Mutiny lead to a change in the way India was governed?

India • 657

Anti-British Protest

After World War I more and more Indians began demanding the end of British rule. A lawyer named Mohandas K. Gandhi became the most important leader of this Indian independence movement.

Gandhi and Nonviolence Place Gandhi reached out to the millions of Indian peasants. He used a strategy of nonviolent mass protest. He called for Indians to peacefully refuse to cooperate with the British. Gandhi led protest marches and urged Indians to **boycott**, or refuse to buy, British goods. Many times the police used violence against marchers. When the British jailed Gandhi, he went on hunger strikes. Gandhi's determination and self-sacrifice attracted many followers. Pressure grew on Britain to leave India.

✔ **READING CHECK:** Do you know how India came under British control?

Independence and Division

Region After World War II the British government decided to give India independence. The British government and the Indian National Congress wanted India to become one country. However, India's Muslims demanded a separate Muslim state. Anger and fear grew between Hindus and Muslims. India seemed on the verge of civil war.

Finally, in 1947 the British divided their Indian colony into two independent countries, India and Pakistan. India was mostly Hindu. Pakistan, which then included what is today Bangladesh, was mostly Muslim. However, the new boundary left millions of Hindus in Pakistan and millions of Muslims in India. Masses of people rushed to cross the border. Hundreds of thousands were killed in rioting and panic.

✔ **READING CHECK:** Do you know why India was divided when it became independent?

▲ Mohandas Gandhi was known to his followers as the Mahatma, or the "great soul."

Section Review 2

Define Sanskrit, sepoys, boycott

Working with Sketch Maps On the map you created in Section 1, label Delhi, Calcutta, and Mumbai. What bodies of water are important to each of these cities?

Reading for Content Understanding

1. Region What factors made the Mughal Empire one of the most powerful states in the world?

2. Movement How did the English East India Company gain control of most of India?

3. Place Who was the most important leader of the Indian independence movement, and what was his strategy?

You Be the Geographer: CRITICAL THINKING

4. Movement Why was the British colony of India divided into two countries?

Organizing What You Know

5. Copy the following time line. Use it to mark important events in Indian history from 2500 B.C. to A.D. 1947.

2500 B.C. ————————————— A.D. 1947

Reading Check

To check on how well you know the important parts of a textbook, answer the following questions by referring to the key parts of the textbook you are now using, called *The Holt Reader.*

Test Practice

Circle the correct answer.

1. The **copyright page** is in the front of the book, usually the page after the main title page. Here is where you will find the date the book was published. What is the copyright date of this textbook?

   A 2000
   B 2001
   C 2002
   D 2003

2. The **table of contents** is found in the front of a textbook. According to the table of contents of this textbook, how many chapters are in Part 1 of the book?

   F 5
   G 6
   H 7
   J 8

3. In *The Holt Reader,* what is found in **Part 2**?

   A Literary selections
   B Index of Authors and Titles
   C Table of Contents
   D Informational selections

4. The "Walk Through the Book" section in the front of the book provides information about the different features that are found throughout the book. What feature is *not* in the "Walk Through the Book" section?

   F Before You Read
   G Types of Literature
   H Quick Questions
   I Types of Notes

5. In *The Holt Reader,* what is found in **Part 3**?

   A To the Student Letter
   B Test Practice
   C Table of Contents
   D Copyright Page

Eeking Out a Life

Structure and Purpose of a Newspaper Article

The **purpose** of a newspaper article is to give you factual information about current events. A good informational article in a newspaper provides detailed answers to the questions *who? what? when? where? why?* and *how?*

Many newspaper articles are structured in what's called an **inverted**—or upside-down—**pyramid** style.

The article begins with a **summary lead,** a sentence or paragraph that gives the **main idea** of the story—this is usually the most important idea or detail in the story. It is followed by the less important details of the article.

Some articles begin with a lead that simply grabs your interest in a topic. Such a lead does not summarize but instead describes an interesting situation or fact related to the story. Here are some additional elements in the **structure** of a news article:

- **Headline:** the catchy boldface words that tell you what the article is about.
- **Subhead:** additional boldface words in smaller type under the headline, which add details about the article.
- **Byline:** the name of the reporter who wrote the article.
- **Dateline:** the location where the article was reported and the date on which the information was reported.
- **Lead:** the sentence or paragraph that begins the news article.

You'll have a chance to fill out your own inverted pyramid after you read the following newspaper article.

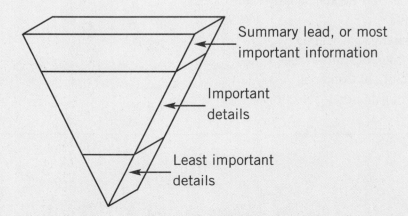

Summary lead, or most important information

Important details

Least important details

Matt Surman

Eeking Out a Life

IDENTIFY

What are the most important details you learn in this **summary lead**?

_____

_____

_____

_____

_____

_____

_____

_____

_____

_____

_____

INTERPRET

Re-read lines 13–26. Circle the details that suggest that Sunny Jim is probably not a wild rat.

_____

_____

_____

_____

_____

_____

Who knows what trials the rat named Sunny Jim endured in his days alone in the wilderness?

Was he chased by voracious[1] owls? beset by marauding[2] gangs of streetwise sewer rats? Did he yearn for a child who had lost him on a day's outing?

His new owners—Hayley Huttenmaier and Nachshon Rose—can only guess. The little rat that they rescued, housed, and fed isn't talking, of course. And now Rose isn't sure he wants to find out about the past of the rat they have named
10 Sunny Jim if that means the owner is going to come forward. Rose, in fact, has become attached to this sweet, squirming, don't-call-him-vermin little guy.

All the former veterinary hospital employee knows is that he was returning from a short hike through Corriganville Park one Tuesday when a bundle of fur scampered across the parking lot. He followed, saw it stick its nose out of a little burrow, and then—bit by bit—come to perch on his shoe.

"I was kind of concerned that if I didn't catch him, he would probably be eaten," Rose said. "He probably couldn't
20 have been out there more than a day."

The rat wasn't wearing any tags. There were no remnants of a leash. But he had to be a pet: Just look at the white and brownish-gray markings, his docile[3] —could one go so far as to say friendly?—behavior, his clean fur, and diminutive[4] size. Clearly this was not one of those sooty, dirt-brown outdoor creatures known as _Rattus rattus_.

So, he brought the rat home, and there, he and his fiancee, Huttenmaier, welcomed the rat into their family of two dogs and three cats. Now, Sunny Jim has his own room—well, a
30 cabinet actually—with a cubbyhole formed by bricks, a handful of toys, a soft bed of wood shavings, and regular meals.

Huttenmaier insisted that they place an ad seeking its owner. "My theory is a kid took him out to play and lost

---

1. **voracious** (vô·rā′shəs) _adj._: extremely hungry; eager to eat a lot of food.
2. **marauding** (mə·rôd′iŋ) _adj._: roving in search of something to take or destroy.
3. **docile** (däs′əl) _adj._: manageable.
4. **diminutive** (də·min′yo͞o·tiv) _adj._: very small; tiny.

him," she said. But so far they have received no calls. While Huttenmaier feels a bit for the poor owner, Rose doesn't want to give Sunny up. He thinks a mom forced her kid to abandon the creature when she realized there was a rodent hiding in a bedroom.

Which brings up the question: Isn't owning a rat found in
40 the woods—even one with a cute glossy face, busy little hands, and a slippy short tail—a little worrisome?

"We can't turn down a cute face," Huttenmaier explained.

And experts agreed: Sunny Jim is almost certainly not a tree-dwelling, bubonic-plague carrying, skinny wild rat. He is closer to man's best friend.

"Oh, rats are like little dogs," said Louis Stack, membership director of the Riverside-based American Fancy Rat & Mouse Association, whose members raise show rats the way purebred owners raise show dogs. "They can sit on your shoulder and
50 watch TV with you."

And indeed, rat lovers are not shy about their enthusiasm. The Web hosts scores of sites extolling[5] *Rattus norvegicus*—the pet rat, domesticated about 100 years ago in England—and dispelling what they call misinformation about the cleanliness of their pets.

"There are people who are fanatical about rats," Stack said. "There are . . . all kinds of newsletters." Huttenmaier and Rose have no intentions of going that far.

They are just happy to offer little Sunny a home, a sense of
60 safety—disregarding one little incident with a curious cat—and a chance to take it easy for a while.

And just maybe, there is a chance for a Rat Pack. "We might even get him a friend," Huttenmaier said.

INTERPRET

What makes Huttenmaier and Rose especially good guardians for their newly adopted friend?

---

5. extolling (ek·stōl′iŋ) *v.*: praising highly.

Inverted Pyramid

Many newspaper articles have a structure that follows that of an inverted pyramid. First the most important information is given, then important details, and then less important details.

Now that you've read "Eeking Out a Life," fill out the inverted pyramid below with details from the article.

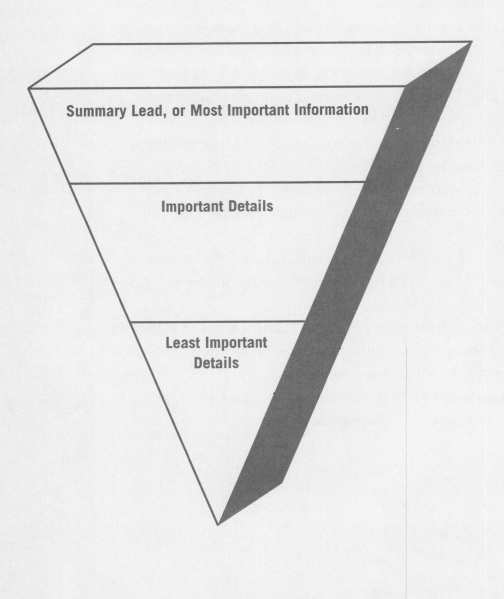

Summary Lead, or Most Important Information

Important Details

Least Important Details

Reading Check

1. What is the **purpose** of a newspaper article?

_____

2. Summarize the information from the article on pages 182–183 that answers the questions *who? what? when? where? why?* and *how?*

_____

_____

3. The **headline** title of this article contains a **pun,** which is a play on word meanings. What two words, both pronounced "eek," is the headline playing with?

_____

Test Practice

Circle the correct answer.

1. The **structure** of a newspaper article is said to be similar to an —

A octagon
B inverted pyramid
C oval
D upside-down T

2. The **dateline** of the article on page 000 names which city?

F Salt Lake City
G Des Moines
H Buxton
J Simi Valley

3. The **subhead** of the article tells you that —

A something is eeking out a life
B a couple has adopted a stray rat
C the rat may have beeen chased by an owl
D rats have become popular

4. The **byline** of the news article shows it was written by —

F George G. Toudouze
G Nachshon Rose
H Matt Surman
J Sunny Jim

5. The **lead** of this article —

A is an attention grabber
B makes a serious statement about dangerous rats
C answers *who? what? where? when?* and *how?*
D presents the story's main idea

6. The **main idea** of this article is —

F a couple loves its adopted rat
G rats can't live with people
H keeping a rat at home is dangerous
J the rat population is a problem

What's *Really* in a Name?

Perspective: How We Look at Life

Perspective refers to the way we look at a subject. Take the subject of school uniforms. Some people's perspective on that subject is negative. They think children should be free to dress the way they wish. Other people have a positive perspective on school uniforms. They think uniforms help equalize children and do away with clothes competition.

All writers have perspective on their subjects. O. Henry's perspective on life is clear in the story "After Twenty Years" (see page 69). He sees life as offering us choices between honest and dishonest behavior. He comes down in favor of honesty, even when friendship is at stake.

You may have thought about pros and cons of school uniforms yourself. Fill out the chart below with positive and negative perspectives on the issue of school uniforms.

School Uniforms

Positive	Negative
Uniforms do away with clothes competition.	Students should be free to dress the way they wish.

What's Really in a Name?

HELLO
my name is
Jack

by Joan Burditt

HELLO
my name is
Jack

(see page 69 for a story by him)

see page 69

(see page 69 for a story by him)

IDENTIFY

Why does the writer feel uncomfortable around Patsy (lines 1–6)?

_____

_____

_____

_____

_____

_____

PREDICT

Re-read lines 7–14. What do you think the writer's **perspective,** or viewpoint, on changing names will be?

_____

_____

_____

_____

_____

_____

_____

_____

IDENTIFY

Underline the reason why William Sydney Porter changed his name to O. Henry (lines 22–31).

Patsy seemed like a movie star before she really became one. She was my sister's friend, and her presence made me hide behind the plants in the living room. I didn't want to talk to her. I just wanted to watch her. She was only in the sixth grade, but she had an air of sophistication that I had never experienced in my seven years.

After we all grew up, Patsy moved to New York and then to Los Angeles. I began to see her on television. Then I saw her in movies. At the end of one movie, I searched the closing credits
10 for her name, but it wasn't there. So I called my sister and said, "I can't believe they left Patsy's name off the credits." My sister said, "They didn't. She changed her name. "I hung up the phone feeling confused. To me Patsy would always be Patsy. Why would she need a new name?

Patsy had given herself a pseudonym.[1] Although it sounds like a bad disease, it's not. A pseudonym is a made-up name. (*Pseudo* comes from a Greek word that means "fake.") For writers a pseudonym is also called a pen name. William Sydney Porter, the famous short story writer, called himself O. Henry
20 (see page 69 for a story by him). Mark Twain's name was really Samuel Clemens.

People have all sorts of reasons for using pseudonyms. It's easy to see why William Sydney Porter had one. He spent more than three years in jail for stealing money from a bank where he had worked. Although the evidence of his crime remains questionable, the damage to his reputation was done. As an ex-convict, he might have had a hard time getting his books published. So he changed his name. One story is that the name *O. Henry* came from his cat. When he called the family cat, he
30 yelled, "Oh, Henry." Another story has it that he got the name from his prison guard. The guard's name was Orrin Henry.

Sometimes writers give themselves pen names because their publishers ask them to. It might have been hard to sell a shoot-'em-up western if your name was Archibald Lynn Joscelyn. Change that name to Al Cody (think of Cody, Wyoming, and

1. **pseudonym** (s$\overline{oo}$′də·nim′) *n.*

Buffalo Bill Cody), however, and you've got a winner. The romance writer Elaine Carr is really a man named Charles Mason.

The main reason for taking a pseudonym is that it just sounds better. It's more appealing and memorable. Which has a better
40   ring—Charles Lutwidge Dodgson or Lewis Carroll? Reginald Kenneth Dwight or Elton John? Ralph Lifshitz or Ralph Lauren? Norma Jean Baker or Marilyn Monroe?

So why am I still troubled today that the beautiful and talented Patsy changed her name? I assumed that by adopting a new name, Patsy was trying to get rid of her past—her old friends, the neighborhood, even the scrawny seven-year-old kid who gazed at her from behind the plants.

Patsy, Norma Jean, Reginald—they probably all had good reasons for choosing new names. I hope when they changed their
50   names, they held on tight to their roots. I agree with writer James Baldwin, who said, "Know from whence you came. If you know from whence you came, there are absolutely no limitations to where you can go."

EVALUATE

Re-read lines 38–42. Underline one reason the writer gives for why someone would use a pseudonym. Would you change your name for the same reason? Why or why not?

_____

_____

_____

INTERPRET

Put into your own words the **author's perspective,** or point of view, on changing names.

_____

_____

_____

_____

_____

_____

_____

_____

_____

_____

_____

Perspective Chart

We reveal our **perspectives,** or views, on a subject in almost everything we write. After you read "What's *Really* in a Name?" fill in the chart below. Begin by identifying the position statement, in which the writer reveals her perspective on her subject. (Note: Position statements don't always appear at the beginning of an essay.) Then, fill in the Detail boxes. Cite the facts, reasons, or expert opinions that support the writer's perspective.

Detail That Supports Position

_____

_____

_____

_____

Detail That Supports Position

_____

_____

_____

_____

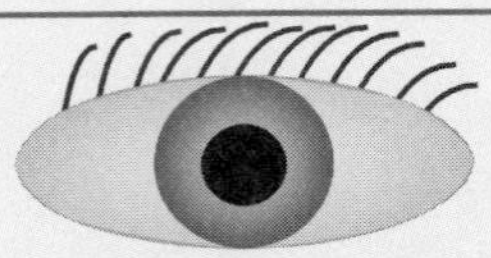

Position Statement or Perspective

_____

_____

_____

_____

Detail That Supports Position

_____

_____

_____

_____

Detail That Supports Position

_____

_____

_____

_____

Reading Check

1. What is a pseudonym? What is another expression for pseudonym?

_____

_____

2. According to this writer, what is the main reason people take pseudonyms?

_____

_____

3. Explain how the quote from James Baldwin at the end of the essay supports the writer's feelings about pseudonyms. _____

_____

Test Practice

Circle the correct answers.

1. The writer of this essay believes that —

A people should feel free to change their names

B it's important to remember where you came from

C William Sydney Porter was guilty of stealing money

D writers should use pseudonyms if they want to sell books

2. A writer's **perspective** is —

F his or her point of view on a subject

G a story the writer tells to entertain readers

H a sequence of related events

J the words a writer chooses

3. This essay was written in order to —

A explain a process

B describe a place

C compare several ideas

D express an opinion

4. In the quote "If you know from whence you came, there are absolutely no limitations to where you can go," the word *whence* means —

F where

G how

H there

J whether

5. The writer's *perspective* was *most* influenced by —

A Whoopi Goldberg

B her sister's friend Patsy

C James Baldwin

D William Sydney Porter

Buddies Bare Their Affection for Ill Classmate

Summarizing: Putting It All in a Nutshell

Have you ever found yourself rambling on and on about something that's happened to you, and your patient but now frustrated listener finally says, "Enough already—just give it to me in a nutshell"? What your friend's asking for is a summary. A **summary** restates the main events or main ideas of a text in a shorter form than the original.

Summaries are useful because they can help you remember the most important points in material you've just read. They're especially handy if you're doing research from a number of sources. Reviewing your summaries will show you how one source differs from another.

Before *you* write a summary, read the text carefully to decide what details to include and what to leave out. An example of a text and its summary appear below. After you've read "Buddies Bare Their Affection for Ill Classmate," you'll have a chance to collect information and write your own summary.

Sample Text

Middle school students in Japan take entrance exams to get into high school. The exams are very demanding, and students study every day, including weekends, for months before the test. Parents, teachers, students, and communities focus on the upcoming test. If students fail the test, they go to a "cram school" and retake the test the next year.

Summary

In Japan, entrance exams to high school are so difficult and important that students spend months preparing for them. Everyone gets involved, and students who fail go to a special school to prepare to take the test again.

OCEANSIDE, CAL., MAR. 19 (Associated Press) — In Mr. Alter's fifth-grade class, it's difficult to tell which boy is undergoing chemotherapy. Nearly all the boys are bald. Thirteen of them shaved their heads so a sick buddy wouldn't feel out of place.

"If everybody has their head shaved, sometimes people don't know who's who. They don't know who has cancer and who just shaved their head," said eleven-year-old Scott Sebelius, one of the baldies at Lake Elementary School.

10   For the record, Ian O'Gorman is the sick one. Doctors recently removed a malignant tumor from his small intestine, and a week ago he started chemotherapy to treat the disease, called lymphoma.

"Besides surgery, I had tubes up my nose. I had butterflies in my stomach," said Ian, who'll have eight more weeks of chemotherapy in an effort to keep the cancer from returning.

Ian decided to get his head shaved before all his hair fell out in clumps. To his surprise, his friends wanted to join him.

"The last thing he would want is to not fit in, to be made 20 fun of, so we just wanted to make him feel better and not left out," said ten-year-old Kyle Hanslik.

Kyle started talking to other boys about the idea, and then one of their parents started a list. Last week, they all went to the barbershop together.

"It's hard to put words to," said Ian's father, Shawn, choking back tears as he talked about the boys. "It's very emotional to think about kids like that who would come together, to have them do such a thing to support Ian."

The boy's teacher, Jim Alter, was so inspired that he, too, 30 shaved his head.

Ian left the hospital March 2. Although he has lost twenty pounds and is pale, he is eager to get back to the business of being an eleven-year-old playing baseball and basketball. "I think I can start on Monday," he said.

— from the *Austin American-Statesman*

IDENTIFY

Circle the name of the boy who actually needs chemotherapy and underline why he needs it.

INTERPRET

Re-read lines 19–21. Underline the reason the "baldies" shaved their heads.

INFER

List some things that Ian will do as he begins getting "back to the business of being an eleven-year-old."

Summarizing: Putting It All Together

The graphic organizer below can be used to collect information for your summary. You may wish to fill in the graphic organizer as you read the newspaper article, Buddies Bare Their Affection for Ill Classmate.

Then use the information in the graphic organizer to write a summary paragraph on the following page.

Main Events

Doctors remove tumor from Ian O'Gorman

↓

He starts chemotherapy

↓

↓

↓

The Writer's Main Point

Summary of "Buddies Bare Their Affection for Ill Classmate"

An article from the *Austin American-Statesman* tells the story of fifth-grader Ian O'Gorman who is undergoing chemotherapy.

_____

_____

_____

_____

_____

_____

_____

Test Practice

Circle the correct answer.

1. According to the opening paragraph, what's difficult to tell about the boys in Mr. Alter's class is who —

    A is the brightest student
    B is undergoing chemotherapy
    C once had the longest hair
    D Ian O'Gorman is

2. The main reason the boys shaved their heads was to —

    F look unusual
    G show individuality
    H act original
    J show support

3. Kyle Hanslik got the idea of shaving his head because —

    A he liked the way Ian looked
    B he didn't want Ian to be made fun of
    C he was protesting Ian's illness
    D he wanted to confuse the teacher

4. Who else was surprisingly inspired to shave his head?

    F Mr. Alter
    G Ian's dad
    H Kyle's dad
    J Ian's doctor

Gentlemen of the Road

Analyzing Causes and Effects

You know from experience that one thing leads to another. If you sleep through your alarm, you know you'll be late for school and you'll miss your favorite class—English. Sleeping through your alarm is a **cause**—it makes something happen. An **effect** is what happens as a result of some event—you're late for school and miss English.

You could go on. Being late for English class causes you to have to make up the time after school. Making up the time causes you to miss tryouts for football. Missing tryouts causes you to lose the chance to impress a certain girl. So you lose the girl, and it all can be traced to sleeping through an alarm.

When you read a text and ask, "Why did this happen?" and "What happened because of this?" you are asking about causes and effects. To find causes and their effects, look for signal terms such as *cause, effect, resulted in, so, thus*, and *because*.

See the example to the right of a cause-and-effect chart. You may also wish to turn to page 200, and fill out the cause-and-effect charts as you read.

Cause and Effect

What Happened
Some people in England got very rich. Others got poorer.

↓

Effect
Government built new toll roads for the rich to travel.

↓

Effect
Highwaymen held up stagecoaches and carriages to get money.

↓

Effect
Highwaymen . . .

Gentlemen

of the Road

Mara Rockliff

IDENTIFY

Re-read lines 1–37. Find and circle another name for the highwaymen. Why were they known by this name?

_____

_____

_____

_____

_____

_____

_____

_____

_____

_____

_____

_____

_____

_____

_____

INTERPRET

Underline the social conditions that contributed to the rise of the highwaymen. (lines 12–22).

_____

_____

_____

_____

Why did people once think of highwaymen, the bandits (like Bess's beloved) who robbed travelers in seventeenth- and eighteenth-century England, as gentlemen?

To answer that question, first look at these facts. The seventeenth and eighteenth centuries saw the rise of a very wealthy class in England. England became a nation of haves and have-nots. The rich dressed in silks and velvets. Men and women wore huge powdered wigs. The rich lived on vast estates. They traveled to London for rounds of parties in the winter-spring
10 season and spent summers in seaside towns, where gambling was a favorite pastime.

As the wealthy became richer, the conditions of the poor grew worse. Because the government did not care about their welfare, the poor lived in filthy slums in cities and in miserable conditions in farms and towns. In the worst years, 74 percent of the children in London died before the age of five. These were the social conditions that contributed to the rise of the highwaymen.

In addition, newly built toll roads ran through the countryside, connecting towns and villages. These improved
20 roads brought out more travelers—rich ones. The highwaymen could stop the private carriages and the stagecoaches that used the toll roads and rob the passengers.

The highwaymen called themselves gentlemen of the road, and some people agreed—sometimes even their victims! How did they come by this surprising reputation?

Some people saw the highwaymen not as criminals but as the new Robin Hoods because they gave to the poor what they had stolen from the rich (or part of it).

Another reason why people thought of these bandits as
30 gentlemen was that they looked the part. Most highwaymen came from poor families or, at best, middle-class ones. But once they turned to a life of crime, they could afford to dress in style. They wore high-heeled boots that went all the way to the hip, fancy shirts, long, elegant coats, and wide-brimmed hats with feathers. With their dashing clothes and fine horses these former footmen, butchers, and cheese sellers might have been mistaken for aristocrats.

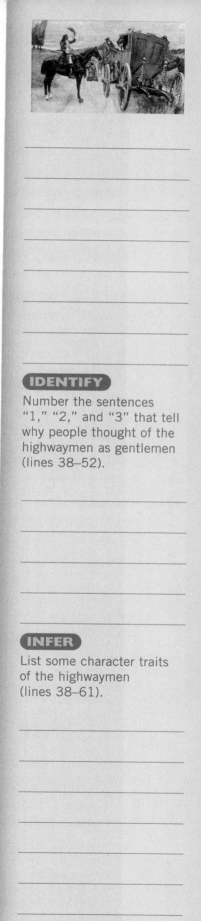

Some highwaymen tried to act like gentlemen as well. Many would never point a gun at a lady or search her for valuables, and sometimes they'd let women they robbed keep items of sentimental value. Highwaymen loved their horses too and took pride in earning the loyalty of their steeds by treating them well.

Some highwaymen politely begged their victims' pardon as they relieved them of their money and jewels. Others took only what they felt they needed and returned the rest to their owners.

In one account a robbery victim was upset about losing his beloved watch. He offered the highwayman two guineas instead, along with a promise not to turn him in to the authorities. The highwayman agreed, and they went off together to the man's home. The money changed hands, the two men shared a bottle of wine, and after many courteous words on each side, the highwayman galloped off.

Even when captured and sentenced to hang (the usual punishment for robbery in those days), some highwaymen tried to behave like gentlemen. They were too proud to cry or beg for mercy from the authorities they defied. After the noose was tied around their neck, some threw themselves off the scaffold rather than wait for the wagon they stood on to be pulled from beneath them. For those who romanticized the highwaymen in stories and song, this final act showed scorn for the corrupt authorities and courage in the face of death.

IDENTIFY

Number the sentences "1," "2," and "3" that tell why people thought of the highwaymen as gentlemen (lines 38–52).

INFER

List some character traits of the highwaymen (lines 38–61).

Cause-and-Effect Charts

A **cause** is a force or an event that makes another event happen. An **effect** is what happens as a result of the cause. A cause may have several effects. For example, a lower speed limit on highways may lead to fewer accidents and more speeding tickets being issued. An effect may have several causes. For example, fewer car accidents may be due to lower speed limits and safer car designs.

As you read "Gentlemen of the Road," think about why things happen, and also how something that happens causes other things to happen. Then, complete the two charts below with details from the selection.

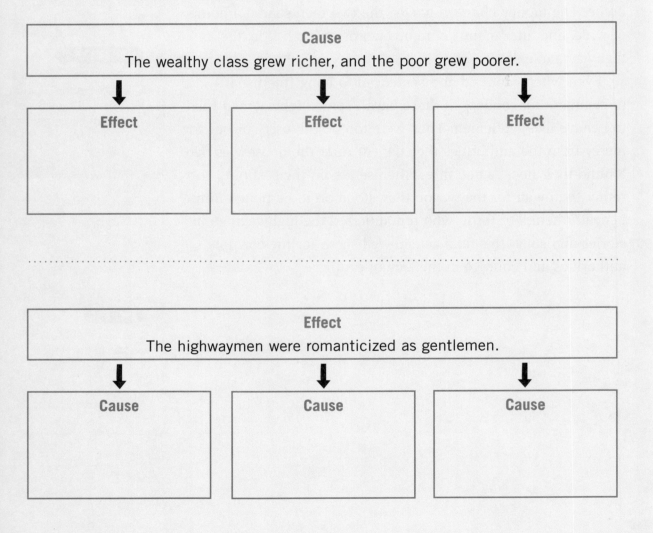

Cause
The wealthy class grew richer, and the poor grew poorer.

Effect	Effect	Effect

Effect
The highwaymen were romanticized as gentlemen.

Cause	Cause	Cause

Reading Check

Test Practice

Circle the correct answer.

1. This article suggests that all of the following might have **caused** the rise of the highwayman *except* the —

   A worsening conditions of the poor

   B rise of a very wealthy class

   C use of capital punishment

   D newly built toll roads

2. What **caused** people to see the highwaymen as the new Robin Hoods?

   F They rode horses and used bows and arrows.

   G They robbed from the rich and gave to the poor.

   H They lived in Sherwood Forest.

   J They wore Robin Hood outfits.

3. The highwaymen were able to dress in style because —

   A they were wealthy aristocrats

   B they took advice from their victims

   C their crimes made them wealthy

   D they were interested in fashion

4. Some highwaymen didn't beg for mercy from the hangman because of their —

   F pride

   G fear

   H mercy

   J shame

5. Which of the following statements does *not* explain why some people thought of the highwaymen as gentlemen?

   A The highwaymen behaved like gentlemen.

   B They treated women well.

   C They gave to the poor.

   D They came from rich families.

6. In the next-to-the-last paragraph the writer uses the word <u>guineas</u>. In the same paragraph she provides a context clue explaining what guineas are. What are they?

   F money

   G jewels

   H chickens

   J cattle

The Fall of the House of Poe?

Clarify Your Understanding

Take Notes

When you read informational material actively, a lot goes on in your head.

- You connect what you read with your own experiences and knowledge.
- You ask yourself questions and make predictions.
- You challenge the text.
- You reflect on its meaning.

Jotting down notes will help you understand and remember what you read. Here's what to do:

- **Be organized.** Use a simple outline form to jot down the information or ideas that you think are most important. (See the box for a sample outline form.)
- **Be brief.** Keep your notes short, simple, and clear. Write only words and phrases that will help you focus on the most important information.
- **Underline or circle information.** It may be useful to highlight certain information directly in the text, but don't do it in a book that doesn't belong to you, and don't get carried away. If everything is highlighted, then it's hard to tell what's most important.

When you read this selection about a house Edgar Allan Poe once lived in, be sure to jot down key details on the lines in the margin beside the story.

Outlining

Outlining can help you uncover the skeleton that holds the text together. An outline highlights main ideas and supporting details. Here's an example of an informal outline about an earthquake:

Main Idea
Earthquake occurred in Alaska
Supporting Details
Roads buckled
Houses split in two
Earth split open

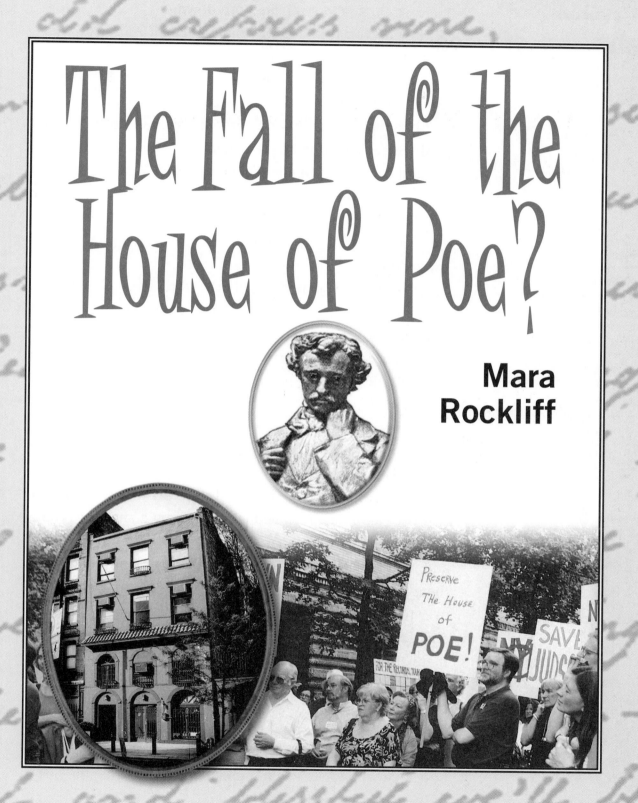

The Fall of the House of Poe?

Mara Rockliff

IDENTIFY

Pause at line 14. What is the most important detail you've read so far? Write it down below.

_____

_____

_____

_____

INFER

Underline the steps Poe's fans took to save the building (lines 15–20).

_____

_____

IDENTIFY

Complete this **outline** of the paragraph that begins with line 24:

I. NYU's reasons for tearing down the house where Poe had lived

A. Poe did not live there for long.

B. _____

_____

_____

C. The house had drastically changed over time.

D. _____

_____

_____

Think of your favorite place in the world, the place where you've spent some of the happiest hours of your life.

Now, think about it being torn down.

How do you feel? Terrible, right? If Edgar Allan Poe were alive today, scholars say, that's the way he might feel about the fate of the boardinghouse he once lived in at 85 Amity Street in New York City's Greenwich Village.

More than a century and a half has passed since Poe died. Amity Street was long ago renamed West Third Street, and the
10 former boardinghouse now belongs to New York University. For years the university used it for classrooms and offices. But in 1999, NYU officials announced that they would be tearing the house down to make room for a new building for their law school.

Loyal Poe fans joined neighborhood residents in vigorously protesting the university's plan. They wrote letters, circulated petitions, and organized a rally attended by several hundred supporters chanting, "No, no, Poe won't go." They read aloud from "The Raven," the poem that made Poe famous, and chanted
20 its famous refrain: "Nevermore!"

"It always mystified me why there was not a gold plaque outside the house," one Poe scholar said. "It is a genuine literary landmark."

New York University disagreed. Its representatives argued that Poe (along with his young wife, Virginia, and her mother) may have lived at the boardinghouse for as little as six months and that he had not written any of his more important works there. They also said that the house had changed drastically over the years, leaving no traces of Poe's residence. They even
30 questioned whether the current building was the same one that had stood there in 1845, when Poe moved in. One NYU representative concluded, "This is not a building that remembers Poe."

The protesters researched the university's claims. They studied all kinds of documents, from letters and recollections of people who knew Poe to public records showing the history of the neighborhood.

Judging from dates and addresses in Poe's surviving correspondence, including a valentine given to him by Virginia in 1846, it seems probable that Poe lived there for less than a
40   year. But that may have been longer than he stayed at any of the other eight places where he lived in Manhattan, all of which have already been torn down.

But the months he spent at 85 Amity may have been the happiest in Poe's short and troubled life. The boardinghouse was close to Washington Square Park, where his young wife, who was dying of tuberculosis, could breathe fresh air into her ailing lungs. That would have been his last full year with his beloved Virginia.

Professionally Poe was at the height of his career. He had
50   finally achieved what he called "the one great purpose of my literary life"—writing and editing his own literary magazine, the *Broadway Journal*. He also had published *The Raven and Other Poems*, and he had written dozens of essays and short stories, including his famous detective story "The Facts in the Case of M. Valdemar." Poe was completely absorbed in his writing, sometimes spending as many as fifteen hours a day at his desk.

The house where all that happened, it turned out, was indeed the house that the university planned to demolish. Detailed city
60   atlases in the Maps Division of the New York Public Library show that although the name of the street has changed, the house numbers have not. Eighty-five West Third was 85 Amity. The house, according to tax ledgers in the New York City Municipal Archives, was built in 1836—nearly a decade before the Poe family moved in.

On September 29, 2000, after examining the evidence on both sides, State Supreme Court Judge Robert E. Lippmann dismissed the case, saying he had no legal authority to prevent NYU from tearing down the Poe house. This prompted an NYU
70   spokesman to add, "The Tell-Tale Heart does not beat beneath the floorboards of this building." Preservation groups planned to appeal the decision.

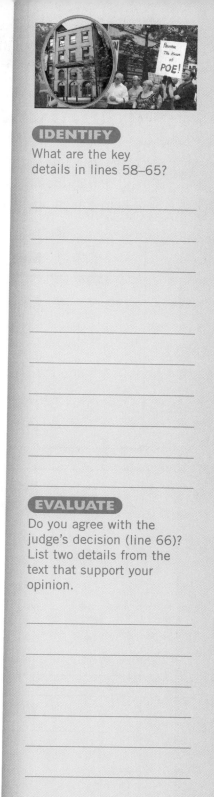

IDENTIFY

What are the key details in lines 58–65?

_____

_____

_____

_____

_____

_____

_____

EVALUATE

Do you agree with the judge's decision (line 66)? List two details from the text that support your opinion.

_____

_____

_____

_____

_____

_____

_____

_____

Main Idea Note Cards

Clarify your understanding of "The Fall of the House of Poe?" by taking notes on what you read. Fill in the note cards below with the main ideas from the text. Then, use your notes to help you complete the outline on page 207.

Note Card 1	**Note Card 2**
Note Card 3	**Note Card 4**
Note Card 5	**Note Card 6**

Outline

Now that you've taken notes on the article, complete the blanks in the following outline.

I. NYU officials plan to tear down Poe house in order to build a new law school.

II. Poe fans and residents protest.

    A. They wrote letters and circulated petitions against the university's plan.

    B. _____

    _____

III. NYU argues against protesters.

    A. Poe lived there for less than six months.

    B. _____

    _____

    C. _____

    _____

IV. _____

    A. They studied letters, public records, and other documents.

    B. _____

    _____

    C. _____

    _____

    D. They found that the house NYU wanted to destroy was the house where Poe had lived.

V. _____

Reading Check

Test Practice

Circle the correct answer.

1. Which of the following statements is an **opinion**, not a fact?

    A Poe wrote *The Raven and Other Poems.*

    B Poe's young wife died of tuberculosis.

    C All the other places in Manhattan that Poe lived in have already been torn down.

    D "This is not a building that remembers Poe."

2. The judge who dismissed the case did so because he —

    F had no legal authority to prevent NYU from tearing down the house

    G believed NYU was doing the right thing

    H did not like the protesters

    J did not think the protesters had a good case

3. What announcement did NYU officials make in 1999?

    A They discovered Poe lived in the house on Amity Street for less than a year.

    B They were tearing down Poe's old home to build a law school.

    C They were taking the protests of Poe's fans under advisement.

    D They would build the new law school elsewhere.

4. What action did Poe's fans take in response to NYU's announcement?

    F They wrote poems in tribute to Poe.

    G They filed a lawsuit against NYU.

    H They protested against the university's plan.

    J They put up a gold plaque outside Poe's house.

5. When Poe said he achieved "the one great purpose of my literary life," he was referring to —

    A living at 85 Amity Street with Virginia

    B writing *The Raven and Other Poems*

    C turning his attention to his wife's illness

    D writing and editing his own literary magazine

6. Which of the following would *not* be included in an outline of the article?

    F Poe definitely lived at the house on Amity Street.

    G The judge dismisses the case.

    H Preservation groups plan to appeal.

    J There are other law schools in New York City.

Vocabulary: Words to Own

Latin Roots

Many English word roots come directly or indirectly from the Latin language. A word **root** is a word or word part from which other words are made. Learning some of the main word roots derived from Latin will give you a key to understanding the meaning of many English words.

Words with Latin Roots
circulated
petitions
representatives
absorbed
demolish

Practice

Match each word in the box above with the Latin word it comes from. Can you find an additional word with the same origin and use it in a sentence?

Latin Word	Meaning	Word Bank	Additional Word
petere	"to seek"		
demoliri	"to pull down; destroy"		
circulari	"to form a circle"		
absorbere	"to suck in"		
repraesentare	"to be again"		

It Just Keeps Going and Going . . .

Finding the Pattern

The article you are about to read follows an organizational pattern called a **cause-and-effect chain.** This pattern is built around a series of causes and effects. Each event **causes** another event to happen. The event it causes is called an **effect.** In this article a little mistake starts a chain reaction. Soon a chain of causes and effects has turned a minor mishap into a big mess.

Writers of cause-and-effect articles often use **transitions** to show how one idea is connected to another. These transition terms help the reader follow the cause-and-effect pattern.

Cause-and-Effect Terms	
after	so
as a result	then
because	therefore
consequently	since

Read "It Just Keeps Going and Going . . ." once all the way through. Then, read it a second time and keep track of the cause-and-effect chain by filling out the organizer on page 214.

It just keeps Going and Going . . .

Joan Burditt

IDENTIFY

Read the first paragraph, and underline the topic of this article. Then, circle the names by which "this monster" is known.

IDENTIFY

Circle the words in lines 7–16 that describe the **effects** of the computer virus.

CAUSE AND EFFECT

What happens because the answer key is wrong?

_____

_____

_____

CAUSE AND EFFECT

What is the **effect** of the full trash can?

_____

_____

_____

IDENTIFY

Circle the instructions on the sticky note (lines 31–33).

_____

_____

_____

_____

_____

It is a human-made monster. No one can escape the reach of its tentacles, which can extend not just across a room but also around the entire planet. It gets worse. This monster, known by names such as the Brain, Crusher, Grog, and the Creeper, can quickly reproduce and shut down entire systems. This is no science fiction or fantasy creature. It's a computer virus.

The effects of computer viruses range from pesky system crashes to life-threatening situations, but experts disagree on how serious they really are. In fact, information and opinions
10 on viruses are spreading as fast as the viruses themselves. *Encarta Encyclopedia* defines a computer virus as a "self-replicating computer program that interferes with a computer's hardware or operating system (the basic software that runs the computer)." That doesn't sound too bad, but think about the term *self-replicating*. That means that it keeps making copies of itself over and over again.

Here's an explanation of how a computer virus works, based on a model by the computer scientist Eugene Kaspersky.

A teacher is working at his desk at the end of the
20 day. He finds mistakes in the midterm answer key, so he tosses it into the trash. Since the trash can is overflowing, the answer key falls onto the floor.

Then the teacher feels a headache coming on and goes home. The custodian comes to empty the trash, sees the answer key on the floor, and picks it up. He puts it back on the teacher's desk. But now, at-
30 tached to the answer key is a sticky note

that says, "Copy two times, and put copies in other teachers' boxes."

The next day the teacher stays home because he has the flu. As a result, a substitute is called to the school. The first thing the substitute

sees is the answer key with the note stuck to it. So she copies it twice for each teacher

40 and puts the copies into the teachers' boxes. She leaves the sticky note on the answer key so they will see that the absent teacher wanted them to get the copies.

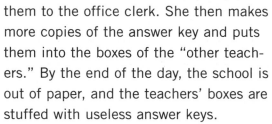

When the other teachers find the two copies of the answer key with the instructions to copy them twice and distribute them, they give them to the office clerk. She then makes

50 more copies of the answer key and puts them into the boxes of the "other teachers." By the end of the day, the school is out of paper, and the teachers' boxes are stuffed with useless answer keys.

CAUSE AND EFFECT

What **causes** a substitute teacher to come to school? What **effect** does the substitute create?

_____

_____

_____

_____

_____

_____

_____

This model resembles what happens with a computer virus. The difference between the answer-key situation and a computer virus lies in motivation. The teacher didn't plan to cause chaos in the school. The whole mess was just a series of unfortunate causes and effects. On the other hand, computer

60 viruses are created by people who have all kinds of motives, none of them good. The effects are the corruption of massive amounts of important information as well as the cost of billions of dollars in lost productivity every year.

Developers of antivirus programs are gaining on the virus villains, making it easier to detect a virus before it spreads and causes a path of destruction. Nonetheless, watch what you put in your computer . . . and in your trash.

EVALUATE

Did the answer-key situation help you understand how a computer virus works? Explain.

_____

_____

_____

_____

_____

_____

_____

_____

_____

Cause-and-Effect Chart

Sometimes a series of causes and effects create comedy. For example, say a man slips on a banana peel. Then, because he slipped on the banana peel, he crashes into a wall, causing a flowerpot to fall on his head.

   After reading "It Just Keeps Going and Going . . . ," re-read the section that gives the example of a teacher working at his desk. Find the causes and effects that are presented in the passage. Link the causes and effects using the chart below.

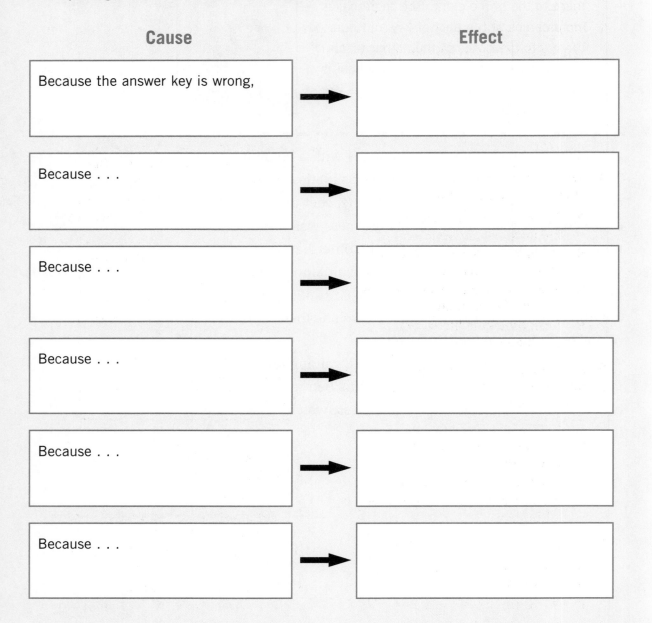

Cause	Effect
Because the answer key is wrong,	
Because . . .	
Because . . .	
Because . . .	
Because . . .	
Because . . .	

Reading Check

1. Which two main events cause the answer-key confusion to spin out of control?

_____

2. Make a list of all the cause-and-effect words in this article. _____

_____

3. According to the article, what are the effects of computer viruses? _____

_____

4. Imagine you submitted this article to an editor of a newspaper. The editor tells you to get a new title. What would you call it? _____

Test Practice

Circle the correct answer.

1. Which of the following sentences contains a **cause** and an **effect**?

A The computer she wanted was the most expensive one.

B The salesperson agreed to throw in a monitor for free.

C Since the monitor was free, she bought the computer.

D I can't imagine life without computers.

2. According to the article, which of the following statements is a major **effect** of computer viruses?

F Computers are ruined.

G Billions of dollars and a lot of information are lost.

H Some viruses ruin networks.

J A computer will do everything it is told to do.

3. This article is mainly about —

A problems with computers

B how to kill a virus

C the history of computers

D how computer viruses work

4. The causal chain below shows some of the important **causes and effects** in the story about the answer key.

> Cause: Because the teacher stays home with the flu . . .

> Effect: a substitute is called to the school.

> Cause:

> Effect: every teacher gets two copies of the wrong answer key.

Which of these statements belongs in the blank *Cause* box?

F The substitute is unsure about what to do.

G The substitute follows the instructions on the sticky note.

H The substitute tells all the teachers the answer key is wrong.

J The substitute helps the office clerk with all the extra copying.

Cellular Telephone Owner's Manual

Structure and Purpose of an Instructional Manual

With all the electronic products available today, it's useful to know how to read an instructional manual. The **purpose** of an instructional manual is to help you operate and care for a specific device, such as a cordless phone or a hand-held Internet appliance. Many instructional manuals have a **structure** like that of a small textbook.

Use these strategies in order to make the best use of an instructional manual:

- Scan the **table of contents** of the manual to get an idea of the topics covered.
- If you don't see the topic you're looking for, turn to the **index,** located in the back of the manual. This is an alphabetical list of the topics and the page numbers on which they appear.
- Become familiar with the parts of the device. An instructional manual usually includes a **diagram** showing you the important parts of the device and explaining their functions.
- Read the **directions** carefully, and keep referring to the actual device as you read.
- Do the directions have **steps**? Follow them in order. Read all the directions for a procedure before you move on to the next one.
- Make sure you understand any special abbreviations or symbols. You may find definitions and meanings in the manual's **glossary**— an alphabetical list of special terms and their definitions.
- Look for a regular mail address and an **e-mail address** as well as a customer service **phone number** or **Web site** where you can get additional help from the manufacturer.

Cellular Telephone Owner's Manual

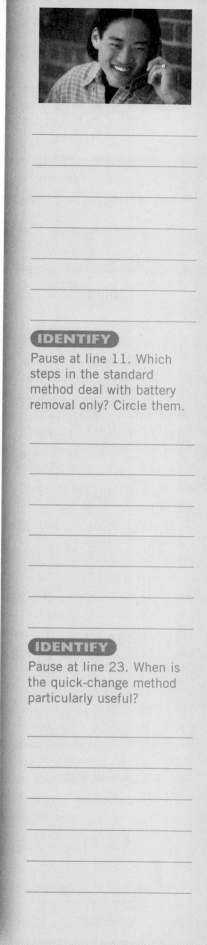

Battery Removal and Replacement

There are two ways to remove and replace your telephone battery—the standard method and the quick-change method.

Standard Method

1. Turn off your telephone.
2. Depress the latch button on the rear of the battery, and slide the battery pack downward until it stops.
3. Lift the battery clear to remove.
4. To reinstall, place the battery pack on the unit so that its
10   grooves align, and slide upward (in the direction of the arrows on the back of the phone) until it clicks into place.

Quick-Change Method

1. Advise the party you are talking to that you are about to change batteries.
2. Remove the battery from the telephone.
3. Put on the spare battery.
4. Press PWR. This will return you to your telephone call. You will have only five seconds to complete this action before your telephone call is terminated.

20 The quick-change method allows you to remove your telephone battery at any time and replace it with a charged spare battery during a telephone call. This is especially useful if you receive the "low battery" message (or an audible tone) during a call.

It is a good idea to practice this procedure a few times before using it during an actual phone call.

IDENTIFY

Pause at line 11. Which steps in the standard method deal with battery removal only? Circle them.

IDENTIFY

Pause at line 23. When is the quick-change method particularly useful?

Checklist

To make sure you have followed directions in a manual completely, create a checklist for yourself. Turn each step in the manual into a question to ask yourself at each stage of the process. Complete each question starter with a step from the cell phone manual.

Standard Method
1. Did I _____ _____
2. Did I _____ _____
3. Did I _____ _____
4. Did I _____ _____

Quick-change Method
1. Did I _____ _____
2. Did I _____ _____
3. Did I _____ _____
4. Did I _____ _____

Reading Check

1. According to the owner's manual, how many methods are there for changing the battery? _____

2. Why would a cell phone user need this information?

Test Practice

Circle the correct answer.

1. The **main topic** of the section of the manual on page 217 is —

A removing and replacing the battery

B making and receiving calls

C using the phone to send e-mail

D using the phone in out-of-state networks

2. In which part of the manual would you look to find the pages on which the topic of ringer volume appears?

F Diagram

G Glossary

H Index

J Cover

3. In which part of the manual would you look to find the meaning of the abbreviation _LCD_?

A Table of contents

B Glossary

C Index

D Cover

4. The first step in the standard method is to —

F remove the battery

G tell the person you're speaking with to call back

H turn off the phone

J turn off the "low battery" message

5. The first step in the quick-change method is to —

A put in the spare battery

B remove the battery

C tell the person you're speaking with that you're going to change the battery

D ask the person you're speaking with to call you back after you've changed the battery

6. After you put in the spare battery using the quick-change method, your call will be terminated unless you —

F press PWR within five seconds

G deposit twenty-five cents

H charge the telephone battery

J press 0 for further assistance

How to Change a Flat Tire

Understanding Explanations

Technical directions are step-by-step instructions that explain how to accomplish mechanical tasks. The technical directions in the instructional manual may have taught you how to operate your new cell phone. Technical directions can also instruct you how to repair mechanical devices you are using. You may have followed them when you removed and oiled the wheels on your in-line skates or when you cleaned the sprockets on your bicycle.

You're probably too young to drive a car, but you're certainly not too young to be thinking about it. Driving can give you a new independence, but it also gives you new responsibilities. Any number of things can go wrong with your car, and it's up to you to fix them—or get them fixed. You won't be expected to repair the engine, but you can fairly easily fix one of the most common automobile emergencies: a flat tire. A flat is something every driver will have to face someday. To be prepared, study the directions on the next page.

Before you read, think about what you know about changing a flat tire. Write the information on the lines below. Then write down what you would like to learn from this passage. Refer to your chart after you've read the directions to see if your questions have been answered.

There are many parts involved in changing a flat tire.

I know that changing a flat tire involves . . .

_____

_____

_____

I would like to find out . . .

_____

_____

_____

How to Change a Flat Tire

Before you can change a flat tire on your car, you first have to realize that the tire is flat. You might come out of your house in the morning and see the wheel rim resting on the road with the tire spread around it. You'll know right away the tire's flat. How can you tell, though, if it goes flat while you are driving? A first clue is that your car starts to pull to the right or the left even though you aren't turning the steering wheel. Another clue is that passing motorists honk and point as they drive by. Yet another clue is that the car starts bouncing up and down
10 and making a loud thumpity-thump-thump sound.

When you suspect you have a flat tire, follow these procedures:

1 Park the car as far off the road as possible. Put the car in park (if you have an automatic transmission) or in gear (if you have a standard transmission), turn off the engine, and put on the emergency brake. Turn on your car's flashing lights. Now, get out and look at your tires. If you have a flat, put out
20 emergency triangles or, at night, flares. (It's a good idea to carry warning triangles and flares in your trunk at all times in case of an emergency.)

lug wrench

spare tire

lug nuts

jack

screwdriver

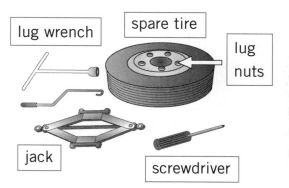

2 Remove the spare tire from the trunk. Also take out the jack, the lug wrench, and related tools.

IDENTIFY

Underline the different ways that you know you have a flat tire (lines 6–10).

INFER

When changing a flat tire, why should the car be parked as far off the road as possible? (line 13)

IDENTIFY

List the tools needed to change a flat tire.

INFER

Read lines 35–38. Circle a lug nut in the picture. What is a lug nut? What is it used for?

INFER

Underline the one thing you should never do, according to lines 50–51. Why shouldn't you do this?

30 **3** Remove the wheel cover from the flat tire, using a screwdriver or the end of the jack handle.

4 Loosen the lug nuts with the lug wrench, but do not remove them. Most lug nuts loosen counterclockwise.

40 **5** Position your jack. Different makes of cars come with different types of jacks, so check your owner's manual to learn how to use your jack. Make sure the jack is sitting on a solid, flat surface.

6 Lift the car with the jack until your flat tire is two or three inches off the ground.
50 *(Never lie under the car when it is on the jack!)*

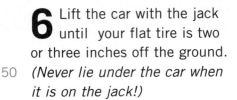

7 Now, finish unscrewing the lug nuts. Put them inside the wheel cover so you don't lose them.

8 Remove the flat tire, and replace it with the spare tire. Replace the lug nuts, and tighten them by hand.

60 **9** Lower the jack until the spare tire is firmly on the ground. Remove the jack. Firmly tighten the lug nuts with the lug wrench. Work diagonally—tighten one on the top, then one on the bottom; one on the left, then one on the right; and so on.

70

10 Place the flat tire, the wheel cover, and all your tools in the trunk. As soon as you can, drive to a garage or a tire repair shop to get the tire fixed or replaced. You never want to be without a spare, because you never know when you'll get another flat!

INFER

What is a spare tire? Where would you get the spare tire?

_____

_____

_____

_____

INTERPRET

The directions tell you to work diagonally. Underline what is meant by "working diagonally." Draw arrows in the space below to create a visual representation of working diagonally.

_____

_____

_____

INTERPRET

Underline the most important statement in Step 10.

_____

_____

_____

_____

_____

_____

_____

Chronological Sequence Chart

Technical directions involve a **step-by-step process.** Following the steps in order is an important part of the process. Create a set of travel directions for motorists to use as a quick reference in case of an emergency. Summarize the steps in the passage, "How to Change a Flat Tire," and fill in the sequence chart below. Try to use a phrase or simple sentence in each box to summarize the different steps.

Topic: How to Change a Flat Tire

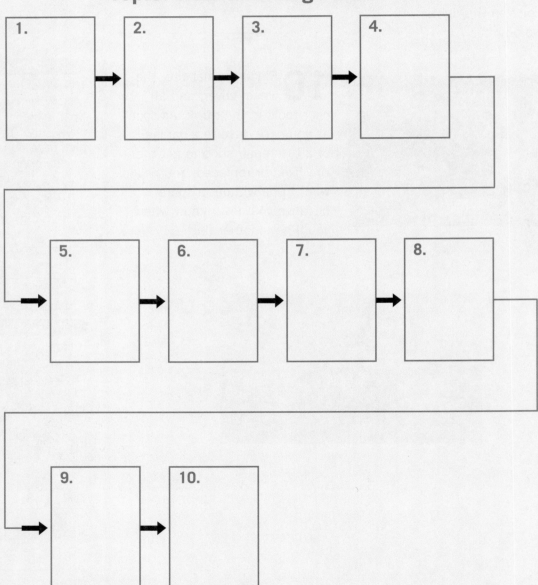

Reading Check

1. How can you tell you have a flat tire? List three clues.

   _____

2. List the tools needed to fix a flat tire.

   _____

3. What should you do as soon as you can after you've changed your flat tire?

   _____

Test Practice

Circle the correct answer.

1. When you think you have a flat tire, what should you do first?

   A Drive the car to your family's garage.

   B Call your parents, and ask them to pick you up.

   C Park the car as far off the road as possible.

   D Look out your window to see if the tire's flat.

2. The best tool for loosening the lug nuts is —

   F a screwdriver

   G a lug wrench

   H a jack

   J your hand

3. You should lift the car with the jack until —

   A you can fit comfortably underneath the car

   B the car is two to three feet in the air

   C the flat tire is two to three inches off the ground

   D the flat tire comes off the wheel

4. When you remove the lug nuts, you should —

   F let them fall to the ground

   G put them in the wheel cover

   H throw them away

   J feed them to a squirrel

5. After you have changed a flat tire, what should you do next?

   A Call your parents to let them know what happened.

   B Drive to a garage to get the flat tire fixed.

   C Continue where you were going before you got the flat.

   D Throw away the flat tire.

Public Documents

Locating Information in Public Documents

Public documents supply citizens with information that may be of interest to them. Public documents can relate to schools, churches, government agencies, the courts, libraries, and fire and police departments, to name just a few.

Typically, most citizens do not read the public documents put out by the government, the military, and nonprofit agencies or groups. Instead, they read **newspaper articles** that report on the documents. Whether you read a document itself or a newspaper account of its contents, public documents exist to tell you what is happening in your world.

All public documents have one thing in common: They inform people (you) about things you might need or want to know. Public documents are all about information. Let's follow one person's experience in finding information she needs by using some public documents.

Meet Sam (Miss Samantha Sallyann Lancaster, and don't even think about calling her anything but Sam, thank you very much). Anyone who knows Sam for five minutes knows two things about her: She's smart, and she can beat anyone, anything, anywhere on her BMX bike. That's usually where you can find her if she isn't doing homework or attending dance class. So imagine Sam's excitement when she comes across the **announcement** on page 227 in her favorite biking magazine.

Casting Call

If you've been looking for the right break to get into motion pictures, this may be your chance. StreetWheelie Productions is casting fresh talent for an upcoming action movie.

To audition you must
- be a charismatic, awesome, off-the-wall male or female individualist
- be an expert at making your BMX-type bike do whatever you want it to do
- have your own bike
- look like you're between the ages of twelve and fifteen
- meet the requirements for a permit to work in the entertainment industry if you are under age eighteen
- be living in or near San Francisco during July and August 2002

Auditions will be held in
Golden Gate Park, San Francisco
Saturday, May 25, 2002
10:00 a.m. to 5:00 p.m.
Bring your bike.

See you in the movies!

10

IDENTIFY

Underline the name of the company making the casting call.

_____

_____

_____

_____

INFER

Re-read the requirements for an audition (lines 4–12). What do you think each person will need to do for the audition?

_____

_____

_____

INTERPRET

Circle the city where the auditions will take place. What should someone who wants to audition bring to the audition?

_____

_____

_____

_____

Locating Information: An Article

Sam thinks, "Cool!" This may be for her, but she wants more information. An **Internet search** using the key words *StreetWheelie Productions* and *San Francisco* yields this **article** from *Hollywood Beat*, a newsmagazine.

Hollywood Beat

Shhhhhh!

Here's a little secret for you. Remember Bilbo Baggins, the lovable little hobbit who saved Middle Earth from the Powers of Darkness in J.R.R. Tolkien's classic novel? Well, that little hobbit's about to get radical. *Hollywood Beat* has discovered that StreetWheelie Productions is developing an out-of-sight version of this tale, and Middle Earth will never be the same.

10   Set in San Francisco, the hobbits are bike-riding dudes who, in order to save their world, oppose an endless stream of baddies who ride BMX bikes. The principal character, Bilbo, is a nerdy innocent who finds himself at the center of (Middle) Earth-shaking events. The result? Batman meets Mr. Rogers.

Sources closest to the production say that there is some big talent interested in the project. As of yet, nobody's talking, but remember . . . you'll hear all about it first on *Hollywood Beat.*

IDENTIFY
Write down the kind of movie Sam will be auditioning for.

INFER
Underline what makes the BMX bike an important part of the movie (lines 8–13).

RETELL
Re-read lines 8–13. **Retell** what the movie is about.

Filling Out the Application

Study the application below to find out what Sam will need to do to get permission to work in a movie.

STATE OF CALIFORNIA
Division of Labor Standards Enforcement

APPLICATION FOR PERMISSION TO WORK IN THE ENTERTAINMENT INDUSTRY

THIS IS NOT A PERMIT   ❑ NEW   ❑ RENEWAL

PROCEDURES FOR OBTAINING WORK PERMIT

1. Complete the information required below.
2. School authorities must complete the School Record section below.
3. For minors 15 days through kindergarten, please attach a certified copy of the minor's birth certificate. See reverse side for other documents that may be accepted.
4. Mail or present the completed application to any office of the Division of Labor Standards Enforcement for issuance of your work permit.

Name of Child	Professional Name, if applicable
Permanent Address Number Street City State Zip Code	Home Phone No.

School Attending						Grade
Date of Birth	Age	Height	Weight	Hair Color	Eye Color	Sex

Statement of Parent or Guardian: It is my desire that an Entertainment Work Permit be issued to the above-named child. I will read the rules governing such employment and will cooperate to the best of my ability in safeguarding his or her educational, moral, and physical interest. I hereby certify, under penalty of perjury, that the foregoing statements are true and correct.

Name of Parent or Guardian (print or type)	Signed Daytime phone #

SCHOOL RECORD

❑ I certify that the above-named minor meets the school district's requirements with respect to age, school record, attendance, and health.
❑ Does not meet the district's requirements and permit should not be issued.

Authorized School Official	Date	
School Address	School Telephone	(School Seal or Stamp)

HEALTH RECORD

COMPLETE THIS SECTION IF INSTRUCTED TO DO SO OR IF INFANT UNDER ONE MONTH OF AGE

Name of Doctor   Address   Telephone Number

I certify that I am Board Certified in pediatrics and have carefully examined

and, in my opinion: He/She is physically fit to be employed in the production of motion pictures and television. If less than one month, infant is at least 15 days old, was carried to full term, and is physically able to perform.

Signature   M.D.   Date

Approved DLSE 277 Rev. 03/99

INFER

Who needs to fill out this application?

IDENTIFY

What two things under "School Record" make this application unique to each child's school?

INTERPRET

Underline the two things a doctor has to certify. Why is this an important part of the application?

Information-Locator Wheel

Write the number of each item from the Information Bank in the area that shows the kind of document where the information can be found.

Information Bank

1. age of character Sam might play
2. age at which you can work in entertainment in California
3. how the actor playing the part should look
4. title of the book that StreetWheelie Productions is making into a movie
5. name of a main character in the movie
6. types of people who must declare that Sam can work in the entertainment industry
7. requirements for trying out for a part in the movie
8. Sam's birth date
9. time and place of audition
10. the city where the movie will be set

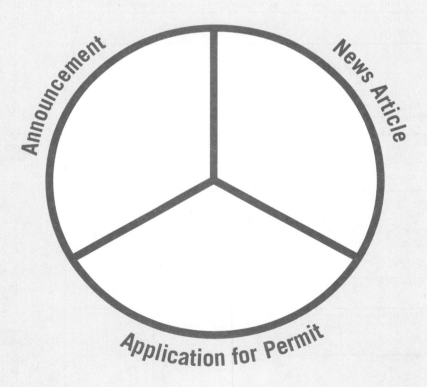

Reading Check

1. What is the most important purpose of a **public document**?

_____

2. Where and when will the auditions be held?

_____

3. What special talent must people have to audition for this part?

_____

4. What will the movie be about?

_____

Test Practice

1. The fact that the advertisement appeared in Sam's favorite biking magazine suggests that the casting agents are especially interested in kids who can —

A read magazines
B act a little crazy
C follow directions
D ride a bike

2. If Sam is hired to play a part, she will be working during —

F May and June
G June and July
H July and August
J August and September

3. Sam is probably auditioning to play —

A a hobbit
B Mr. Rogers
C a goodie
D Bilbo Baggins

4. Sam is confident that she will qualify for a **work permit.** To do so, she will need all of the following *except* —

F the full support and help of her parent or guardian
G a statement of good health from a doctor
H a statement from her school that she has met the district's requirements for her grade level
J permission from her school to be absent when necessary

5. If Sam wanted to find out more about StreetWheelie Productions, her *best* choice would be to —

A search the Internet using the key words *StreetWheelie Productions*
B look in an encyclopedia under "Film Industry"
C read *The Hobbit* again
D post a question on her school's electronic bulletin board

PART 3   STANDARDIZED TEST PRACTICE

Literature

Informational Materials

DIRECTIONS

Read the following story. Then, read each question on page 235 and circle the letter of the best response.

The Dinner Party
Mona Gardner

The country is India. A colonial official and his wife are giving a large dinner party. They are seated with their guests—army officers and government attachés[1] and their wives, and a visiting American naturalist[2]—in their spacious dining room, which has a bare marble floor, open rafters, and wide glass doors opening onto a veranda.

A spirited discussion springs up between a young girl who insists that women have outgrown the jumping-on-a-chair-at-the-sight-of-a-mouse era and a colonel who says that they haven't.

"A woman's unfailing reaction in any crisis," the colonel says, "is to scream. While a man may feel like it, he has that ounce more of nerve control than a woman has. That last ounce is what counts."

The American does not join in the argument but watches the other guests. As he looks, he sees a strange expression come over the face of the hostess. She is staring straight ahead, her muscles contracting slightly. With a slight gesture she summons the Indian boy standing behind her chair and whispers to him. The boy's eyes widen; he quickly leaves the room.

Of the guests, none except the American notices this nor sees the boy place a bowl of milk on the veranda just outside the open doors.

The American comes to with a start. In India, milk in a bowl means only one thing—bait for a snake. He realizes there must be a cobra in the room. He looks up at the rafters—the likeliest place—but they are bare. Three corners of the room are empty, and in the fourth the servants are waiting to serve the next course. There is only one place left—under the table.

His first impulse is to jump back and warn the others, but he knows the commotion would frighten the cobra into striking. He speaks quickly, the tone of his voice so arresting that it sobers everyone.

"I want to know just what control everyone at this table has. I will count to three hundred—that's five minutes—and not one of you is to move a muscle.

---

1. **attachés** (at′ə·shāz′) *n.:* diplomatic officials.
2. **naturalist** *n.:* person who studies nature by observing animals and plants.

Those who move will forfeit[3] fifty rupees.[4] Ready!"

The twenty people sit like stone images while he counts. He is saying ". . . two hundred and eighty . . ." when, out of the corner of his eye, he sees the cobra emerge and make for the bowl of milk. Screams ring out as he jumps to slam the veranda doors safely shut.

"You were right, Colonel!" the host exclaims. "A man has just shown us an example of perfect control."

"Just a minute," the American says, turning to his hostess. "Mrs. Wynnes, how did you know that cobra was in the room?"

A faint smile lights up the woman's face as she replies: "Because it was crawling across my foot."

---

3. **forfeit** (fôr′fit) *v.*: give up as a penalty.
4. **rupees** (roo′pēz) *n.*: Indian money, like dollars in the United States.

---

1. The **setting** of this story is colonial —
   A America
   B India
   C Africa
   D Australia

2. Which of the following events in the **plot** of the story happens first?
   F The American challenges the guests to remain still.
   G A cobra is attracted to milk.
   H The hostess whispers to a servant.
   J The colonel argues with a girl.

3. What **later event** explains the strange expression on the hostess's face?
   A A cobra has crawled across her foot.
   B She dislikes the colonel's biased opinions about women.
   C The servant is not doing his job.
   D She sees a cobra on the veranda.

4. What **later event** explains why the boy places the milk on the veranda?
   F The colonel's speech bores him.
   G The American sees a cobra.
   H A cobra makes for the milk.
   J The American proposes a challenge.

5. What event marks the **climax** of the story?
   A The argument between the girl and the colonel ends.
   B The boy places a bowl of milk on the veranda.
   C The American begins to count.
   D The cobra emerges, and screams ring out.

6. The **resolution** of the story shows all of the following *except* that the —
   F colonel was right
   G colonel was wrong
   H young girl was right
   J hostess is brave

DIRECTIONS

Read the story. Then, read each question on page 237 and circle the letter of the best response.

Here is a portion of a story set in Antigua, an island that is part of the West Indies. The narrator is a young girl named Annie John, who has for a while wanted to play with another girl she calls the Red Girl.

from The Red Girl

Jamaica Kincaid

The Red Girl and I stood under the guava tree looking each other up and down. What a beautiful thing I saw standing before me. Her face was big and round and red, like a moon—a red moon. She had big, broad, flat feet, and they were naked to the bare ground; her dress was dirty, the skirt and blouse tearing away from each other at one side; the red hair that I had first seen standing up on her head was matted and tangled; her hands were big and fat, and her fingernails held at least ten anthills of dirt under them. And on top of that, she had such an unbelievable, wonderful smell, as if she had never taken a bath in her whole life.

I soon learned this about her: She took a bath only once a week, and that was only so that she could be admitted to her grandmother's presence. She didn't like to bathe, and her mother didn't force her. She changed her dress once a week for the same reason. She preferred to wear a dress until it just couldn't be worn anymore. Her mother didn't mind that, either. She didn't like to comb her hair, though on the first day of school, she could put herself out for that. She didn't like to go to Sunday school, and her mother didn't force her. She didn't like to brush her teeth, but occasionally her mother said it was necessary. She loved to play marbles, and was so good that only Skerritt boys now played against her. Oh, what an angel she was, and what a heaven she lived in! I, on the other hand, took a full bath every morning and a sponge bath every night. I could hardly go out on my door-step without putting my shoes on. I was not allowed to play in the sun without a hat on my head. My mother paid a woman who lived five houses away from us sevenpence a week—a penny for each school day and twopence for Sunday—to comb my hair. On Saturday, my mother washed my hair. Before I went to sleep at night I had to make sure my uniform was clean and creaseless and all laid out for the next day. I had to make sure that my shoes were clean and polished to a nice shine. I went to Sunday school every Sunday unless I was sick. I was not allowed to play marbles, and, as for Skerritt boys, that was hardly mentionable.

1. Which of the following **character** traits does the narrator apply to the Red Girl?
   A She is a careful dresser.
   B She spends too much time on her hair.
   C She is unconcerned about her appearance.
   D She is always clean and neat.

2. All of the following **traits** are characteristic of the narrator *except* —
   F she envies the Red Girl's freedom
   G she much prefers her own life to that of the Red Girl
   H she obeys her mother
   J she dresses neatly and wears clean shoes

3. From the narrator's vivid description of the Red Girl, you can **infer** that the narrator —
   A is repulsed by the Red Girl
   B wants to help the Red Girl
   C longs to be more like the Red Girl
   D doesn't want to be friends with the Red Girl

4. The narrator tells us directly how she feels about the Red Girl when she says —
   F "She took a bath only once a week. . . ."
   G "She didn't like to go to Sunday school. . . ."
   H "I was not allowed to play in the sun without a hat on my head."
   J "Oh, what an angel she was, and what a heaven she lived in!"

5. In this passage from "The Red Girl," the narrator uses all of the following methods of **characterization** *except* —
   A stating character traits directly
   B describing actions
   C quoting speech
   D describing appearance

DIRECTIONS

Read the two selections, "Home" and "Gold" (see page 240). Then, read each question on pages 240–241 and circle the letter of the best response. Some of the questions will ask you to think about how the selections are alike.

Home
Gwendolyn Brooks

What had been wanted was this always, this always to last, the talking softly on this porch, with the snake plant in the jardiniere in the southwest corner, and the obstinate slip from Aunt Eppie's magnificent Michigan fern at the left side of the friendly door. Mama, Maud Martha, and Helen rocked slowly in their rocking chairs, and looked at the late afternoon light on the lawn and at the emphatic iron of the fence and at the poplar tree. These things might soon be theirs no longer. Those shafts and pools of light, the tree, the graceful iron, might soon be viewed possessively by different eyes.

Papa was to have gone that noon, during his lunch hour, to the office of the Home Owners' Loan. If he had not succeeded in getting another extension, they would be leaving this house in which they had lived for more than fourteen years. There was little hope. The Home Owners' Loan was hard. They sat, making their plans.

"We'll be moving into a nice flat somewhere," said Mama. "Somewhere on South Park, or Michigan, or in Washington Park Court." Those flats, as the girls and Mama knew well, were burdens on wages twice the size of Papa's. This was not mentioned now.

"They're much prettier than this old house," said Helen. "I have friends I'd just as soon not bring here. And I have other friends that wouldn't come down this far for anything, unless they were in a taxi."

Yesterday, Maud Martha would have attacked her. Tomorrow she might. Today she said nothing. She merely gazed at a little hopping robin in the tree, her tree, and tried to keep the fronts of her eyes dry.

"Well, I do know," said Mama, turning her hands over and over, "that I've been getting tireder and tireder of doing that firing. From October to April, there's firing to be done."

"But lately we've been helping, Harry and I," said Maud Martha. "And sometimes in March and April and in October, and even in November, we could build a little fire in the fireplace. Sometimes the weather was just right for that."

She knew, from the way they looked at her, that this had been a mistake. They did not want to cry.

But she felt that the little line of white, sometimes ridged with smoked purple, and all that cream-shot saffron would never drift across any western sky except that in back of this house. The rain would drum with as sweet a dullness nowhere but here. The birds on South Park were mechanical birds, no better than the poor caught canaries in those "rich" women's sun parlors.

"It's just going to kill Papa!" burst out Maud Martha. "He loves this house! He *lives* for this house!"

"He lives for us," said Helen. "It's us he loves. He wouldn't want the house, except for us."

"And he'll have us," added Mama, "wherever."

"You know," Helen said, "if you want to know the truth, this is a relief. If this hadn't come up, we would have gone on, just dragged on, hanging out here forever."

"It might," allowed Mama, "be an act of God. God may just have reached down and picked up the reins."

"Yes," Maud Martha cracked in, "that's what you always say—that God knows best."

Her mother looked at her quickly, decided the statement was not suspect, looked away.

Helen saw Papa's coming. "There's Papa," said Helen.

They could not tell a thing from the way Papa was walking. It was that same dear little staccato walk, one shoulder down, then the other, then repeat, and repeat. They watched his progress. He passed the Kennedys', he passed the vacant lot, he passed Mrs. Blakemore's. They wanted to hurl themselves over the fence, into the street, and shake the truth out of his collar. He opened his gate—the gate—and still his stride and face told them nothing.

"Hello," he said.

Mama got up and followed him through the front door. The girls knew better than to go in too.

Presently Mama's head emerged. Her eyes were lamps turned on.

"It's all right," she exclaimed. "He got it. It's all over. Everything is all right."

The door slammed shut. Mama's footsteps hurried away.

"I think," said Helen, rocking rapidly, "I think I'll give a party. I haven't given a party since I was eleven. I'd like some of my friends to just casually see that we're homeowners."

Gold

Pat Mora

When Sun paints the desert
with its gold,
I climb the hills.
Wind runs round boulders, ruffles
5   my hair. I sit on my favorite rock,
lizards for company, a rabbit,
ears stiff in the shade
of a saguaro.[1]
In the wind, we're all
10 eye to eye.

Sparrow on saguaro watches
rabbit watch us in the gold
of sun setting.
Hawk sails on waves of light, sees
15 sparrow, rabbit, lizards, me,
our eyes shining,
watching red and purple sand
     rivers stream down the hill.

I stretch my arms wide as the sky
like hawk extends her wings
20 in all the gold light of this, home.

---

1. **Maud Martha in "Home" and the speaker of "Gold" share strong feelings about —
   A   nature
   B   houses
   C   robins
   D   porches

2. In "Home," Mama, Maud Martha, and Helen are upset because —
   F   their house is more expensive than a flat
   G   Mama has been working too hard
   H   their friends won't come to see them
   J   they may be losing their home

3. In "Home," Brooks writes that Mama's "eyes were lamps turned on." This is an example of —
   A   a simile
   B   a metaphor
   C   a definition
   D   rhyme

4. What place is home to the speaker of the poem?
   F   A favorite rock
   G   A house with a porch
   H   The desert
   J   A nice flat

---

1. **saguaro** (sə·gwär′ō) *n:* a huge cactus found in the southwestern United States and northern Mexico.

5. At the end of the story and the poem, the characters and the speaker regard their homes with a feeling of —

A disappointment
B anger
C worry
D contentment

6. In "Home," Brooks writes that Maud Martha "tried to keep the fronts of her eyes dry." This means that Maud Martha is —

F near tears
G cleaning her glasses
H wet all over from the hose
J having trouble with her vision

7. Mama says she is tired of doing "that firing." Based on clues in the story, what do you guess that <u>firing</u> means here?

A Losing a job
B Starting a fire
C Cooking
D Cleaning

8. Brooks describes Mama's eyes as "lamps turned on." Which words from "Gold" mean the same thing?

F "our eyes shining"
G "we're all / eye to eye"
H "sails on waves of light"
J "I stretch my arms"

9. The following words are in both selections. Which is the **key word** in both selections?

A purple
B light
C sky
D home

10. Which statement *best* expresses the **theme** of both the story and the poem?

F Home is a place we associate with special feelings.
G Homelessness is a terrible problem.
H It's a relief to have a nice house of one's own.
J The out-of-doors makes the best kind of home.

DIRECTIONS

Read the following materials. Then, read each question on page 243 and circle the letter of the best response.

Structure and Purpose of Informational Materials

SIGN

TEXTBOOK

CHAPTER 2 | **Biomes: World Plant Regions**

What is a biome? A plant and animal community that covers a very large land area is called a **biome.** Plants are the most visible part of a biome. If you looked down on the United States from space, you would see various biomes. The forests of the eastern United States would appear green, while the deserts of the Southwest would be light brown.

NEWSPAPER ARTICLE

B2

Hatteras Lighthouse Completes Its Move

BUXTON, N.C., July 9 (AP)—As onlookers clapped and cheered, the Cape Hatteras Lighthouse slid today onto the concrete pad where its caretakers hope it will stand for another century, a safe distance from the thundering Atlantic surf.

INSTRUCTIONAL MANUAL

page 32

Looking Up Synonyms for a Word in a Document
1. Select the word in the document.
2. Choose Utilities Thesaurus (Alt,U,T), or press the THESAURUS key (Shift+F7).
3. Look through the list of synonyms in Synonyms. Scroll through the list if necessary.

Command for Thesaurus
Utilities Thesaurus or THESAURUS key (Shift+F7)
    Lists alternative words
    for the selection

Thesaurus: English (US)   ? X

Looked Up: Replace with Synonym:
Important   significant   Replace

Meanings: significant   Look Up
significant (adj.)   substantial
pompous (adj.)   consequential   Cancel
Antonyms   considerable
Related Words   meaningful   Revise
    material
    momentous

1. Which statement explains the difference between the **purpose** of a textbook and the purpose of a newspaper article?

    A   A textbook has an index, a glossary, and graphic features, while a newspaper article has an inverted pyramid structure.

    B   A textbook has a table of contents and an index, while a newspaper article has a headline, a dateline, and a byline.

    C   A textbook gives lots of information about a big subject, while a newspaper article gives information about a current event.

    D   A textbook has many pages, while a newspaper article is usually one page long or less.

2. In comparing the **structure** of a textbook and the structure of an instructional manual, you could say that —

    F   they both have a table of contents, a glossary, an index, and graphic features, but a textbook is much longer

    G   a textbook presents information about a big subject, but an instructional manual presents information about how to operate and use a device

    H   a textbook is something you use in a classroom, but a manual is something you use at work or at home

    J   a textbook is something your school gives you to use, but a manual comes with something you buy

3. In the **textbook** excerpt the word biome means —

    A   a community of plants growing in a forest

    B   plants and sand that are found in desert areas

    C   the coastal areas of the United States as seen from outer space

    D   a plant and animal community that covers a large area

4. The **instructional manual** shown on page 242 gives instructions on how to —

    F   find biomes

    G   move a lighthouse

    H   look up synonyms

    J   use the Internet

5. The **sign** shown on page 242 indicates a place to —

    A   eat

    B   sleep

    C   buy knives and forks

    D   buy gas

6. The **newspaper article** on page 242 shows all of the following features *except* a —

    F   byline

    G   dateline

    H   summary lead

    J   headline

DIRECTIONS

Read the following article. Then, read each question on page 245 and circle the letter of the best response.

Mongoose on the Loose

Larry Luxner

In 1872, a Jamaican sugar planter imported nine furry little mongooses from India to eat the rats that were devouring his crops. They did such a good job, the planter started breeding his exotic animals and selling them to eager farmers on neighboring islands.

With no natural predators—like wolves, coyotes, or poisonous snakes—the mongoose population exploded, and within a few years, they were killing not just rats but pigs, lambs, chickens, puppies, and kittens. Dr. G. Roy Horst, a U.S. expert on mongooses, says that today mongooses live on seventeen Caribbean islands as well as Hawaii and Fiji, where they have attacked small animals, threatened endangered species, and have even spread minor rabies epidemics.

In Puerto Rico there are from 800,000 to one million of them. That is about one mongoose for every four humans. In St. Croix, there are 100,000 mongooses, about twice as many as the human population. "It's impossible to eliminate the mongoose population, short of nuclear war," says Horst. "You can't poison them, because cats, dogs, and chickens get poisoned, too. I'm not a prophet crying in the wilderness, but the potential for real trouble is there," says Horst.

According to Horst, great efforts have been made to rid the islands of mongooses, which have killed off a number of species, including the Amevia lizard on St. Croix, presumed extinct for several decades. On Hawaii, the combination of mongooses and sports hunting has reduced the Hawaiian goose, or nene, to less than two dozen individuals. . . .

Horst says his research will provide local and federal health officials with extremely valuable information if they ever decide to launch a campaign against rabies in Puerto Rico or the U.S. Virgin Islands.

1. In 1872, a Jamaican sugar planter imported nine mongooses to —

   A keep snakes away from his farm
   B serve as pets for his young children
   C eat the rats that were ruining his crops
   D breed them for their fur

2. Because the mongooses didn't have any natural predators in that part of the world, their population —

   F diminished
   G exploded
   H fluctuated
   J declined

3. The mongooses' biggest threat to humans is that they —

   A spread rabies
   B outnumber humans
   C kill their pets
   D threaten endangered species

4. You would be *most* likely to find this information about mongooses in a —

   F chemistry book
   G collection of stories
   H travel guide
   J magazine on nature

5. The following diagram shows some important information about the **causes and effects** of bringing mongooses to Jamaica.

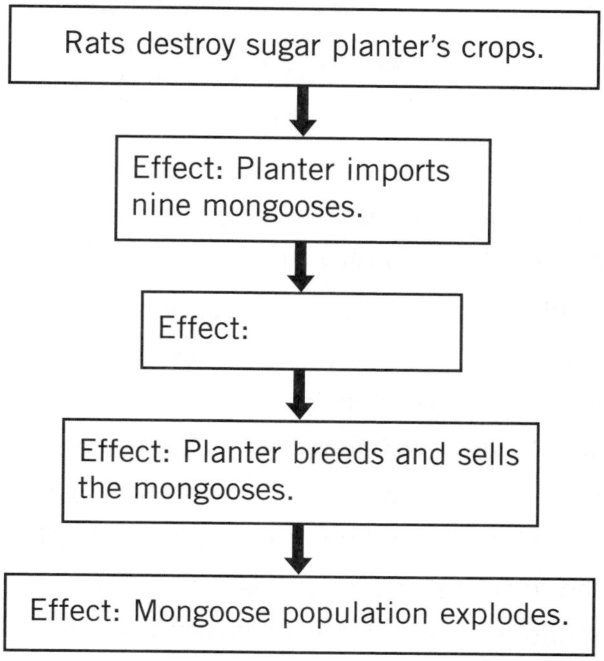

   Rats destroy sugar planter's crops.

   ↓

   Effect: Planter imports nine mongooses.

   ↓

   Effect:

   ↓

   Effect: Planter breeds and sells the mongooses.

   ↓

   Effect: Mongoose population explodes.

   Which of these events belongs in the third box?

   A Mongooses do a good job getting rid of rats.
   B Mongooses threaten the Hawaiian goose.
   C Mongooses destroy other species.
   D Mongooses are difficult to study.

DIRECTIONS

Read the following article. Then, read each question on page 247 and circle the letter of the best response.

Can We Rescue the Reefs?

Ritu Upadhyay from *Time for Kids*

1 Time is running out to stop the destruction of coral reefs.

2 Under the clear blue sea, bustling communities of ocean creatures live together in brightly colored, wildly stacked structures called coral reefs. These silent, majestic underwater cities are home to four thousand different species of fish and thousands of plants and animals. For millions of years, marine creatures have lived together in reefs, going about their business in their own little water worlds.

3 But danger looms. At an international meeting on coral reefs in October 2000, scientists issued a harsh warning. More than one quarter of the world's reefs have been destroyed. Unless drastic measures are taken, the remaining reefs may be dead in twenty years. "We are about to lose them," says Clive Wilkinson of the Coral Reef Monitoring Network.

Precious Underwater Habitats

4 The destruction of coral reefs, some of which are 2.5 million years old, would have a very serious impact on our oceans. Though coral reefs take up less than 1 percent of the ocean floor, they are home to 25 percent of all underwater species. Wiping them out would put thousands of creatures at risk of extinction. It would also destroy one of our planet's most beautiful living treasures.

5 Though it's often mistaken for rock because of its stony texture, coral is actually made up of tiny clear animals called coral polyps. Millions stick together in colonies and form a hard outer shell. When coral die, their skeletons are left behind, and new coral build on top. The colonies eventually grow together, creating large reefs. Reefs grow into complex mazelike structures with different rooms, hallways, holes, and crevices for their inhabitants to live in. Over the years the ancient Great Barrier Reef off Australia's coast has grown to be 1,240 miles long!

1. Which of the following statements best summarizes the writer's **perspective** in "Can We Rescue the Reefs?"

   A   The outlook for coral reefs is hopeless.

   B   Global warming is a threat to the whole earth.

   C   Saving endangered coral reefs is very important.

   D   Coral reefs are beautiful little worlds within the oceans.

2. Paragraph 2 contains words and phrases such as "bustling communities," "underwater cities," "home," "going about their business," and "their own little water worlds." The writer uses those words and phrases to —

   F   make coral reefs seem like human societies

   G   describe coral reefs the way a scientist would describe them

   H   tell where coral reefs are located

   J   describe how coral reefs are formed

3. In paragraph 3, the writer supports her position by —

   A   describing her personal fears about the reefs

   B   quoting an expert on the issue

   C   telling a brief story about the development of coral reefs

   D   giving reasons why coral reefs are beautiful

4. Which statement is an example of a **statistic**?

   F   "Time is running out to stop the destruction of coral reefs."

   G   "Coral is actually made up of tiny clear animals. . . ."

   H   "Reefs grow into complex mazelike structures. . . ."

   J   "More than one quarter of the world's reefs have been destroyed."

5. Which of the following is a statement of **fact**—something that can be proved to be true?

   A   Coral is the most beautiful thing in the sea.

   B   Over the years the ancient Great Barrier Reef has grown to be 1,240 miles long.

   C   Coral reefs must be saved.

   D   Coral reefs are fascinating.

6. The writer's **purpose** in this article is to —

   F   inform

   G   describe

   H   persuade

   J   all of the above

7. According to the article, why are coral reefs important?

   A   They attract tourists.

   B   They are home to 25 percent of all underwater species.

   C   They are very old.

   D   They grow into complex mazelike structures.

DIRECTIONS

Read the following speech. Then, read each question on page 249 and circle the letter of the best response.

Looking for Heroes

A Speech to the Graduating Class of Lakeville Middle School

Our world, freshly beginning a new age, is a long way from the time of King Arthur. We have no fighting knights, no daring rescues of damsels, no more brave souls who think only of others above all else. We have no loyalty, no honor, no chivalry. All we have are the stories and thus, some distant memories of what the world used to be and will never be again.

If you believe that, I've got some oceanfront property in Oklahoma to sell you.

We have to change the way we think about heroes. We've just been looking in all the wrong places. Let's dismiss King Arthur and the knights of the Round Table for just a moment and go on our own quest to find our own heroes.

So, turn off the TV. Shut down the computer. Put away the magazines. Just watch life with me for a few moments.

First, we'll journey to Abilene, Texas. As we walk down the sidewalk, I want you to notice that elderly man walking towards his car. He's just an ordinary man, and it seems as if there is nothing special about him. But over fifty years ago on his forty-third Air Force mission escorting bombers over occupied Europe, his plane's engine quit at thirty thousand feet. The plane plunged 26,000 feet before he could get the engine started again. He eventually had to bail out and spent six months in hiding. He was then turned over to the Gestapo and spent three months in prison. This pilot, Bill Grosvenor, is one of about 93,000 American prisoners of war who returned alive from Europe after World War II.

Next, we fly to Seattle, Washington. As we pull up to St. Joseph's Catholic Church, I want you to notice the woman carrying a large bag and hurrying up the steps. Her name is Jeannie Jaybush, and she created the Baby Corner, an organization that last year gave away about $1,000,000 worth of baby items to families in need. About 12 percent of Seattle's homeless population is made up of children who are five years old and younger, according to the City of Seattle's Human Services Department. Because of the efforts of Jaybush, these children now have some of the basic necessities that are needed to grow and be healthy.

If we had more time, we could fly to Duluth to visit a woman who is caring for her husband, one of the fourteen million Americans who have Alzheimer's disease. We could stop in Chicago, where a child with cancer lives each day fully. We could also land in Los Angeles, where a bilingual child is teaching his parents to read in English.

We'll stop our search for now, but let yours continue. Keep looking, and let your heart lead you to the heroes of today. I'll promise you, they're a lot easier to find than oceanfront property in Oklahoma.

1. The main **assertion** in this speech is —
   A there were more heroes in the old days
   B our world is full of heroes
   C we need more heroes like King Arthur
   D it is impossible to find heroes in today's world

2. Which of the following statements from the speech is an **accurate** piece of evidence that can be proved?
   F "About 12 percent of Seattle's homeless population is made up of children who are five years old and younger. . . ."
   G "We have to change the way we think about heroes."
   H "We have no loyalty, no honor, no chivalry."
   J "We've just been looking [for heroes] in all the wrong places."

3. Suppose a listener responded to this speech by saying, "Heroes are usually males who are recognized by most of the population." This would be an example of —
   A accurate evidence
   B appropriate evidence
   C adequate evidence
   D stereotyping

4. The speech supports its assertion mainly with —
   F statistics
   G quotes from experts
   H examples of people considered heroic
   J stereotypes

ACKNOWLEDGMENTS

For permission to reprint copyrighted material, grateful acknowledgment is made to the following sources:

Américas, bimonthly magazine published by the General Secretariat of the Organization of American States in English and Spanish: From "Mongoose on the Loose" by Larry Luxner from *Américas,* vol. 45, no. 4, July/August 1993, p. 3. Copyright © 1993 by Américas.

The Associated Press: "Buddies Bare Their Affection for Ill Classmate" from *Austin American-Statesman,* March 19, 1994. Copyright © 1994 by The Associated Press.

Susan Bergholz Literary Services, New York: "Names/Nombres" by Julia Alvarez. Copyright © 1985 by Julia Alvarez. First published in *Nuestro,* March 1985. All rights reserved.

The Estate of Gwendolyn Brooks: "Home" from *Maud Martha* by Gwendolyn Brooks. Copyright © 1993 by Gwendolyn Brooks. Published by Third World Press, Chicago.

Don Congdon Associates, Inc.: "The Naming of Names" by Ray Bradbury from *Thrilling Wonder Stories.* Copyright © 1949 by Standard Magazines, Inc.; copyright renewed © 1976 by Ray Bradbury.

Dial Books for Young Readers, a division of Penguin Putnam Inc.: "The Flight of Icarus" from *Stories of the Gods and Heroes* by Sally Benson. Copyright 1940 and renewed © 1968 by Sally Benson.

Farrar, Straus & Giroux, LLC: From "The Red Girl" from *Annie John* by Jamaica Kincaid. Copyright © 1985 by Jamaica Kincaid.

Henry Holt and Company, Inc.: "The Runaway" from *The Poetry of Robert Frost,* edited by Edward Connery Lathem. Copyright 1951 by Robert Frost; copyright 1923, © 1969 by Henry Holt and Company, Inc.

Houghton Mifflin Company: "Bargain" from *The Big It and Other Stories* by A. B. Guthrie. Copyright © 1960 by A. B. Guthrie. All rights reserved.

Patricia Lauber: "When the Earth Shakes" from *Earthquakes: New Scientific Ideas About How and Why the Earth Shakes* by Patricia Lauber. Copyright © 1972 by Patricia Lauber.

The Los Angeles Times: "Eeking out a Life" by Matt Surman from *The Los Angeles Times,* July 8, 2000. Copyright © 2000 by The Los Angeles Times.

Pat Mora: "Gold" by Pat Mora. Copyright © 1998 by Pat Mora. Originally published by Harcourt Brace in *Home: A Journey Through America* by Thomas Locker and Candace Christiansen.

Random House UK Ltd: "Narcissus" (retitled "Echo and Narcissus") from *Tales the Muses Told* by Roger Lancelyn Green. Copyright © 1965 by Don Bolognese. Published by The Bodley Head.

The Saturday Review: "The Dinner Party" by Mona Gardner from *The Saturday Review of Literature,* vol. 25, no. 5, January 31, 1941. Copyright © 1941 by General Media Communications, Inc.

Scribner, a division of Simon & Schuster: "A Day's Wait" from *Winner Take Nothing* by Ernest Hemingway. Copyright 1933 by Charles Scribner's Sons; copyright renewed © 1961 by Mary Hemingway.

Amy Tan and Sandra Dijkstra Literary Agency: "Fish Cheeks" by Amy Tan. Copyright © 1987 by Amy Tan. Originally appeared in *Seventeen Magazine,* December 1987.

Piri Thomas: "Amigo Brothers" from *Stories from El Barrio* by Piri Thomas. Copyright © 1978 by Piri Thomas.

Time, Inc.: "Can We Rescue the Reefs?" by Ritu Upadhyay from *Time for Kids,* vol. 6, no. 9, November 10, 2000. Copyright © 2000 by Time, Inc.

Mel White: "A Mason-Dixon Memory" by Clifton Davis, slightly adapted from *Reader's Digest,* March 1993. Copyright © 1993 by Mel White.

Abbreviations used: (tl) top left, (tc) top center, (tr) top right, (l) left, (lc) left center, (c) center, (rc) right center, (r) right, (bl) bottom left, (bc) bottom center, (br) bottom right.

Page 3, (c) Dinodia/Omni-Photo Communications, (bc), Michael Fogden/ Photo Researchers; 23, Ralph A. Reinhold /Animals Animals; 27, (rc) Jack Parsons/ Omni-Photo Communications; (lc), Image Copyright ©2003 Photodisc Inc.; 35, (rc), Sepp Seitz/Woodfin Camp, (c), Derik Murry/The Image Bank; 41, Image Copyright ©2003 Photodisc Inc.; 49, Courtesy of the author, (inset) Bill Eichner/Algonquin Books; 69, Grace Davies/Omni-Photo Communications; 77, St. Frederick High School yearbook; 87, Culver Pictures; 103, HRW Illustration; 119, Amos Zezner/Omni-Photo Communications; 127, Image Copyright ©2003 Photodisc Inc.; 131, Steve McCutchen; 141, (c), Image Copyright ©2003 Photodisc Inc. (bkgd), Dr. E.R. Degginger; 149, (tr), R. Blansjar/West Stock, (bkgd), Image Copyright ©2003 Photodisc Inc.; 155, HRW Illustration; 169, (tl), Joe McDonald/CORBIS, (bkgd), Image Copyright ©2003 Photodisc Inc.; 175, HRW Library;181, Joe McDonald/ CORBIS; 187, (c), Image Copyright ©2003 Photodisc Inc., (lc), Bill Bachman/Photo Network/PictureQuest, (bkgd), Image Copyright ©2003 Photodisc Inc.; 193, (tr), AP Wide World Photos, (bkgd), Image Copyright ©2003 Photodisc Inc.; 197, (c), North Wind Pictures, (coins), British Museum/The Bridgeman Art Library, (bkgd), Image Copyright ©2003 Photodisc Inc.; 203, (c), Art Today, (bc) (bkgd), Michael J. Deas; 211, Image Copyright ©2003 Photodisc Inc.; 217, (c) (bc), Bob Daemmrich/Stock Boston/ PictureQuest, (bkgd), Image Copyright ©2003 Photodisc Inc.; 221, Image Copyright ©2003 Photodisc Inc.

AUTHOR AND TITLE INDEX